WOODCARVING ILLUSTRATED

WOODCARVING ILLUSTRATED

Roger Schroeder
and
Paul McCarthy

Stackpole Books

WOODCARVING ILLUSTRATED

Copyright © 1983 by Stackpole Books

Published by
STACKPOLE BOOKS
Cameron and Kelker Streets
P.O. Box 1831
Harrisburg, PA 17105

Printed in the U.S.A.

Library of Congress Cataloging in Publication Data

Schroeder, Roger, 1945–
  Woodcarving illustrated.

  1. Wood-carving—Technique. I. McCarthy, Paul,
1942–   . II. Title.
NK9704.S37 1983   736′.4   82-19626
ISBN 0-8117-2271-6 (pbk.)

To Lil and Diane

Contents

PART ONE

Materials and Techniques for Woodcarving

1

An Introduction to Woodcarving

Another carving book? Already there are books for bird carvers, animal carvers, books for whittlers, chip carvers, and ship carvers. So what's the fuss about this one? We believe a good illustration is worth a thousand wood chips. That's why we wrote *Woodcarving Illustrated*.

Each of our ten projects will take you step-by-careful-step from a block of wood to a finished carving. We'll tell you how to cut out the project, what tools to use, what finishes to apply.

The second project, a tiny shorebird called the least sandpiper, takes over fifty steps to make it look realistic with feathers, legs, and glass eyes. Why so many? The answer lies in the material you're working with. Wood is a medium that's difficult to control and master because it is vague. Its grain can be prominent or invisible. The wood itself can twist, warp, dull your tools with resins and silicates, ruin and even break them. But most important to consider, woodcarving is subtractive. Once you remove a piece of wood, there is no putting it back. You have to be precise, then, and think ahead. That is what we have found, and that is why we have so many steps.

In spite of its limitations, there are outstanding things being done today in wood as shown in illustrations 1 and 2. Illustration 1 was actually carved from a solid block of pine with only the pipe added. Can the average woodcarver do this kind of work? We think he can if he has a thorough understanding of the wood he is working with, a knowledge of a few basic tools and how to sharpen them, plus persistence.

Age is certainly not a limitation. Illustration 3 shows eleven-year-old Chris Thibodeau carving away on a squirrel, one of his very first projects.

Before you turn to the projects section, read the information we have provided in the first seven chapters. Did you know that a dull tool is usually more dangerous than a sharp one? What would you think if we told you that motor oil is the best thing to store your paint brushes in? Suppose you have a piece of hardwood like oak that you want to carve. We will tell you to try pine instead. Believe it or not, it is more difficult to master.

In addition to offering enough information for anyone who has never picked up carving tools to do so and carve any of our projects, we have also given advice and tips we have not found in print anywhere else. This way, the experienced carver can benefit too. And since all these projects are originals, designed by Paul McCarthy, we feel this is a book for all carvers, regardless of experience.

We have arranged our ten projects not so much in order of difficulty as in order of interest. There is a great fascination for carved birds in this country, so one of the early projects is a sandpiper decoy. This will require only four tools: a jackknife, a parting tool, a half-round gouge, and a fishtail gouge. Then you can progress to the realistic sandpiper. Farther on, you will have the opportunity to carve other animals including a whale and a beaver, plus projects like a cutting board, a doorknocker and a gold panner.

In our chapter on tools and how to use them, we have limited you to five basic ones, including the jackknife. Two are called gouges, one a chisel, one a parting tool. It is possible you could do all the projects in this book with just the knife, but we do not advise it. The next chapter will tell you how to sharpen tools and keep them that way.

For all our carvings we recommend pine or basswood. We have found they are available, they are still inexpensive, and they are workable. Yet, there may be trees in your backyard or in the woods nearby or in the local lumber mill you would like to carve. Our chapter on wood offers useful, no-nonsense

1. This New England seafarer was carved by artist Armand LaMontagne from a solid block of pine, including the watch cap and cableknit sweater. (Photograph by Joseph Avarista.)

2. Two pintail ducks taking off from water were carved from basswood by South Carolina bird sculptor Gilbert Maggione. (Courtesy of the Ward Foundation.)

information about woods like walnut, oak, maple, and mahogany.

What's next after you have bought your tools, sharpened them, and you have found the wood you want to carve? We have an entire chapter on how to cut the wood to size, how to glue it and hold it down, and how to work from the patterns that accompany each project.

Chapter 6 tells you how to finish that carving you have labored on so long. You will find suggestions on stains, polyurethanes, even such unusual finishes as gold leaf and bronzing powders.

What we do not offer in this book is a lot of ceremony. We do not burn wood at an altar, we do not invoke the spirits of our ancestors. Instead, the emphasis is on technique and progress.

This does not mean we have not learned from the past. Woodcarving is one of the oldest art forms in human evolution, and one of the oldest in this country. When the early settlers came to America, they found lots of trees, something that was becoming scarce in European countries like Great Britain. And trees meant wood for houses, furniture, ships, and carvings. But the heyday of woodcarving came in the first half of America's nineteenth century when most of the people doing it were shipcarvers. They were turning out sternboards and quarterboards, figureheads and eagles. But by the end of that century, wooden ships turned to iron. And by the middle of the twentieth century, even wood furniture was replaced by glass, brass, and plastic.

We believe that today there is both time and a need again to do something

3. An eleven-year-old carving student of Paul McCarthy, Chris Thibodeau, carves a squirrel with a jackknife. (Photograph by Gil Snapper.)

creative and difficult; that there is more to leisure time than working on the lawn. We think woodcarving, which is having a revival, fills those needs.

When we started writing this book, we talked to a traveling salesman who learned our carving techniques. Why did he take up carving? we asked him. It gave him something to keep himself occupied and out of trouble, he responded. A piece of wood and a knife, he added, were the only companions he needed.

Woodcarving is, then, something you can take with you outside the house or even out of the country. That is why someone wrote that all you need to be a carver is a knife, a sharpening stone, a chunk of wood, and an idea.

Wherever you carve them, we hope that many of these projects trigger those pleasurable feelings the outdoors can give us. Picture the sandpiper you carve running through the mild surge of beach water in search of food. And

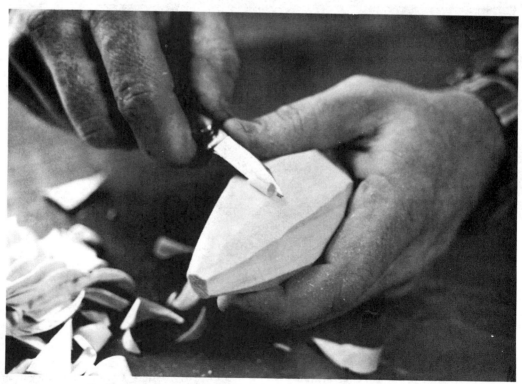

4. Technique is exemplified by carving with a jackknife.

5. Progress is exemplified by the evolution in wood of a bird.

imagine the cold stream the wooden gold panner searches in for his precious metal.

After you have finished *Woodcarving Illustrated* and have removed thousands of wood chips meticulously from the blocks or cutouts, we hope you have not only learned and progressed, but also that you have become hooked on woodcarving.

2

The Tools and How
to Use Them

Here are four rules every woodcarver should know about tools.

1. The more expensive a tool is, the better is its steel.

2. A carving tool is meant for separating or cutting the wood away, not busting or breaking it out.

3. Little tools are for little projects. Big tools are for big projects.

4. A tool should be held so it is controlled with both hands.

The Steel

It has been said a cheap tool is good for one thing: cutting string. What makes a good tool? It is the steel, and tools with high carbon steel are what we use. Regardless of the kind of knife, chisel, or gouge you purchase, Swiss steel is considered the best. It holds a sharp edge, it is not brittle, and it rarely breaks.[1] Illustration 6 shows a variety of Swiss-made tools. Their octagonal

---

[1]Chapter 7 lists a mail order supplier of Swiss tools.

6. All these tools are Swiss-made.

handles are an added feature. Better than round handles, their shape means less likelihood of the tool slipping out of your hands, so the control is good.

Are stainless steel tools worthwhile? For working outdoors in the rain or for kitchen work where the steel could rust, they are fine, but for maintaining a sharp edge they are worthless.

Cutting

When you first tried carving meat with a knife, you probably tried tearing it apart instead of slicing it. The same holds true for wood. By definition carving is the shaping and refining of a medium. The wood you are working with may wear out your tools, may respond with an iron tenacity, may separate contrary to the way you want it to, but there should never be any excuse for going at your carving project the way you would take a stump out of the ground. You may need a lot of patience and persistence, but you must learn how to make controlled cuts to remove what wood you want.

Tool Size

Another problem carvers face is having the right tool. Just as you would not use a sledgehammer to put a nail into the wall, neither would you want to use a cumbersome tool on a small hand-held piece of wood. When you get to our projects, we will show you profiles of the tools we used to carve them.

Holding the Tool

Once you have the right-size tool, the next question is, How do you hold it? One of the most difficult tools to handle is the jackknife. There is no tool

7. *Clockwise from upper left:* **a half-round gouge, a parting tool, a carver's chisel, a fishtail gouge, the jackknife.**

8. *Left to right:* **A macaroni tool, a back-bent gouge, a forward-bent gouge, a skew chisel.**

that can get you into more trouble if you do not know what both hands are doing at all times. We will explain to you shortly how to hold the jackknife and how not to hold it. And we will do the same for the other tools you will need for our projects. Plus, we have simplified things a step further. None of the projects will require a mallet. That is reserved for big pieces like statues and totem poles. Instead, you will learn how to brace and hold each tool with both hands to remove wood.

The Tools

The tools you will need for the projects are pictured in illustration 7. They are the jackknife, the carver's chisel, the parting tool, the half-round gouge, and the fishtail gouge. We will refer to the last four as push tools.

A problem with push tools is that if you were to add up all the sizes and shapes, you would find well over a thousand different ones! Chisels can be

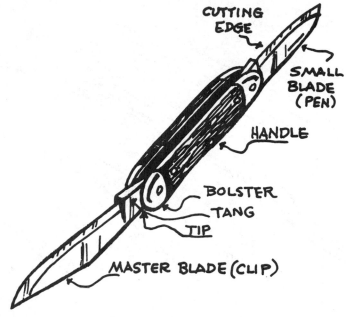

CUTTING EDGE

SMALL BLADE (PEN)

HANDLE

BOLSTER

TANG

TIP

MASTER BLADE (CLIP)

9. The jackknife and its parts.

straight or skewed, gouges can have straight shafts or flared ones, can be bent forwards or backwards, can look like spades or fishtails, can be cornered right or left, can vein, gouge, part, or flute. Illustration 8 shows some of the odd-looking tools on the market. To make things more complicated, their sizes or cutting edge widths are usually metric (anywhere from 1 mm to 50 mm), and the cutting edges have curves called sweeps which are shaped differently. These sweeps are given numbers ranging from 1, which would describe a flat or straight chisel, to 15, which has a deeply V-shaped cutting edge. And add to this the fact that these numbers may not be uniform from one tool company to another.

The Jackknife

Though it is the most difficult to handle, the jackknife is the most versatile tool in woodcarving. Illustration 9 shows the knife and what its parts are called. Many small projects such as birds, animals, and folk figures can be done almost exclusively with the jackknife because it is good for getting into small areas and crevices that are almost impossible to reach with your other tools.

There are, however, many kinds of knives with a variety of different blades. Some blades are skewed; some are spear-pointed. There are pen blades, clip blades, fixed, and folding blades. The most common are shown in illustration 10. The pen blade, shorter than most other blades, has a sharp point, and it is helpful in doing close, detailed work. A longer blade on many jackknives is the clip blade, a useful one for roughing out a project and reaching into deep crevices. Still another common blade is the sheep's foot, which is usually shorter than the clip blade and has the advantages of both the clip and pen blades. Because of its straight cutting edge, it is good for making V-shaped cuts.

The kind of jackknife we use is shown in illustration 11. It has a clip blade that measures 2 inches, a pen blade that is 1⅜ inches, and a sheep's foot blade that is 1⅜ inches long. But don't feel limited by these dimensions. This knife is for an average-size hand, and larger jackknives can be purchased.

Some carvers use fixed-bladed knives. We have found that with most of them that either the handle is too big or the blade is too short. After grinding the steel to get an edge on it, the life expectancy is literally too short.

Since the second project in this book, the least sandpiper, is done almost entirely with the jackknife, we will relate the use of the knife to that carving. Begin by grasping the wood cutout in your fingers, pushing it into your palm while leaving your thumb as free as possible, as in illustration 12. With the jackknife in the other hand, place that free thumb at the base of the blade, opposite the tang, shown in illustration 13. This thumb is used as the center

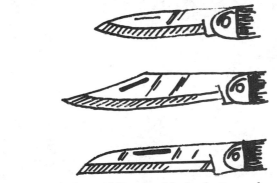

10. *Top,* pen blade; *middle,* clip blade, *bottom,* sheep's foot blade.

11. A typical jackknife.

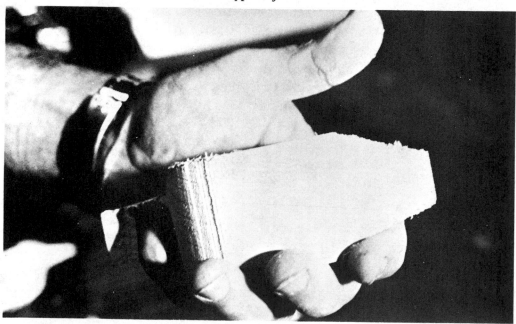

12. Holding the wood cutout.

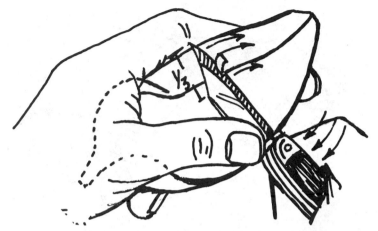

13. Carving away from you with the jackknife.

point for a pivot or lever. Use your knife-holding hand to pivot the blade on your thumb so the cutting edge is moving forward in small arcs. Notice the direction of the arrows in illustration 13. You will feel how the knife hand guides the cut.

Once you feel comfortable with holding your project with just the fingers and palm of one hand and the knife in the other, you will be able to use your thumb for more than a pivot point. Now try pushing with your thumb. This way, while your knife hand is pulling, your thumb will be pushing, allowing you to make longer cutting strokes.

Notice also in illustration 13 that only a portion of the knife's cutting edge is used. It is the upper third of the blade that is doing the carving. This is the ideal part of the blade because it gives you the best cut with the least effort, owing to the leverage of the thumb.

Let's make our first rule of thumb based on this procedure. Whenever possible, carve away from yourself. This is the best way to keep from getting cut.

Here is some other advice. Don't put too much pressure on the blade with that thumb. You will either risk cutting yourself, or you will take too much wood away. Another precaution is not letting the blade point disappear into the wood. When this happens, it could emerge anywhere, even in a finger.

Sometimes, contrary to our rule of safety about carving away from yourself, you will have to carve toward your body. If this is the case, grasp the cut-

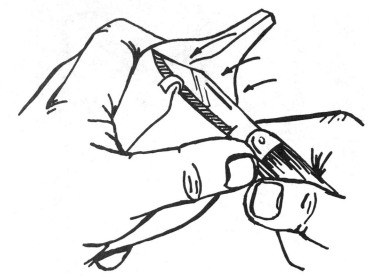

14. Carving toward you with the jackknife.

out as you did before, the wood pressed into the palm, the fingers wrapped around the wood. But this time, place your free thumb against the front of the tang but not on the cutting edge. Work the knife toward you with your knife hand, while pushing against the tang with that thumb. See illustration 14. If you keep a little pressure on your thumb at all times and work the knife toward your hand, this will almost always prevent slipping.

Occasionally you will need to cut straight down into the wood with the point of the knife, and it is dangerous because the knife can slip. To be safe, you will need that thumb again. Grasp the wood as you have done before, and, with the guidance of your thumb on the back of the blade, direct the point of the knife to the area where you are making the straight-down cut. Illustration 15 shows how to do this. Once the point has penetrated to the proper depth, keep your thumb on the back of the blade and push it along while exerting downward pressure. It is a difficult procedure to get used to, but once you do, you will be able to make uniform depth cuts safely.

We would like to illustrate the wrong way to carve our projects. What is traditionally called the paring cut, illustration 16, is best left for putting points on spears and peeling fruit. Though you may not cut yourself, you will prob-

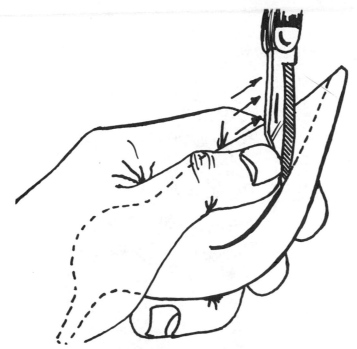

15. Carving straight down with the jackknife.

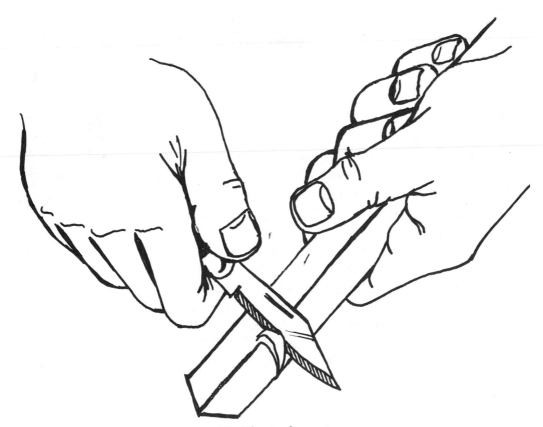

16. The paring cut.

17. The draw cut.

ably take too much or too little wood away because you do not have both hands controlling the blade. And then there is the draw cut shown in illustration 17. This was probably used by students of the past to put graffiti on desks. It is similar to our straight-down cut except it is one-handed. If you exert too much downward pressure the knife can fold up into your hand. Also, the control is limited because, without the other hand as a guide, the knife can wobble from side to side.

Although the topic of grain is usually reserved for the chapter on wood in a carving book, we have to stop and mention it here. Regardless of the tool you are using, you have to be aware of the grain's direction. Illustration 18 shows the top and side views of the sandpiper and how the grain runs in the wood. If you carve against the arrows, you stand a great chance of splitting off a piece of wood as illustration 19 shows.

Here is a rule to learn. Start from the thickest or biggest part of the carving

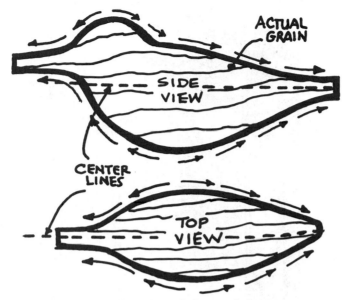

18. The grain direction of the sandpiper cutout.

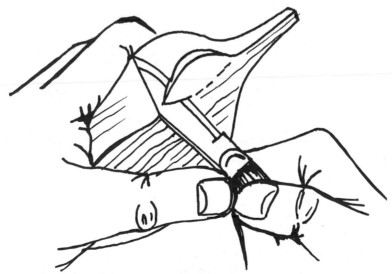

19. Carving against the grain, or "uphill," can cause a large piece of wood to split off.

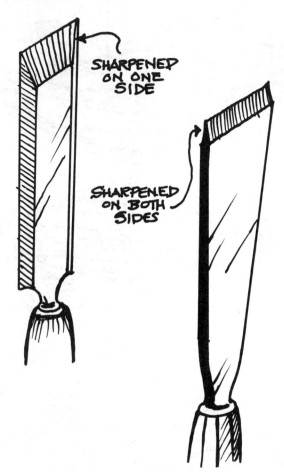

SHARPENED ON ONE SIDE

SHARPENED ON BOTH SIDES

20. *Left,* a typical carpenter's chisel; *right,* the carver's chisel.

and work down. Think of this in terms of a hill. When you are going down the hill, you are going with the grain. When you are going up the hill, you are going against the grain.

The Carver's Chisel

A carver's chisel differs from a carpenter's chisel because it has a cutting edge sharpened on both sides of the blade. Illustration 20 shows both chisels. Also, the carver's chisel is thinner at the cutting edge and makes crisper, cleaner cuts than the bulkier carpenter's chisel, which is good for removing wood for door hinges.

We use the carver's chisel for rounding convex surfaces efficiently and quickly. This is a procedure we use with the pineapple, Project 1. We also use the carver's chisel for making stop cuts. A stop cut establishes a wall of wood. That wall sets up a boundary so adjoining wood can be removed with the same tool or a different one. To remove that adjacent wood cleanly, however, the stop cut should go slightly below the area you want to remove.

The best way to make a stop cut is to direct the tool's cutting edge with one hand and use the other hand to push the chisel straight down. Downward pressure and a slight back-and-forth rocking motion, as in illustration 21, will cut the wood cleanly.

The philosophy behind holding the chisel is the same as that behind the jackknife. Have both hands controlling the tool. With a chisel or the other

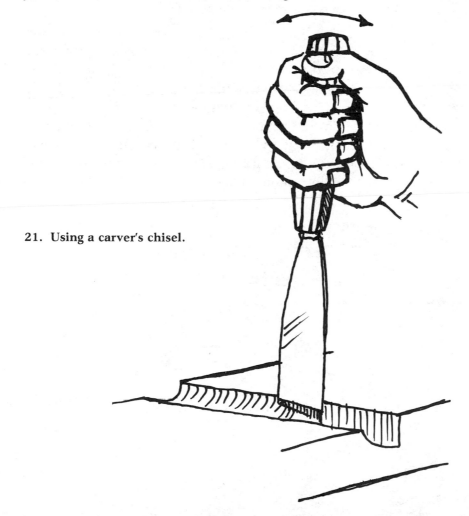

21. Using a carver's chisel.

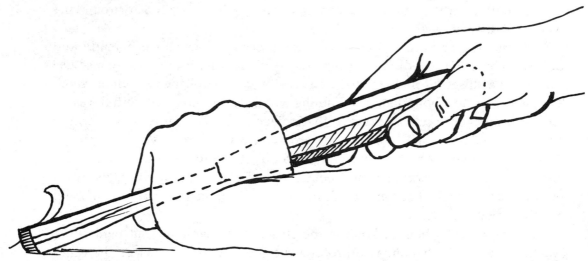

22. The correct way to hold a pushtool.

push tools, you can think in terms of positive and negative pressure. In illustration 22 you can see how the tool is held. We grasp the tool handle in one hand, placing the end in the palm. With the other hand, we grasp the tool so the third or ring finger wraps around where the steel shank and handle meet. The back hand acts as the guide and the power, while the other hand, with its wrist firmly on the work surface, acts as a brake. This way you can remove wood in four-to-five-inch strokes without lifting that wrist from the work surface. Note the arced arrow in illustration 23.

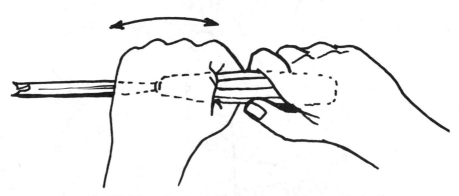

23. Making short cutting strokes with a pushtool.

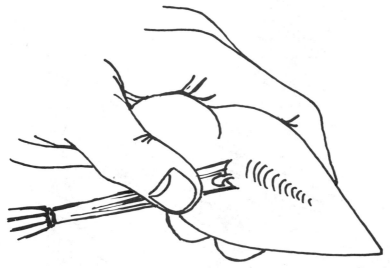

24. Using a pushtool, a gouge in this case, with a hand-held project.

Sometimes you will need a pushtool for a hand-held project. Notice in illustration 24 how the bird cutout is held as if you were carving with a jack-knife. The free thumb is placed on the shank of the pushtool for control. Again, the rule of thumb is not violated, for each hand is controlling the tool, one hand pushing, the other acting as a brake.

The Parting Tool

The parting tool, also called redundantly the V-parting tool, is really two chisels joined at an angle. And, like a chisel, it makes incisions in the wood. The advantage of this tool is that you have two cutting edges to work with, and with those edges you can outline a design or make V-shaped cuts for decoration.

The disadvantage comes when you make a turn in the wood. For while one cutting edge of the parting tool may be going with the grain, the other will be going against it. Result: frayed or rough edges on the cut as shown in illustration 25. To correct this problem you should begin by making narrow cuts, then reverse the direction of the cuts and make them slightly wider.

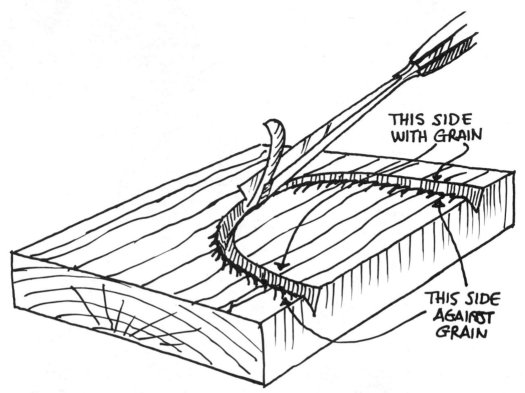

THIS SIDE
WITH GRAIN

THIS SIDE
AGAINST
GRAIN

25. The problem with using a parting tool—frayed or rough edges may result.

Parting tools, like your chisels, come in different sizes. The V can be very narrow or very wide, ranging from the size of one cutting edge from 1 mm to 30 mm.

Half-Round Gouges

We call the gouges we use half-rounds because their cutting edges have the arc of a circle. They also have parallel sides that run along the shank to the cutting edge. Ranging in size from ⅛ inch wide to 1½ inches wide, they are used for removing wood that fits the curvature or sweep of the tool. Sometimes they are used for hollowing bowls, for example, and sometimes they are used for cutting grooves or just accenting a background.

The Fishtail Gouge

The name of this tool derives from its shape. Coming from the handle, the steel is narrow but broadens at its end to the shape of a fish's tail. It is an ideal tool for trimming, smoothing, and light cutting, especially where you do not want the wood to have deep gouges. In fact, it is particularly useful for leaving a fairly flat surface after gouging. The big advantage is its blade area. With that wide cutting edge and narrow shank, you can get the tool into narrow places and sometimes even slide it in sideways.

Illustration 26 shows how this tool plus the chisel and a half-round gouge are used to relieve or raise a star in wood. The first step is going completely around the star with a half-round gouge. Then the carver's chisel is used to make a stop cut around the star, one slightly deeper than the area to be removed. The third step is to remove the background wood with a fishtail gouge by pushing it into the wall made by the stop cuts.

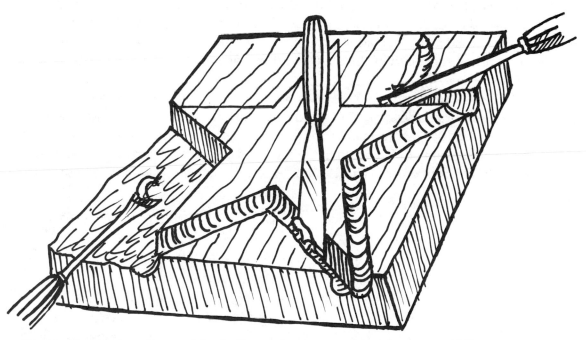

26. Carving a star. *Upper right,* half-round gouge outlines the star; *middle,* carver's chisel makes a stop-cut; *lower left,* fishtail gouge removes or flattens background to raise the star.

CORNERS OF CUTTING EDGE REMAIN OUT OF WOOD

27. *Right,* **a half-round gouge buried in the wood;** *left,* **the gouge's cutting edges are out-side the wood.**

Whatever tool you need to use, you cannot go too deeply into the wood. Suppose, for example, you got both corners of your half-round gouge buried in the wood as in illustration 27. If you continue to push, you will end up break-ing the wood away instead of carving it. Here, then, is our rule of thumb: Keep at least half the depth of the blade's cutting edge outside the wood. Illustration 27 also shows this.

Here is some final advice on tools. Do not leave them in your car, your basement, or your garage. Tools with high-carbon steel are meant to be kept in a dry place. But just to make sure they stay dry, keep them oiled lightly with some household oil. If you do notice they have pitting or rust, use oil and steel wool to clean them up. There is no reason, then, why they should not last a lifetime.

3

Sharpening

There is a famous wood sculptor who is fond of saying, "A dull tool is the wrong tool." We could not agree more. And, in fact, a dull tool is a dangerous tool. Why? If your tools are not properly sharpened, you start to hack away at the wood using unnecessary force. If you should slip, and your hands are not where they should be, you stand a good chance of getting cut.

Basic Elements

Before you begin to get that keen edge so needed on a carving tool, here are six terms you should be familiar with: grinding, bevel, hollow ground, wire edge, honing, and temper.

Grinding

Grinding is that first step in sharpening. What happens is that you remove steel from the tool to leave an edge. This has traditionally been done on a turned-by-hand or motor-driven wheel that can be made of aluminum oxide, carborundum, or sandstone. The sparks you see flying away on a grinding wheel that has a tool put to it are the ground-off metal particles.

Bevel

The bevel or cutting edge is what the grinding wheel is supposed to leave on the steel. The longer or steeper the bevel, the keener the edge. The shorter it is, the blunter the edge.

Hollow Ground

The hollow ground is caused by the shape of the wheel as it grinds away steel to make the bevel. The larger the wheel, the flatter your hollow ground will be. The smaller the diameter of the wheel, the more concave the hollow ground will be. The old-timers used enormous grinding wheels turned by hand for axes and adzes, large tools that needed long but flattened hollow grounds.

Wire Edge

The wire edge, even after grinding, is what will keep the tool dull. The action of the wheel causes the steel at the end of the tool to bend over toward you, however slightly. In most cases, if you run your finger along the cutting edge after grinding, you can feel the wire edge.

Honing

Honing is the removal of that wire edge to leave a keen edge on the steel. Traditionally, honing has been done on flat stones, leather, and buffing wheels.

Temper

Temper refers to the hardness or inner strength of the steel. Most beginning sharpeners let the tool get too hot from the action of the grinding wheel. When this happens and the end of the tool turns blue or darkens, as in illustra-

28. The darkened end of a carpenter's chisel that was ground too hot and has lost its temper.

tion 28, the temper has been lost. And so will your own because the tool's edge will repeatedly bend over as you carve.

The Grinder

We do not think it is possible to get much carving done without the electric grinder. Almost any place that sells tools will sell grinders. One with a six-inch diameter stone is the best for most tools since it leaves a hollow ground that is not too concave. Plus, it is available and not too expensive. But why not use a flat stone to take away the steel? First, it is more difficult to maintain the angle of the bevel on a stone than it is on a wheel rotating at thousands of RPM's. Second, the wheel makes hundreds of "strokes" for every one you could possibly make by hand on a flat stone. In fact, you will actually end up putting a groove in the stone with constant use!

Most grinders come with two arbors and a grinding wheel on each, one with a medium grit or cutting surface, and one with a fine grit. The fine wheel has a greater tendency to heat the steel too much and burn the edge off, affecting the temper. The medium wheel, we have found, does a better job of grinding the steel away to leave a keen edge. We also recommend you put a buffing pad on the grinder by removing the fine grit wheel. The buffer should be six inches in diameter and at least an inch thick. You may need to put two thin ones together to get that thickness. With the application of a rouge compound to the buffer you can hone your tools by literally polishing off the wire edge. Illustration 29 shows a typical setup.

Using a grinder, like learning to use a carving tool, takes practice. And the question people invariably ask is, How do you hold the tool to the wheel? First, all push tools have to be held toward the ceiling, which is against the downward rotation of the wheel. Have one hand holding the tool by its handle and the other with its thumb against the shank about halfway between the edge and the handle. Place the rest of those fingers against the grinder housing as in

29. This grinder has a grinding stone on the left, a one-inch-thick buffing pad on the right.

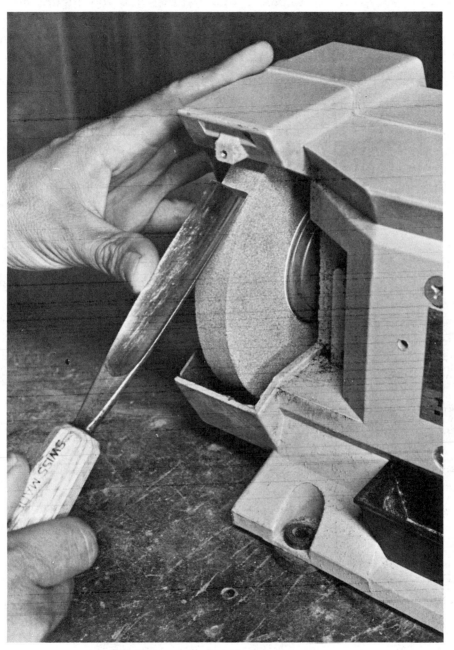

30. The proper way to grind a gouge.

illustration 30. All grinders come with a tool rest, and you might want to use this to rest the tool-holding hand on.

The advantage of having the thumb on the steel is that you have not only more control, but you can also feel the temperature of the steel. If the steel gets too hot, you are in danger of losing the temper. Certainly, this is a literal rule of thumb.

The solution for a tool getting too hot (but not blueing at the end) is water. Simply douse the tool in a trough of water (many grinders have them attached between the wheels). This dunking should be done every fifteen or twenty seconds anyway.

One of the first mistakes people make with the grinder is that they take the tool off the wheel every few seconds to look at how the steel is being ground away. There is no way you can maintain the same bevel by doing that without a lot of practice. Another mistake is not keeping the tool moving against the rotating wheel. You must keep it moving side-to-side with a light, even pressure. If you do not, you will end up cutting a groove in the steel or flattening it if it is a gouge. But do not go to the extreme edges of the wheel.

That back and forth motion will be the same whether you are grinding a straight chisel, a gouge, or a parting tool, though with curved tools it is going to be more of a side-to-side, rocking motion.

Getting the right bevel is the most difficult aspect of sharpening. First, grinding too high on the wheel will make too much of a hollow ground, leaving the cutting edge too brittle. Grinding too low will make the edge too blunt. These bevels are shown in illustration 31. To make things more frustrating, if the bevel is too steep, the keen edge will be too thin or brittle, owing to that hollow ground effect. And if the bevel is too blunt, you will not be able to cut through the wood.

The rule we follow is that the heavier the tool, the farther back you can make the bevel, and the lighter the tool, the shorter the bevel. However, a long bevel can be good for finely detailed work in difficult-to-get-at areas.

We should mention here that the most difficult tool to sharpen is the parting tool. This is because the angle at the bottom has to be as carefully sharpened as the sides. The best advice we can give is to sharpen one cutting edge at a time, then round the bottom of the V with a rocking motion on the wheel until it is balanced with the sides. You cannot leave the sides either protruding or lower than the V-bottom as shown in illustration 32.

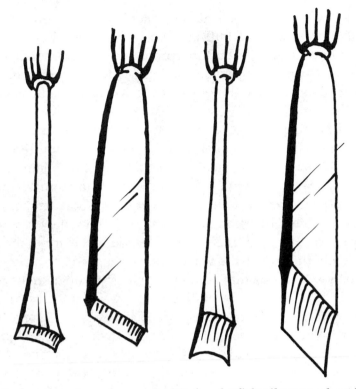

31. *Left to right:* long bevels on a carver's chisel and a fishtail gouge, short bevels on the same tools.

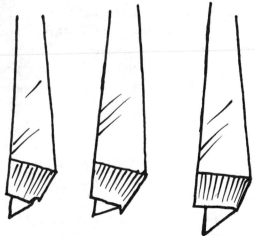

32. *Left,* properly ground parting tool; *middle and right,* improperly ground tools.

Once the bevel on your tools has been achieved, it is time to get rid of that wire edge. This is where the buffing wheel takes over. Before you can buff, however, you have to apply a buffing compound to the revolving cloth wheel. Compounds usually come in stick form, with different compounds having different cutting actions. The red or jeweler's rouge as it is called is probably the one you will use most often.

Instead of holding the tool toward the ceiling when buffing, hold it down toward the floor with the direction of the wheel as shown in illustration 33. Sticking the tool directly into the wheel could cause it to jam in the machine and that could leave you with a broken hand. But doing it properly, you should buff both sides of the tool. Try two or three short strokes on each side.

The most common question people ask us is how they can tell when the tool is really sharp. Here is a trick we use. As you will learn in the next chapter on wood, usually the harder the wood, the closer the consistency of its grain. So a hard wood will allow a dull cutting edge to go through it, leaving a smooth cut. This is not so with a soft wood like pine. Its wood fibers will tear loose if a dull tool tries to pass through it, especially if you carve across the grain at a right angle or if you carve the end of the board where the end grain is. But a tool with a keen edge will make a cut as smooth as glass, one you can see by the reflection of light off its surface or feel by rubbing your finger along the area where the wood has been removed.

Will a tool stay sharp for any length of time? It may take less than an hour for your tool to get dull, depending on the kind of wood you are carving. So expect to do a fair amount of regrinding and rebuffing if you have a big project.

Another thing to be aware of is that nearly all purchased carving tools, especially the knives, rarely come well honed. In fact, they may not even be ground properly. Be prepared, then, both to regrind and rehone them.

Sharpening the Jackknife

Though we did suggest you use the grinder and buffing setup for all your tools, we feel an exception can be made with the jackknife by using flat stones to grind and hone.

The first thing you need to know is something about flat stones. They can be artificial or man-made, can be described as coarse, medium, or fine, can be hard or soft. We recommend any medium to coarse whetstone (one that can

33. Putting a gouge to the buffing wheel on a grinder.

be lubricated so it can carry away metal particles) for the initial grinding of your knife. But there is only one stone we use for the final honing, and that is the hard Arkansas stone. This is a natural stone, white in color with very fine grain. There is a stone called the soft Arkansas stone, but this will not get the knife blade as sharp as you need it. Illustration 34 shows the stone we use.

Beginning, then, with the medium or coarse whetstone, lay your knife blade flat and rock it back and forth until you feel where the beveled edge is. Once you have the feel of this slight angle (as it must be because a jackknife blade is so thin), apply some light machine oil to the stone. A household oil, even baby oil, will do the job. You can adjust your knife edge to the oiled stone by using a slicing motion. This is done by pushing the knife along the stone from the point of the blade to the tang. But instead of simply going back and forth with the blade, you want to make an oval motion, clockwise or counter-

34. A hard Arkansas stone in its own box; jackknife for size comparison.

35. Grinding and honing a jackknife on a sharpening stone.

clockwise, as in illustration 35. While working the knife in small ovals, be sure there is more pressure exerted on the stroke cutting into the stone and less pressure moving away. You will get rid of more of the wire edge this way. Continue this process by counting twenty-five strokes on each edge. Then reduce the number to twenty, then fifteen, then one or two. This initial honing on a medium or coarse stone will take the place of the grinder in getting the desired bevel.

The next step is to get to a fine stone (here you can use a hard Arkansas stone) and repeat the above instructions. Continue using an equal number of strokes on each bevel until you see a fine wire line on the cutting edge. By applying more pressure on your down stroke, the wire edge will cut itself away. Remove that bit of steel from the stone by wiping with a rag and continue honing until all the wire edge is gone.

Now you can check the keenness of the blade on a piece of wood, preferably the end grain of a piece of pine. If the blade does not cut cleanly, rehone it.

These steps may take an hour or more, but we think they are better than grinding the jackknife, which will make the knife smaller and smaller very shortly. Also, you can restore the edge quickly by going back to the hard Arkansas stone and stroking the blade a few times on each side. Still, after a period of time, you will lose the original bevel and you will have to start from the beginning.

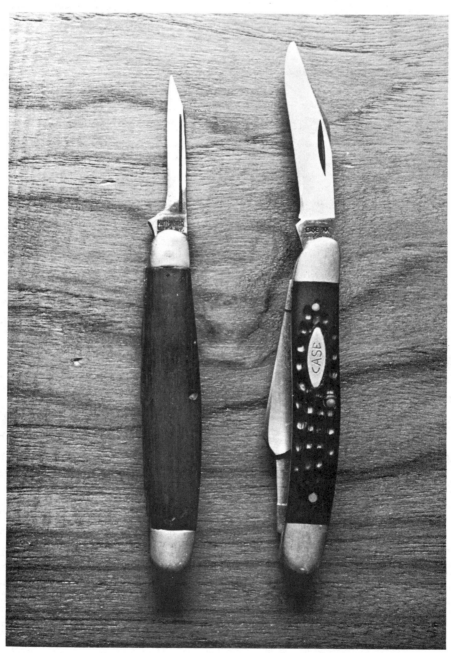

36. *Left*, a ground-thin blade; *right*, a new jackknife blade.

Here are some final thoughts on grinding. Every time you grind a tool, you are changing the shape, no matter how minutely, of the steel. And no matter how much you grind it, it can still be used as a tool. This is especially true of the jackknife. Regardless of how narrow the blade gets because the steel gets ground away, you can still have a use for it. If you use the jackknife a lot, you will soon find that too large a blade cannot turn sharp corners or get into tight areas. But a narrow blade, like the one in illustration 36, will. So do not throw away those ground-thin blades.

The Wood

Wood is a paradox. Some of it is called hard, some soft. Yet balsa, the model-maker's dream wood because of its easy workability, is a hardwood. And hemlock, which holds up your house, is a softwood. There are some pines, all softwoods, that defy carving. And there are oaks, all hardwoods, that when freshly cut, carve like butter.

Many books have been devoted to wood and its properties, and many more will probably be written. We too have thoughts to offer on wood. But since there are thousands of species in the world, we will limit our comments to the handful that seem to appeal to woodcarvers.

We have found that some woods carve better than others. We have also found that you just cannot purchase some woods. Therefore, you have to consider two things before you carve. First, what is the workability of the wood? Second, how available is it?

Before we discuss wood, consider what it is made of. Contrary to surface evidence, it is not solid. Rather, it grows in layers of tissue just as people do. And sometimes these layers twist and intermingle with other layers.

37. The longitudinal section of a red cedar tree.

If you took a section of a tree and cut through it longitudinally, as we did in illustration 37, you would find three main parts—the hard center, or heartwood; the outer ring, or sapwood, which is usually lighter in color; and the bark. Looking at an end section, you would find lines in the form of concentric circles which begin at the center and grow larger and larger until the bark is reached. These are called annual rings. The rings will tell you something about the grain of the wood—does it have a very open grain, which can make carving difficult, or is it a tight grain, which is easier to carve?

Ironically, the heartwood, which is considered the dead wood and serves no purpose other than to provide strength for the trunk, is the ideal part of the tree for carving. The key word here is strength. For the sapwood is the immature or living part of the tree that carries water. Sometimes there will be dissolved substances in that water that remain in the wood and can affect your tools. Teak, heavy with silicates (actual particles of sand), is one example. And it is those silicates that will quickly dull your tools.

Perhaps it is a misnomer to describe some of wood's natural properties as defects. Is it fair to call a knot, which is a portion of a limb or branch, a defect? In illustration 37 you can see the beginning of a limb. But for the sake of the poor carver whose tools cannot seem to go through knots, let's say they are imperfections. We do feel, however, that there is nothing wrong with carving a knot. It is a piece of wood, too, just harder than the rest of the wood. The trick is to carve with the knot. Since branches grow out from a tree (see illustration 38), you will be carving away from the center of the wood; so observe its angle of growth. If you should carve against a knot, it could literally break out from the wood surrounding it.

Resin is another defect of sorts. It is a sticky protective substance found in plants and trees. The problem with resin is twofold. First, it can dull tools and literally gum them up, making them difficult to remove wood. Second, too much resin can make the wood heavier and harder to work with.

Basswood

For people who carve birds, basswood is the choice. With an average weight of twenty-six pounds per cubic foot (white oak is almost double that in weight), it is a lightweight that is very easy to work with carving tools. The grain is so close or tight you can barely see it, making it durable and strong for intricate carvings such as thin bird feathers. One carver we know says it carves like soap since you can carve with or against the grain. Actually, since the heartwood is creamy white in color, it looks like soap. Bird carvers favor it not just for its workability but also for the way it takes paint. Because of its light color and grain tightness, paint will cover it easily and uniformly. This is probably one of the reasons most carousel horses were made from basswood. However, it is not good for staining. Again because of that tight and featureless grain, stains come out a solid color, which is not very appealing.

Since it grows throughout the eastern half of the United States, in an area framed by Maine, Florida, North Dakota, and Texas, it is fairly easy to get. More and more lumber companies are stocking it, and it is still not very expensive. Also, the lumber company stock is usually knot-free.

If you want to look for basswood yourself, the tree which we get it from is called the linden. It grows large with very low-lying limbs and has two differently shaped leaves. Illustrations 39 and 40 show you what to look for.

38. The cross section of a red cedar tree showing the origin of a limb.

39. The linden tree that gives us basswood has been favored for centuries as a shade tree because of its broad, low-lying limbs.

Walnut and Butternut

Walnut has always been prized as a furniture wood, for paneling and even gunstocks because of its coloring and dramatic grain patterns. In America it is called black walnut, though its heartwood ranges from a light brown to a purplish gray-black.

The early American settlers found a plentiful supply of walnut trees, some with enormous diameters of ten feet or more. Regrettably, many were cut down to make way for roads and farms. However, walnut trees can still be found from Massachusetts to Florida, Wisconsin to Texas.

Though its pores are bigger than basswood's, walnut carves beautifully, especially with sharp tools. And it takes every kind of finish, particularly oils.

Another species of walnut is butternut, sometimes called white walnut.

40. The broad and straplike leaves and fruit of the linden tree.

This has a creamy brown color and makes for beautiful carvings when oiled to emphasize the natural color of the wood.

Unfortunately, walnut and butternut are not so easy to come by. And when you do find them in a lumber yard, they can be expensive.

Mahogany

There are many kinds of mahoganies you can come across. Like walnut, mahogany has been favored for furniture and paneling. And it can have dramatic grain patterns. Little of it grows in this country (only in southern Florida), but it can be found in Central and South America, West Africa, and the Philippines.

The heartwood of mahoganies ranges in color from a pale to a reddish brown, while the sapwood runs from white to light brown.

The Central and South American mahoganies, with their tight grains, are good for carving and take stains and oil finishes nicely. Yet some mahoganies, especially the Philippine kind, are tough to work with, "like carving bundles of string," as one carver put it.

The good mahoganies are not so easy to purchase and can be expensive.

Oak

This wood is known by two adjectives that to some extent describe their colors: white and red. The white oak is heavy (it averages forty-seven pounds a cubic foot) and hard to work, but it is favored for flooring, furniture, and especially boats and ships. This oak grows chiefly in the eastern half of the United States. The red oak weighs slightly less and is found generally east of the Great Plains. Primarily, it has been used for flooring, boxes, and crates.

The major difference between the oaks, aside from color, is their porousness. The pores of the white oak are usually plugged, making the wood impervious to liquid; hence, its use in boatbuilding. The red oak, on the other hand, is extremely porous. Illustration 41 compares the end grains of red oak and basswood.

The red oak tends to be like mahogany—too stringy. And the white oak is just plain hard to carve, especially after it has been cut from the tree and has had a chance to age.

41. *Top,* **end grain of red oak;** *bottom,* **end grain of basswood.**

Maple

Maple comes in two varieties: soft and hard. It is found in the eastern half of the United States. Though it is used at times for furniture, it will probably always be used for flooring. Bowling alleys are an easy place to look for maple, especially the hard variety, also called sugar and rock maple.

We would not advise you to carve maple, particularly the rock maple. Using a jackknife, you stand a good chance of cutting your fingers off.

But if you still have the urge to carve maple, it does hold together well, though you have to carve away a tiny piece of wood at a time. Illustrations 42 and 43 show what can be carved in maple. Yet, there are some maples that have bird's-eye figures or curls and stripes in the grain that may require a jack-hammer instead of a jackknife for carving.

42. A pair of cedar waxwings carved in maple.

43. *Lower left,* bluejay feather carved from maple; *upper right,* real feather.

Pine

There are some ninety species of pine growing in North America, and a pine tree can be found just about anywhere in this country. Its uses have been extensive. It has been made into paneling, furniture, flooring, houses, and it has been carved. We find some of it excellent for carving, particularly the kind called Eastern white pine. It is both soft enough to carve and solid enough to hold together. And, as we told you in the chapter on sharpening, pine will indicate just how sharp your tools are. But most important, we like to tell people, it teaches you how to carve.

Compared to basswood, pine has a lot of prominent grain. And, as we pointed out earlier, it is grain that has to be respected, or the wood will quickly assume a mind of its own, which may cause you to ruin what you are carving.

Still, there is strength in Eastern white pine. This is because it grows in relatively cool climates like New England, bringing the annual or growth rings closer together.

There is a pine to avoid and that is sugar pine. Few woods can mess up your tools like this one can because of all the resin in the wood. Not only will your tool edge get dull, but the sides of the tool will build up with the resin, making it nearly impossible to push the tool through the wood. Yet, because of all that sticky substance, sugar pine can be so soft you can dent it with a knuckle. And when a finish is applied to the wood, resin streaks will invariably bleed through.

We do not want to discourage you from trying other woods. Any kind of wood can be carved if you have the time and are willing to endure some frustration. But know something about those properties of wood that include grain, resin, knots, and strength.

We also feel a lot of people forget that when they are buying wood at a lumber company, the wood came from a tree, not the lumber yard. What we are saying is that the wood you want to carve might be growing in your own backyard. There is no reason why, then, if a tree has been cut or blown down, or a limb can be removed, you could not utilize some of that wood. And freshly cut wood, particularly a hardwood, is easier to carve than a piece that has been dried out.

5

Mechanics and Layout

Let's assume you have decided to carve a big eagle like the one pictured partially in illustration 44. But you cannot find a piece of wood big enough. Nor do you want to do all that cutting with handtools. And the pattern you are working with is no bigger than this book!

These are frustrations shared by all woodcarvers who graduate from tiny birds shaped with a jackknife to totem pole-size sculpture. We have provided information that should solve these problems, information known both to professional carvers and furniture makers.

Cutting Out

There is no tool more useful to the woodcarver than the bandsaw. Its continuous blade revolving around two wheels will cut any wood of any reasonable thickness with speed and little waste. These are two things most other cutting tools cannot do. Some carvers try to use a saber saw, a hand-held power tool. It cannot, however, handle thick or small pieces of wood. Nor can

44. This eagle, which is eight feet high at the shoulders, was carved from pine by author Paul McCarthy.

it make a straight cut because the blade tends to drift. The coping saw, recommended by some woodcarvers, is also hand-held. This too does not cut straight, and it will cut through your patience before the wood.

Bandsaws are expensive, and not every carver can afford one, even one that is secondhand. But there are options. Most communities have a woodworking mill or a shop with a bandsaw. For a small fee you can have your wood cut to shape. We suggest, if you are going to be doing a lot of carving, say of birds, to have a number of wood blanks cut out at the same time. If there is no shop around, look for an evening session at a local school that offers woodworking classes. The industrial arts shops usually have excellent equipment. If these two options fail, there is no reason why you cannot shape the piece using handtools such as chisels and gouges. We know of one wood sculptor whose life-size carvings are roughed out with a chainsaw, a tool we would not recommend for our projects.

Gluing Up

After you have found a bandsaw, and you still want to do that big piece, perhaps you just can't find a piece of lumber wide enough or thick enough. Woodcarvers and furniture makers who run into this problem use a method called "gluing up the stock." This means you build up or laminate boards until you get the size lumber you need. It can be done face-to-face for thickness or edge-to-edge for width. Illustration 45 shows the glue lines of wood glued face-to-face to give the size needed for the sculpture. Gluing boards end-to-end, however, is impractical because the open grain at the ends absorbs the glue and there is no bonding strength.

For gluing up stock there are really only two kinds of glue you need, depending on where your piece is to be displayed. For the carving that will be used inside, a water-soluble glue called carpenter's or white glue is ideal. You can use it straight from the container and it will dry fairly clear. For the carving you want to display outdoors, a special glue is needed. It is a waterproof glue called resorcinol, a two-part mixture of liquid and powder. When mixed together, it is extremely strong, but it does have a tendency to set quickly. Care should be taken when mixing the two parts that the mixture is not too dry.

Here are some tricks we have found helpful for gluing up wood. After making sure your surfaces or edges are flat and even, spread the pieces to be

45. This six-foot-high sculpture was laminated with two-inch-thick pine boards and was carved by wood sculptor Joseph Avarista of Rhode Island.

bonded with the glue and let set for a few minutes. Push them together and move them from side-to-side to eliminate glue gaps. Another trick is not to wipe away the glue where it has beaded or dripped across the wood, even with a damp cloth. This will cause the glue to soak into the grain. And if that area is not carved away totally and you want to apply a stain, you will find out that the stain simply will not take. Later, the hardened beads of glue can be pried off with a chisel.

Clamping

Simply stated, gluing requires clamping. This makes for a strong bond while the glue dries or sets. There are three types of clamps we use: the C clamp, the handscrew, and the bar clamp, shown in illustration 46.

A large C clamp can reach pretty far in on the pieces being glued, and it will apply a lot of pressure on a particular area. The handscrew also reaches in fairly far but spreads out the clamping pressure with its large parallel jaws. It

46. *Left,* C clamp; *middle,* bar clamp; *right,* handscrew.

does tend to be bulky and in the way a lot, but you can tighten up a handscrew quickly.

One problem we have faced when gluing pieces of wood together, especially face-to-face, is that they have a tendency to move when clamping pressure is applied. A technique we use is nailing the pieces together before clamping so they do not slip. But this is done only in an area that will be carved away later.

The bar clamp, because of its small jaws, does not do well with pieces of wood thicker than two inches. There is no limit, however, to the number of boards you can glue edge-to-edge because these jaws fit on lengths of pipe that in turn can be fitted together.

Clamps are also useful for holding steady the projects being carved. In illustration 1 of Project 1, you can see how the pineapple is first held with woodscrews to a larger board, which in turn is held to a table or workbench with a C clamp.

What if the piece you are carving is very small or thin, say a half-inch piece of flat lumber? It is too small to clamp directly to a work table and too thin to hold with wood screws. A combination of newspaper and glue will solve the problem. Spread glue on a board larger than the piece to be carved. Put down a page of newspaper on the glue. Then spread glue on the underside of the project and clamp it to the newspapered board, making sure the paper covers the entire bottom of the project. When the glue has dried, you can clamp the board to a table and begin carving. Illustration 47 shows how. When you have finished carving, use a carver's chisel to slice and gently pry the carving away from the board.

Enlarging and Reducing Patterns

It is more the exception than the rule that the patterns you find in a book, even this one, will be the exact size of the carvings you want to make.

The grid method is one way to solve the problem. You will find that all our project patterns have cross-hatching lines called grids. These are provided as references for the outline of the project. By numbering these lines, starting at the lower left-hand corner with a zero and working vertically and horizontally, you can do the same on a larger piece of paper using an equal number of

47. Holding down a thin piece of wood for carving.

squares, but larger. That is, if the squares done in this book are one inch on each side, and if you want to double the pattern size, you will make squares two inches on each side. This is called enlarging from the grid. Notice how our patterns intersect the crosshatched lines or grids. Put a dot at as many of these intersections as you care to. Notice each dot's location in terms of the numbered lines. Find the same place on the enlarged grid. Once you have your points in place, connect the dots, a method not much different from children's books that offer pictures by drawing lines between the dots.

This same method works in reverse. If you come across a pattern, design, or picture that is too large for your carving needs, you can reduce from the grid, using the dot method but making the squares smaller.

Transferring Patterns

Getting a pattern from a page is easy. So you do not mess up the pages of the book, take a piece of tracing paper and trace the pattern. Then, with a sheet of carbon paper between the wood and tracing sheet, redraw the pattern. This will leave a faint outline on the wood that you can go over with a heavy pencil.

However you transfer, saving all of the drawing on the wood is sometimes impossible. In Project 2, the sandpiper, so much wood has to be removed from the sawn-to-shape blank that none of the details would remain. And even if you try drawing in all the feather details after the bird has been rounded, just to carve one layer of feathers will require removing the wood and the penciled-in details for the other layers.

We think you should learn to do freehand much of what you draw on the wood. We are not telling you to discard transferring, but after a while carbon and tracing papers can be a bother. And what if you want to change some details, change our whale's shape slightly or alter our gold panner's features? Suppose a knot in the wood you are carving makes certain design features out of the question? Patterns should never take away the liberty to change and be creative. But be on the safe side and keep that pattern or picture next to you as a reference.

6

Finishing

The carving you have labored at long and hard, the one that kept you going back constantly to the grinder, the one that was just a little too small or too big to make clamping easy, is done. And there you have, with all its delicacy and refinement, a carved piece of wood. Is there still room for improvement? We think so, and feel this chapter on finishes is mandatory.

The idea behind finishing a carving is easy. You want to beautify and enhance the look. You want to give the carving both depth and body. It is the choice of a finish that is difficult. You might decide to apply no more than a wax to the wood. But beyond that, you have stains, paints, dyes, pastes, oils, wood fillers, sealers, and shellacs. And there are no clear-cut rules for what finish goes with what wood. The same piece that might take nothing more than an oil could also be covered with paint.

There have been entire books devoted to just finishing wood, so we do not intend to give you all the options. What we have included here are tips and tricks we have found useful for finishing our carved pieces.

Sanding

There are many projects in this book that need little or no sanding. That has been another reason we have included so many steps for each piece. But for some, you will want not only a clean, smooth look, but also one to which you can apply a finish. The wood has to be smooth to do that properly.

There are several kinds of sandpaper with many different grits or particle sizes that range from coarse to very fine. There is flint paper, garnet, aluminum oxide, silicon carbide. And the coarser the grit, the lower the number of the paper (a coarse grit might be numbered 40 and a very fine grit 600). The kind we use is a red garnet paper. We recommend you buy a good paper like this one since a cheap paper sands off its own grit instead of sanding the wood.

Sandpaper is also needed for many finishes. Usually it is necessary to sand between coats of paint or layers of polyurethane, a clear, plasticlike covering. This makes for a smoother finish and better adhesion between coats. Though some finishers recommend steel wool for this, we do not. Like the grit on your sandpaper, pieces of steel wool, like filings, will come off. Also, like the grit, the steel particles will get into corners, indentations and crevices in the carving. But unlike the grit, if the particles of steel wool are sealed under polyurethane, they are going to rust, making them visible.

Another technique finishers will suggest is using a piece of wood to back up the sandpaper. This is acceptable for flat surfaces but not carvings. A wood block, even a round dowel, can cause unwanted grooves in the wood. But worse, a piece of wood gives you, the sander, no feeling of what you are supposed to be sanding. Sand by hand, then, as pictured in illustration 48. You will soon learn how to use your hand to fit parts of the carving needed to be smoothed.

We also cut our sheets of sandpaper so the strips can be folded over twice as you would a letter, leaving a square piece. What you have is grit to grit, grit to finger, grit to wood, all of which eliminate slipping. The folding also makes the paper stiffer and more durable.

Stains and Varnishes

Many of us have probably used stains and varnishes. They color, enrich, and protect the wood. It is no different with wood carvings. We like to make the stains ourselves because it is not difficult.

48. Sanding with a folded piece of sandpaper.

Universal tinting colors, available at almost all paint stores, are what give the paint in the can its color. Packaged in tubes or small cans, they can be mixed with turpentine to produce not only traditional stains like walnut or oak colors, but also green and red stains or any number of others. These have an especially interesting effect on woods like pine because, when lightly rubbed on the wood, the grain will still show through.

Try mixing a blob of tinting color with turpentine on a pallet. Or just dunk your brush into the turpentine and rub it into the tinting color. Two other advantages are that you will spend less money on the tinting colors than you would on a can of stain, and your tinting colors will last a very long time since so little is needed to make a stain.

Some carvers use acrylics or artist's colors to get the effect of a stain. These also come in tubes, but are mixed with water. We find, however, that they dry too fast, and tend to obscure finely carved details because they build up like a solid coat of paint instead of a stain.

Whether you buy or make your own stain, the question arises, How many coats of stain does the wood need? Wood has the ability to absorb liquids, but only so much. The same is true with a stain. You could put twenty coats of a stain on a piece of pine or oak, and the shade or tint would not change at all.

As for polyurethane, we think the choice comes down to brand names. But whatever kind you buy, you should apply at least two coats of it for a piece displayed indoors and four for outdoor display. Always allow a day between applications for best adhesion. After the first coat, we use a 100 grit sandpaper and sand lightly. After the second, a finer sandpaper, even a 400 grit paper, is used. The rule is, the finer the finish, the finer the sandpaper.

The biggest problem with applying clear finishes, however, is dust. It seems if there is any dust around at all, even on your clothing, your freshly coated piece will pick it up. And dust-free places are hard to find. Our solution is to get a clean cardboard box big enough to cover the carving. An added bonus of this is that the box may deter you from finger-testing the finish to discover whether it is dry.

Paints

Paints will do wonders for a plain wood like basswood and for carvings displayed outdoors. But paints have a tendency to run or form pools and puddles. More effort, then, is going to be needed with your brushing technique. That is one reason we do not use latex paints. They are sure to leave brush marks. What we use are oil-based paints. The ones we buy are the marine, the porch and deck paints, and exterior enamels.

Before we apply any paint, we use two coats of a primer. Since this will raise the grain of the wood, sanding between and after applications is necessary. But the advantage of the primer is that it will dry flat, and it will cover the grain because of its heavy body. This will allow the paint applied later to go on smoothly and evenly with no absorption into the wood.

Brushes

Brushes are a subject all to themselves. We have found every painted project seems to require its own particular brush. If, for example, you are painting a bird, you would not want to use a long skinny bristle brush. That's for holding a lot of paint where a long stroke or line is needed. Instead, you would want to use a brush with shorter bristles since you would not want the bristles to hold too much paint, and you would want to be closer to your work for that fine detail. For that kind of work we use an artist's brush with short, pure bristles that are soft and fine.

Brushes are expensive, however, and need special care to keep them for a long time. Here is how we treat our brushes. We recess a block of wood at a downward angle, as we did in illustration 49. Then we fill the bottom with a clean regular detergent motor oil. The oil will not evaporate, it does not have to be covered, and it will keep the brushes soft and supple indefinitely. When we are ready to use them, we remove the brushes from the motor oil, dunk them in lacquer thinner, wipe them thoroughly, and start to paint.

49. A hollowed out block of wood to hold brushes and motor oil.

Lacquer thinner, we have found, is the best cleaning agent for oil-based paints. Try soaking your brushes in it, and do not forget to get at the particles of paint that get into the heel of the brush (where the bristles join the handle). This is where regular paint thinner is not very effective. Then go back to the motor oil bath.

Sometimes you will need to use big brushes, ones that are two or more inches wide. These will need different care. We wash them with a paint thinner because we have found the lacquer thinner is not as effective where there are so many bristles. Then we lay the brush on a page of newspaper, roll the brush and paper three times, fold the top of the page over, and roll one more time. Next we tear off the excess side paper leaving a piece less than the width of the brush and tuck that torn edge into the folds. The excess paper around the handle is then torn off. Wrapped in newspaper this way, a brush can be set upright in a paint pail filled about an inch deep with paint thinner. The paper will keep the bristles from splaying out, a problem that makes for sloppy painting. When we are ready to use the brushes again, we remove them from the pail, unwrap the newspaper, rinse them in clean lacquer thinner, and dry them off with a clean rag.

Gold Leafing

One of the most brilliant and most difficult finishes to apply is gold leaf, also known as gilding.

There are two kinds of gold leaf that can be purchased from well-stocked artist supply stores. One is an imitation made up of a combination of brass, bronze, and copper. It is sometimes called German foil. The other is real gold, usually 23 karat, but can be as low as 10 karat. The imitation gold leaf has a tendency to tarnish over time, especially outdoors. The second will not tarnish, but it is expensive. Either kind can be purchased in books of very thin gold leaves or sheets.

Whichever you choose to purchase, the leaf should be applied after a primer and sealer like paint and polyurethane have been put down on the wood. But gold leaf will not adhere to the finish without a special adhesive base called a sizing. (We recommend a slow set gold leaf sizing.) The difficulty of applying gold leaf comes when trying to determine when the size is just right for adhesion. If the sizing is too wet, the gold leaf will probably dissolve

50. Removing gold leaf from a page using a bristle brush.

or come out too dull. If the sizing is too dry, the gold leaf will not stick, or it will be patchy. We suggest you use test strips on a piece of finished wood or even glass. Apply the sizing to five or six different areas at the same time. Then apply the gold leaf at different intervals of time, making a note of how long it has been drying. Observe how brilliant or shiny the gold leaf appears. Another test is to rub a finger over the sizing and listen for a squeaky tackiness.

When we finally determine how long it will take for the sizing to set up, we remove a sheet from the book, lay it flat over the drying sizing, and tamp it down with a soft, nylon bristle brush. Illustrations 50 and 51 show how it is done. Areas that might be missed by the gold because the sizing got too dry can be touched up later. We might mention that each page has rouge on it to prevent the gold sheets from adhering to the pages. By rubbing the brush over a blank page you will find you can apply the gold without getting sizing stick-

51. Tamping down the gold leaf with the brush.

ing to the brush. Also, we warn you *never to put a sealer over gold*. It will cause the gold to be lifted off the wood and ruin the finish.

Bronzing

This is an early American technique for decorating furniture and trays. It is still in use today, especially on Hitchcock furniture. Like gold leaf, it offers a metallic sheen, but, instead of coming in leaves, it comes in powder form. This too can be purchased at most artist supply stores.

To apply it, we use a polyurethane base, spreading a thin coat over the areas to be covered. Once this has set up for thirty minutes to an hour, when it will become tacky instead of dry, the powder is applied. You should do it by pouring the powder on a separate piece of paper. Stick a dry brush into a pile of bronzing powder and brush it over the polyurethaned area.

7

Where to Find Supplies

The only place in this country to purchase Swiss-made carving tools is Woodcraft Supply Corp., 313 Montvale Avenue, Woburn, Massachusetts 01888. Most of their business is mail order and a catalog is obtainable by writing to that address. They also sell sharpening tools and stones, finishes, clamps, and books on woodcarving, woodworking, sharpening, and finishing.

Another mail-order company that offers tools, books, finishes, and lumber is Albert Constantine and Son, Inc., 2050 Eastchester Road, Bronx, New York 10461. They have a wide selection of wood and veneer, including walnut, mahogany, oak, and maple, as well as exotic woods like rosewood, zebrawood, and ebony. Write for a catalog.

We believe the best jackknife you can buy is made by Case. It has the best steel of any jackknife we have used, and each knife is inspected for defects. Many hardware stores have them displayed, but if you cannot find one, try writing the company at W.R. Case & Son, Bradford, Pennsylvania 16701.

For a bimonthly magazine called *Chip Chats* that offers photos of carvings, patterns, and news of local carving organizations, write to the National Woodcarver's Association, 7424 Miami Avenue, Cincinnati, Ohio 45243. Membership, which includes the magazine, costs five dollars a year.

The burning tool used for the realistic least sandpiper is called The Detailer. It is manufactured by Colwood Electronics, 715 Westwood Avenue, Long Branch, New Jersey 07740.

If you are interested in bird carvings like the one pictured in illustration 2, a bird carving competition is sponsored annually by the Ward Foundation, Salisbury State College, Salisbury, Maryland 21804.

For cutouts of any of our projects in eastern white pine or basswood, write for a price list to Paul McCarthy's Carving Place, 132 Front Street, Scituate Harbor, Massachusetts 02066.

PART TWO

Projects for Woodcarving

Traditional New England Handcarved Pineapple

Project No. 1

The pineapple was used as a symbol of welcome & hospitality in early new England. History records ships sailing from Nantucket & other New England whaling ports to the south seas in search of whale oil. When the pineapple was discovered it was a strange & exotic fruit never seen by North Americans. Sea Captains would bring this unusual fruit as a prized gift for their families & friends. Upon their return, sometimes after being at sea for 4 or 5 years, they would place a Pineapple on their iron gates. This was public notice that the Captain had returned & was holding open house "Food & drink for all".

Can be used for
Front door
mantle
wall hanging

TOOLS NEEDED
CARVER'S CHISEL
PARTING TOOL (FIG. 29)
HALF-ROUND GOUGE (FIG. 24)

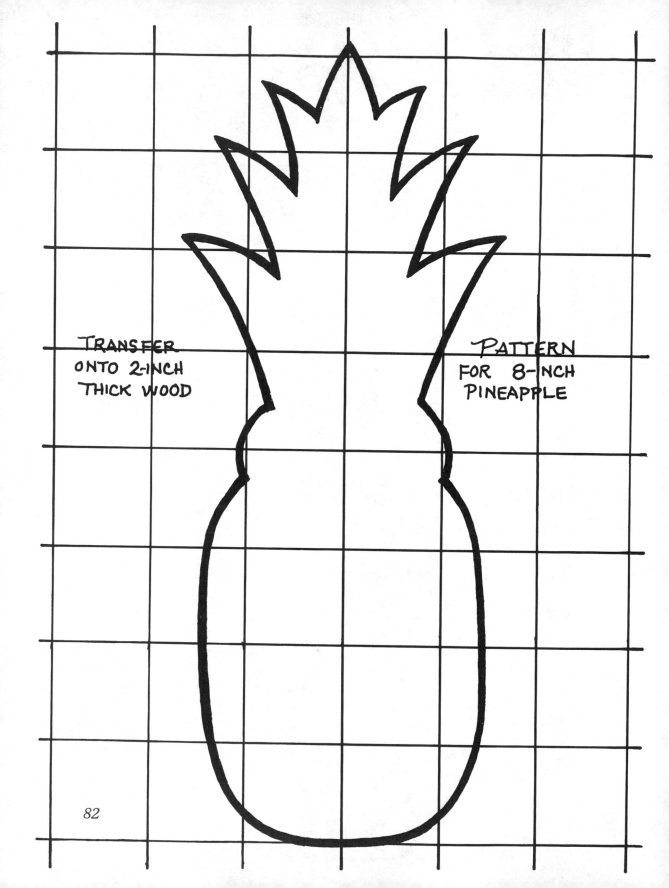

TRANSFER
ONTO 2-INCH
THICK WOOD

PATTERN
FOR 8-INCH
PINEAPPLE

82

STEP 1. SECURING THE WOOD

TO SECURE YOUR CUT OUT PATTERN WHILE CARVING, OBTAIN A PIECE OF 3/4-INCH THICK WOOD A LITTLE LARGER THAN YOUR PINE-APPLE. CENTER YOUR PINEAPPLE ON YOUR BACKBOARD & TRACE ITS OUTLINE ON THE BACKBOARD. DRILL 2 HOLES THROUGH THE BACKBOARD ABOUT 2 INCHES APART WHERE THE MIDDLE OF THE BODY WOULD LAY. SCREW THE PINEAPPLE TO THE BACKBOARD WITH 1½-INCH # 10 WOOD SCREWS (FIG. 1). AFTER THE PINEAPPLE IS SECURED TO THE BACKBOARD, IT WILL BE EASY TO CLAMP YOUR PROJECT TO A BENCH OR TABLE BY CLAMPING THE BACKBOARD. SAVE THIS BACKBOARD TO BE USED ON ANY PROJECTS THAT MAY BE DIFFICULT TO CLAMP.

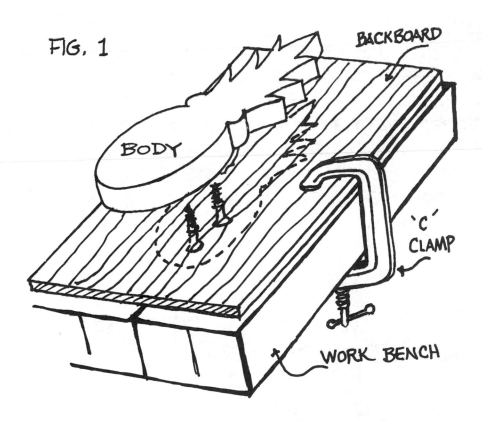

FIG. 1

BACKBOARD

BODY

'C' CLAMP

WORK BENCH

STEP 2. LOCATING THE FROND COLLAR

AFTER YOUR PINEAPPLE IS WELL SECURED TO A BACKBOARD
& CLAMPED TO A BENCH, DRAW LINES ACROSS PINEAPPLE
A TO B TO DESIGNATE FROND COLLAR. THIS FROND COLLAR
WILL REMAIN UNCARVED UNTIL THE BODY & FRONDS ARE
SHAPED (FIG. 2).

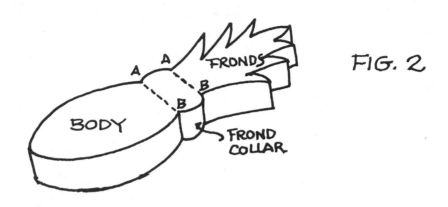

FIG. 2

STEP 3. SHAPING THE BODY

USING A FLAT CARVER'S CHISEL, MAKE A STOP CUT BY CUT-
TING STRAIGHT DOWN AT A 15° ANGLE AT THE FROND COLLAR
(FIG. 3). NOTCH CORNERS BY CARVING TOWARD STOP WITH THE
FLAT CHISEL AT A 15° ANGLE. DO NOT ATTEMPT TO DO THE
COMPLETE NOTCH IN ONE STROKE. MAKE YOUR STOP CUTS &
REMOVE THE WOOD FROM THE NOTCH A LITTLE AT A TIME
WITH MANY STROKES.

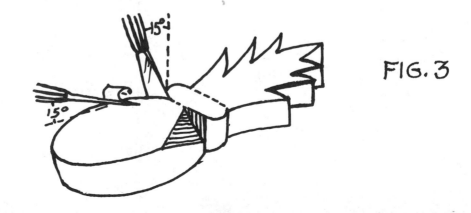

FIG. 3

STEP 4. SHAPING THE BODY (cont'd.)

CONTINUE A STOP CUT STRAIGHT DOWN AT FROND COLLAR (FIG. 4A).
CARVE AWAY WOOD (FIG. 4B) BY CARVING FLAT ON TOP OF PINE-
APPLE BODY, AT AN ANGLE TO A DEPTH OF 3/4 IN. INTO STOP
CUT. REMOVE THIS WOOD A LITTLE AT A TIME. SEE FIG. 5
FOR COMPLETED CUT.

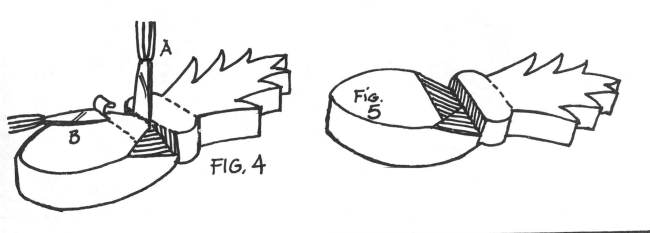

FIG. 4

Fig. 5

STEP 5. ROUNDING THE BODY

DRAW A SLIGHTLY CURVED DOTTED LINE ACROSS THE BOTTOM
OF THE PINEAPPLE (FIG. 6 A TO B). USING A FLAT CHISEL, REMOVE
WOOD FROM OUTSIDE CORNERS & WORK TOWARD CENTER (FIG. 6).
REMOVE WOOD TO FORM A SLIGHT DOME, LEAVING 1/4 INCH AT
THE PINEAPPLE BASE (FIG. 7).

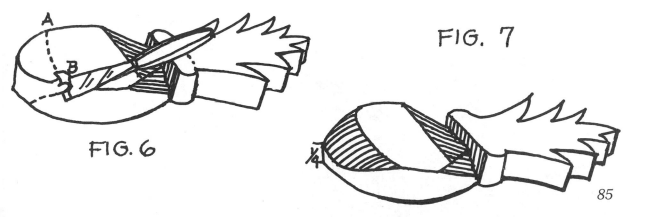

FIG. 6

FIG. 7

STEP 6. ROUNDING THE BODY (Cont'd)

USING A FLAT CHISEL, CARVE BOTH SIDES OF THE PINEAPPLE, REMOVING A FLAT WEDGE (FIG. 8) TO WITHIN ¼ INCH OF THE PINEAPPLE BASE (FIG. 9).

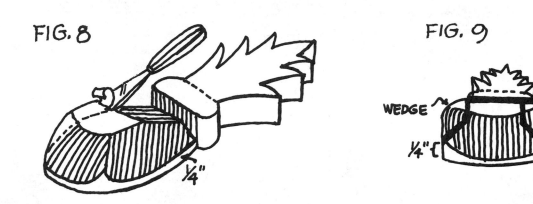

FIG. 8

FIG. 9

WEDGE

¼"

BASE

STEP 7. ROUNDING THE BODY (concluded)

THE STEPS UP TO THIS POINT ENABLE YOU TO FORM AN EVENLY ROUNDED PINEAPPLE BODY. BY REMOVING ALL PROTRUDING ANGLES, YOUR PINEAPPLE BODY SHOULD BE ROUNDING (FIG. 10). CONTINUE CARVING AWAY ALL CORNERS UNTIL YOU HAVE REMOVED ALL FLAT AREAS, BUT DO NOT CARVE AWAY THE ¼-INCH EDGE AT THE BASE. LATER IN CARVING THE DIAMOND PATTERN INTO THE PINEAPPLE BODY, THIS ¼-INCH EDGE WILL HELP PREVENT CHIPPING & SPLITTING OF DIAMONDS AT THE BODY EDGE. THIS EXTRA BULK WILL ALSO ALLOW A LITTLE EXTRA WOOD TO SHAPE EDGE DIAMONDS.

FIG. 10

STEP 8. SEPARATING THE FRONDS FROM THE COLLAR

YOUR PINEAPPLE BODY SHOULD BE COMPLETELY ROUNDED LEAVING A 1/4-INCH EDGE AROUND ITS CIRCUMFERENCE. MAKE A STOP CUT ON LINE A-B & REMOVE WOOD AT AN ANGLE (10°) STARTING AT THE EDGES OF THE FRONDS, WORKING TOWARD THE CENTER UNTIL YOU REACH A DEPTH OF 3/4 IN. AT THE FROND COLLAR (FIG. 11). DO NOT TRY TO MAKE YOUR STOP CUTS TOO DEEP. MAKE SHALLOW STOP CUTS (1/8 INCH), A LAYER AT A TIME, & CARVE AWAY WOOD NO DEEPER THAN THE STOP CUT. IF YOU TRY TO REMOVE THE WOOD DEEPER THAN YOUR STOP CUT, YOU COULD POSSIBLY SNAP OFF THE FROND COLLAR.

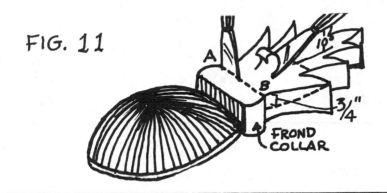

FIG. 11

STEP 9. SEPARATING THE FRONDS (Cont'd.)

AFTER YOU HAVE EXPOSED THE FROND COLLAR, DRAW A LINE ACROSS THE BASE OF THE SECOND SPIKES (FIG. 12 A to B). DRAW A CENTER LINE (FIG. 12 C to D). SHAPE THIS AREA (FIG. 12 AB to D) LEAVING A SLIGHT CONCAVE SHAPE. CARVE THIS AREA DOWN TO AN EQUAL DEPTH AS THE BODY (FIG. 13 SIDE VIEW).

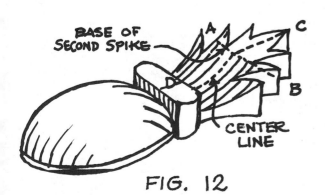

FIG. 12

FIG. 13

87

STEP 10. LOCATING THE CENTER FROND

SKETCH IN A SLIGHTLY CURVED LINE ON BOTH SIDES OF THE CENTER
LINE STARTING AT LINE A.B. (FIG. 14) TO FROND COLLAR. LEAVE
3/8-INCH SPACE ON BOTH SIDES FROM CURVED LINE TO THE EDGE.
THIS IS THE OUTLINE OF A SINGLE FROND WHICH WILL PROTRUDE
FROM THE REMAINING FRONDS.

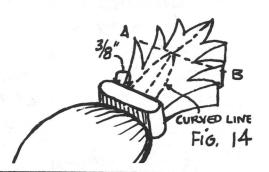

FIG. 14

STEP 11. CARVING THE CENTER FROND

MAKE STRAIGHT-DOWN STOP CUTS AROUND THE CENTER FROND & LOWER
REMAINING FROND AREA, EXPOSING THE CENTER FROND (FIG. 15).
CONTINUE DROPPING AWAY FROM THE CENTER FROND UNTIL THE
SURFACE IS 1/4 INCH LOWER THAN THE BASE OF THE CENTER FROND.
THE REMAINING FRONDS WILL BE CARVED, LAYERING DOWN FROM
THE PRECEDING ONE, UNTIL YOU REACH THE TOP FROND WHICH
WILL BE ONLY 1/4 INCH DEEP (FIG. 16 SIDE VIEW). TO ELIMINATE
MUCH EXTRA WOOD, CARVE FROM THE FROND BASE TO THE TOP
FROND (1/4 INCH DEEP), REMOVING WOOD AT THIS ANGLE (FIG. 16).

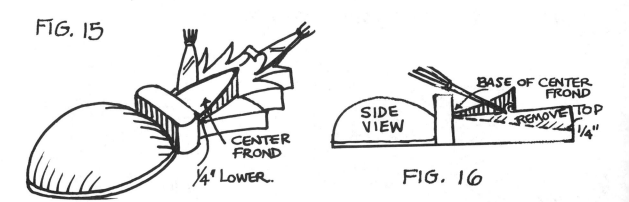

FIG. 15

FIG. 16

STEP 12. LOCATING & CARVING SEPARATE FRONDS

DRAW LINES FOLLOWING THE OUTLINE OF EACH SEPARATE FROND (FIG. 17 A). USING A CARVER'S CHISEL, MAKE STOP CUTS ALONG THESE LINES (FIG. 17 B). DRAW LINES ALONG THE CENTER OF THE EDGES BY SPLITTING THE SIDE OF EACH FROND IN HALF (FIG. 17 C), WITH THE EXCEPTION OF THE TOP FROND, WHICH IS LEFT ALONE. USING A FLAT CARVER'S CHISEL, REMOVE WOOD AT AN ANGLE FROM LINE C TO HIGH POINT A (BASE OF CENTER FROND). THERE ARE 3 SETS OF SIDE FRONDS, EACH OF WHICH IS LOWER THAN THE PREVIOUS SET. AS YOU LOWER EACH SET, YOUR SIDE CENTERLINES (C) WILL ALSO BE LOWER THAN THE PREVIOUS CENTERLINE. EACH SET OF FRONDS SHOULD BE 1/8 – 1/4 INCH LOWER THAN THE PREVIOUS SET. YOU DON'T HAVE TO BE OVER-CAUTIOUS WHEN CLEANING AROUND THE BASE OF THE CENTER FROND NOW. LATER WE WILL REMOVE WOOD FROM BEHIND THE CENTER FROND, GIVING IT A THINNER LOOK.

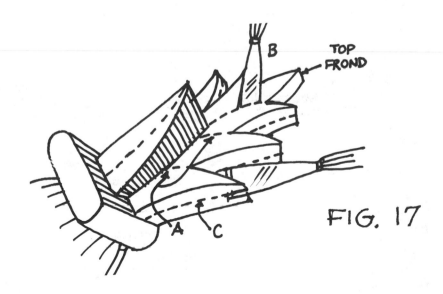

FIG. 17

STEP 13. THE FROND COLLAR & FRONDS

YOUR PINEAPPLE FRONDS SHOULD LOOK LIKE FIG.18. NOW IS THE TIME TO
FINISH SHAPING THE FROND COLLAR. SKETCH A LINE FOLLOWING THE ROUNDED
CONTOUR OF THE PINEAPPLE BODY TO WITHIN ½ INCH OF THE BODY &
FRONDS. REMOVE EXCESS WOOD TO FORM A CURVED SURFACE. AFTER
REMOVING THIS WOOD THE FROND COLLAR SHOULD LOOK LIKE FIG. 19.
ROUND THE FROND COLLAR INTO THE BODY & FRONDS (FIG. 20 A).
ARROWS SHOW ROUNDING DIRECTION. REMOVE SHADED AREA FROM
BEHIND CENTER FROND (FIG. 20) WITH A CARVER'S CHISEL BY CARVING
AWAY A VERY SMALL PIECE & REMOVING THIS PIECE WITH A STRAIGHT-
IN STOP CUT (FIG. 20 B). CONTINUE ENLARGING THIS AREA UNTIL ALL
WOOD IS REMOVED TO COINCIDE WITH SHADED AREA (FIG. 20).
REMOVE WOOD FROM THE BACK OF SIDE FRONDS AT THEIR EDGES AT
AN ANGLE UP TO YOUR SIDE CENTER LINES (FIG. 21). THIS WILL
GIVE EACH SIDE FROND A SHARP STRAIGHT EDGE WHERE THE SIDE
CENTERLINES WERE. THE DEGREE OF ANGLE USED IN REMOVING
THIS WOOD FROM THE BACK OF THE FRONDS DOESN'T MATTER AS
LONG AS A SHARP EDGE REMAINS & EACH FROND ISN'T BULKY LOOKING.

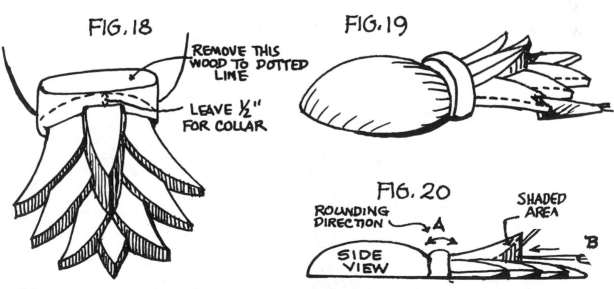

FIG. 18

REMOVE THIS
WOOD TO DOTTED
LINE

LEAVE ½"
FOR COLLAR

FIG. 19

FIG. 20

ROUNDING
DIRECTION — A

SHADED
AREA

SIDE
VIEW

B

STEP 14. FINISHING THE CENTER FROND

THE CENTER FROND WHICH IS STILL FLAT, MUST BE CARVED SO IT FALLS AWAY FROM THE CENTER LINE. START AT THE TIP OF THE CENTER FROND & CARVE EDGE (SIDE) AT ABOUT 15° ANGLE TOWARD THE FROND COLLAR (FIG. 21 A). DO THE SAME TO THE TOP FROND, BEING CAREFUL OF THE DIRECTION OF THE GRAIN (FIG. 21 B).

FIG. 21

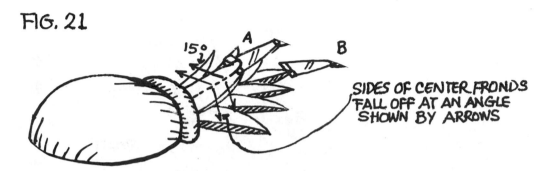

SIDES OF CENTER FRONDS FALL OFF AT AN ANGLE SHOWN BY ARROWS

STEP 15. SEPARATING THE FROND COLLAR BUNDLES

YOUR FRONDS SHOULD NOW LOOK LIKE FIG. 22. THE FROND COLLAR, WHICH IS COMPOSED OF A NUMBER OF CURLED FRONDS, IS CARVED BY CUTTING ¼-INCH WIDE, 'V' SHAPED SLOTS EVERY ⅜ IN. START AT THE CENTER LINE & LINE UP THE FIRST ⅜ INCH BUNDLE WITH THE CENTER FROND & SKIP ¼ INCH BEFORE MARKING IN YOUR NEXT ⅜-INCH BUNDLES, WORKING AWAY FROM THE CENTER. IF YOU END UP WITH ONLY HALF OR PART OF A BUNDLE AT THE EDGE, THAT'S O.K. (FIG 22).

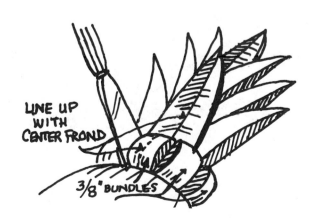

LINE UP WITH CENTER FROND

⅜" BUNDLES

FIG. 22

STEP 16. SHAPING THE FROND COLLAR CURLED FRONDS

EACH OF THESE INDIVIDUAL BUNDLES WILL BECOME A SEPARATE CURLED FROND. TO SHAPE THESE FRONDS, BRING EACH OF THESE BUNDLES TO A POINT ON THE BODY SIDE & CONTINUE THE DEEP 'V' CUT DOWN THE TOP OF THE FROND COLLARS (FIG. 23). CUT DOWN STRAIGHT & REMOVE WOOD FOLLOWING THE CONTOUR OF THE BODY AT THE POINTED FROND END.

FIG. 23

CONTOUR OF THE BODY

POINTED FROND END

STEP 17. CARVING THE CURLED FRONDS

FIG. 24 SHOWS THE ROUNDNESS OF THE GOUGE NEEDED TO CARVE THE FINISHED FROND. CARVE THE CENTER OF EACH FROND BUNDLE CONCAVE WITH YOUR GOUGE, TOWARD THE UPPER FRONDS. STARTING AT THE HIGHEST POINT ON THE FROND COLLAR (WHICH WOULD BE THE CENTER LINE), GO TOWARD THE BODY BY CARVING AWAY FROM THE CENTER LINE (FIG 25 A). WHEN CARVING THE TOP OF THE FROND BUNDLES (FIG. 25B) CONTINUE YOUR CUT RIGHT INTO THE TOP FRONDS, SNIPPING WOOD AS CLEAN AS POSSIBLY AT THE BASE OF THE TOP FRONDS.

FIG. 24

YOU CAN USE A GOUGE ANY SIZE BETWEEN THE SIZES SHOWN BY ABOVE DOTTED LINES.

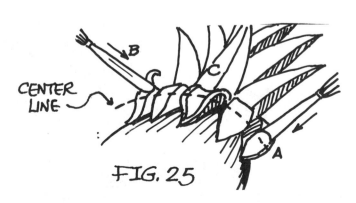

CENTER LINE

FIG. 25

STEP 18. FINISHING THE CURLED FRONDS

WHEN FINISHING THE CURLED FRONDS, THE GROOVE MADE BY YOUR HALF-ROUND SHOULD BE EVEN & SMOOTH. DO NOT CARVE YOUR GROOVE SO IT REACHES THE EDGE OF EACH CURLED FROND. LEAVE ABOUT 1/16 INCH FLAT ON EACH SIDE (FIG. 26). EACH FROND HAS TO BE TRIMMED TO ITS OUTSIDE SHAPE. USE FIG. 26 AS A GUIDE TO SHAPE EACH CURLED FROND.

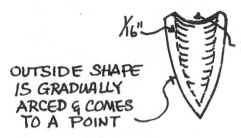

1/16"

OUTSIDE SHAPE IS GRADUALLY ARCED & COMES TO A POINT

FIT GOUGE TO THIS ARC

FIG. 26

STEP 19. LAYOUT OF DIAMOND PATTERN

SKETCH IN CENTERLINE A-B AND CENTERLINE C-D TO ESTABLISH THE CENTER OF THE PINEAPPLE BODY. ALL THE LAYOUT OF THE DIAMONDS WILL DEPEND ON HOW WELL CENTERED YOUR INITIAL LINES ARE. USING THE EXACT CENTER, SKETCH IN 2 SETS OF PARALLEL LINES CROSSING EACH OTHER DIAGONALLY. SKETCH THESE PARALLEL LINES WITH THE CENTER OF THE BODY MIDWAY BETWEEN EACH SET OF PARALLEL LINES. THESE LINES ARE ABOUT 5/8 IN. APART ON THIS SIZE PINEAPPLE & WILL FORM A 5/8-INCH SQUARE IN THE CENTER OF THE BODY (SEE FIG. 27).

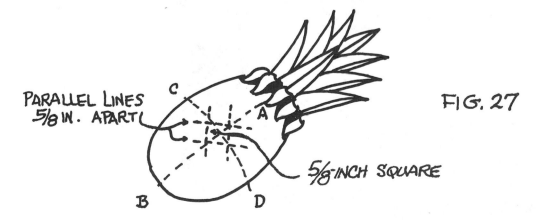

PARALLEL LINES 5/8 IN. APART

FIG. 27

5/8-INCH SQUARE

STEP 20. LAYOUT OF DIAMOND STRIPES

FROM YOUR CROSSED PARALLEL LINES, SKETCH IN CONTINUATIONS OF THESE LINES, BEING SURE THEY CURVE AS YOU GO AWAY FROM THE CENTER OF THE BODY (FIG. 28). BECAUSE THE PINEAPPLE IS ROUNDED, IT WOULD BE A CHORE TO DEVISE A PATTERN FOR THE BODY DIAMONDS. SO GETTING THE PROPER SHAPE, SIZE & ALIGNMENT IS DONE MOSTLY BY EYE. LIGHTLY SKETCH IN YOUR CONTINUOUS LINES STARTING AT YOUR 5/8 INCH CENTER SQUARE. AS YOU GO AWAY FROM THE CENTER THE DIAMONDS BECOME SMALLER, SO YOUR PARALLEL LINES ARE A LITTLE CLOSER TOGETHER. SKETCH IN THE REMAINING LINES (FORMING STRIPES) BY SKIPPING EVERY OTHER ONE. THE REST ARE FILLED IN AFTER A NUMBER OF CORRECTIONS TO GET THE STRIPES BALANCED EQUALLY. AFTER ALL THE STRIPES ARE DRAWN ON THE BODY, DIAMOND SHAPES ARE FORMED WHERE THEY CROSS EACH OTHER. CHECK EACH DIAMOND FOR EQUAL SHAPE. THE DIAMONDS NEAR THE EDGE MAY BE MORE ELONGATED, BUT IF THEY ARE SYM-METRICAL, THAT'S O.K. USE FIG. 28 FOR A GUIDE FOR THE CURVE OF THE STRIPES.

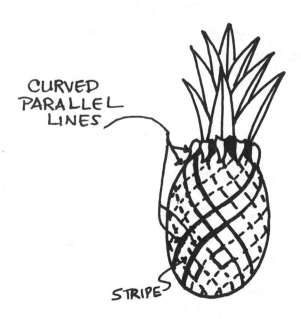

CURVED
PARALLEL
LINES

FIG. 28

STRIPE

STEP 21. CARVING THE STRIPES

USING A 'V' PARTING TOOL, SCORE ALL CRISSCROSSING LINES ¼ INCH DEEP. WORK FROM THE CENTER OF THE BODY OFF THE PINEAPPLE TOWARD THE EDGE AS IF FALLING OFF A HILL (FIG. 29). IF YOU TRY TO SCORE THESE LINES IN ONE DIRECTION IN ONE STROKE, YOU WILL BE GOING AGAINST THE GRAIN FOR HALF YOUR STROKE. EVEN CARVING WITH THE GRAIN, USING A PARTING TOOL, YOU WILL EXPERIENCE TEARING OF THE WOOD ON ONE SIDE OR THE OTHER OF YOUR CUT. NOT TO WORRY, WE HAVE JUST BEGUN TO SHAPE THE DIAMONDS.

FIG. 29

STEP 22. SHAPING THE DIAMONDS

USING A CARVER'S CHISEL, MAKE STRAIGHT-DOWN STOP CUTS IN THE CENTER OF ALL PARTING TOOL GROOVES (FIG. 30). MAKE STOP CUTS (FIG. 30A) & CARVE ONE SIDE OF ALL STRIPES (FIG. 30B). SEE ENLARGED DIAGRAM FIG. 31 FOR RESULTS. NOTICE YOU CARVE AWAY YOUR CENTER LINE. YOU DO NOT START YOUR CUT DIRECTLY ON THE CENTER LINE. IF YOU DO, THE PEAK OF THE DIAMONDS WILL BE TOO HIGH, MAKING YOUR PINEAPPLE LOOK LIKE A HAND GRE-NADE.

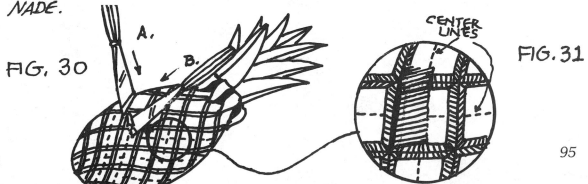

FIG. 30

A.

B.

CENTER LINES

FIG. 31

95

STEP 23. CARVING THE DIAMONDS

YOU ARE NOW READY TO CARVE THE REMAINING 2 SIDES OF EACH DIAMOND. ROUGHLY BRING EACH DIAMOND TO A POINTED PEAK AT THE DIAMOND CENTERS, FORMING SMALL PYRAMIDS, (FIG. 32). BE CAREFUL TO STAY WITH THE GRAIN. IF YOU GO AGAINST THE GRAIN YOU WILL PROBABLY CHIP OR TEAR THE CORNERS OF THE DIAMONDS. ALWAYS FOLLOW THE ORIGINAL PARTING TOOL LINES BY CARVING AS MUCH OF EACH STRIPE IN A LINE. IF YOU TRY TO SHAPE THE DIAMONDS INDIVIDUALLY PRIOR TO CARVING ALL YOUR STRIPES FIRST, YOUR DIAMONDS WILL LOOK CROOKED, & YOU WILL LOSE YOUR SYMMETRICAL STRIPE LINES.

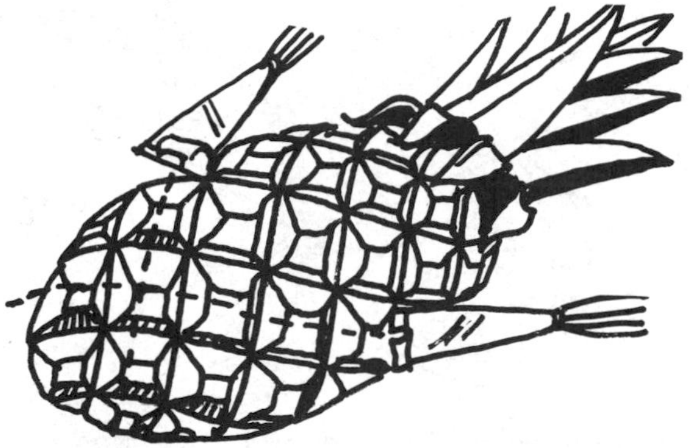

FIG. 32

STEP 24. CARVING THE DIAMONDS (Cont'd)

WITH YOUR CARVER'S CHISEL, MAKE CLEAN STOP CUTS TO SEPARATE THE DIAMONDS CLEANLY. CHECK EACH ANGLE OF ALL DIAMONDS MAKING SURE EACH DIAMOND HAS EQUAL TRIANGULAR SIDES & COMES TO A POINT AT ITS CENTER (FIG. 33). IT IS USUALLY NECESSARY TO RE-CARVE EACH DIAMOND ONE AT A TIME TO MAKE THEM PERFECTLY EQUAL.

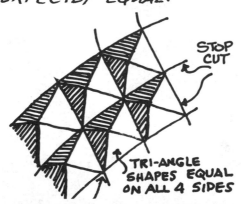

STOP CUT

FIG. 33

TRI-ANGLE SHAPES EQUAL ON ALL 4 SIDES

STEP 25. CARVING THE DIAMONDS (concluded)

TO CLEAN UP THE AREA WHERE THE DIAMONDS MEET THE FROND COLLAR, KEEP THE EDGES (SIDE WALLS) OF EACH CURLED FROND CLEANLY CUT STRAIGHT DOWN, LEAVING A FLAT WALL. CONTINUE TO CARVE AS MUCH OF THE DIAMONDS BETWEEN THE CURLED FRONDS AS YOU CAN REACH (FIG. 34). REMOVE ALL SPLINTERS & LOOSE PIECES OF WOOD BETWEEN THE CURLED FROND WITH THE POINT OF A JACKKNIFE.

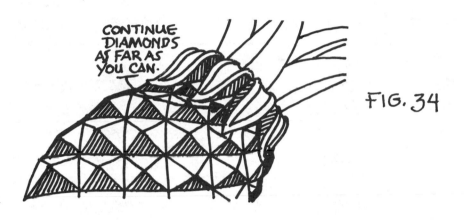

CONTINUE DIAMONDS AS FAR AS YOU CAN.

FIG. 34

STEP 26. CARVING FROND NOTCHES

USING THE PARTING TOOL, CARVE NOTCHES IN THE TOP FRONDS (FIG. 35). CARVE 2 OR 3 GROOVES AT RANDOM ON EACH SIDE OF EACH FROND. DO NOT MAKE THESE GROOVES EQUAL ON BOTH SIDES, CUT THESE TO DIFFERENT LENGTHS & FOLLOW THE SWEEP OF EACH FROND.

FIG. 35

STEP 27. CLEANING UP YOUR CARVING

YOUR PINEAPPLE IS NOW COMPLETELY CARVED. ALL THAT REMAINS IS YOUR FINAL CLEAN UP. CHECK ALL THE DIAMONDS FOR ANY LOPSIDED OR UNEQUAL ANGLES. CLEAN OUT AREAS BETWEEN CURLED FRONDS OF THE FROND COLLAR & WHERE THE FROND COLLAR MEETS THE TOP FRONDS. ANY CHIPS OF WOOD OR SPLINTERS WILL BE DIFFICULT TO REMOVE AFTER YOU HAVE STARTED YOUR FINISHING. CHECK ALL FRONDS & EDGES OF THE BODY DIAMONDS FOR CHIPPED OR BROKEN EDGES. OFTEN IT IS NECESSARY TO RE-CARVE THESE DAMAGED AREAS.

STEP 28. FINISHING

THERE ARE A NUMBER OF METHODS IN FINISHING YOUR PINEAPPLE. IT WILL DEPEND ON WHERE YOU PLAN TO HANG IT. IT WOULD'NT LOOK RIGHT TO HANG A DARK-STAINED PINEAPPLE ON A DARK-STAINED WALL OR DOOR. SELECT YOUR FINISH SO THE PINEAPPLE HAS CONTRAST TO WHERE IT'S TO BE HUNG. TWO DIFFERENTLY COLORED STAINS THAT BLEND WELL TOGETHER ARE WALNUT ON THE BODY & LIGHT OAK ON THE FRONDS & COLLAR. A GREEN STAIN ON THE FRONDS (MADE WITH UNIVERSAL TINTING COLORS - SEE TEXT) & WALNUT ON THE BODY LOOK NATURAL. GOLD LEAF & BRONZING POWDERS CAN ALSO BE USED FOR A RICHER LOOK. WHEN YOU HAVE COMPLETED YOUR FINISHING, PAINT THE EDGES OF THE CURLED FRONDS WITH BLACK PAINT. THIS WILL GIVE MORE DEPTH & HELP CRISP UP THE CONTRAST BETWEEN THE BODY & FRONDS (FIG. 36).

FIG. 36

PAINT EDGES OF FROND COLLAR WITH BLACK

CARVING A
Least Sandpiper

Project No. 2

DECORATIVE
&
DECOY

TOOLS NEEDED

JACKKNIFE
HALF·ROUND GOUGE (FIG. 42)
FISHTAIL GOUGE
PARTING TOOL
ELECTRIC BURNING PEN

·Decorative·
Feather carving
Raised wing tips
Glass eyes
Wood feet & legs
ornamental base

Decoy·
Simplicity with a smooth
body & lustrous finish.
Excellent for a home
decoration

TOOLS NEEDED

JACKKNIFE
HALF·ROUND GOUGE

(FIG. 9)

Least Sandpiper PATTERN

THIS PATTERN WILL MAKE A LIFESIZE CARVING OF A
LEAST SANDPIPER, SMALLEST OF NORTH AMERICAN SHOREBIRDS.
IT IS COMMON THROUGHOUT NORTH AMERICA, SEEN ALONG
MANY BEACHES & MUD FLATS.

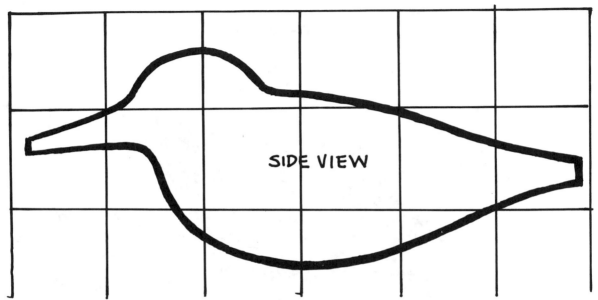

SIDE VIEW

BANDSAW SIDE VIEW FIRST FROM 2-INCH THICK WOOD. THEN
TRANSFER TOP VIEW OUTLINE TO WOOD & SAW TO SHAPE.

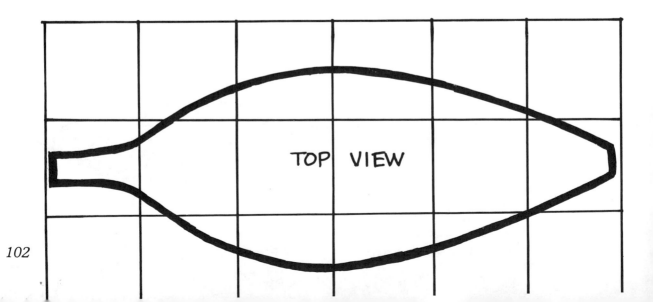

TOP VIEW

THIS PROJECT IS ACTUALLY 2 PROJECTS IN ONE. YOU WILL LEARN HOW TO CARVE A SIMPLE ORNAMENTAL DECOY, THEN ADVANCE INTO CARVING THE MORE COMPLICATED DECORATIVE BIRD.

STEP 1.   SHAPING THE BODY.

WITH A SHARP JACKKNIFE, USE THE CARVING AWAY METHOD, CARVE FROM THE BACK OF THE HEAD & NECK AT A 45° ANGLE TOWARD THE TAIL. DO THIS ON BOTH SIDES OF THE BACK (FIG. 1). DO THE SAME CUT FROM THE BREAST TO THE TAIL ON BOTH SIDES. FRONT VIEW (FIG. 2) SHOWS THE WOOD TO BE REMOVED ON THE 4 CORNERS. THIS WILL LEAVE THE BODY SECTION WITH AN OCTAGON SHAPE. REMOVING THE WOOD EQUALLY ON 4 SIDES WILL ALLOW MORE EQUAL ROUNDING IN THE NEXT STEP. FIG. 3 SHOWS YOU THE RESULTS OF THIS STEP.

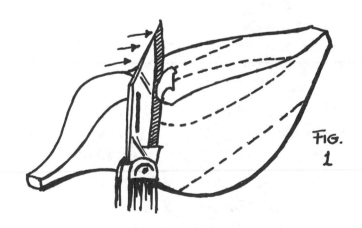

FIG. 1

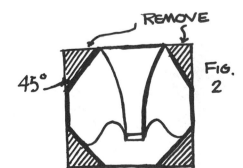

REMOVE

45°

FIG. 2

FIG. 3

STEP 2. ROUNDING THE BODY

EVENLY ROUND THE BODY BY TAKING THE CORNERS OFF YOUR PRECEDING CUTS & CONTINUE TO CARVE AWAY ALL SHARP CORNERS UNTIL THE WOOD FEELS ROUND. AS YOU ROUND TOWARD THE TAIL MAKE THE END OF THE TAIL POINTED. IF THIS CARVING IS DONE PROPERLY THE BODY WILL BE WELL ROUNDED WITHOUT ANY FLAT AREAS OR SAW MARKS AS IN FIG. 4.

FIG. 4

STEP 3. ROUNDING THE HEAD & NECK

TURN YOUR BIRD AROUND & HOLD BODY TO CARVE AWAY ON BREAST. CARVE AT A 45° ANGLE ON BOTH SIDES & REMOVE WOOD FROM BREAST ALL THE WAY TO THE END OF THE BEAK (FIG. 5). BE CAREFUL FOR A CHANGE IN THE GRAIN. IF THE WOOD STARTS SPLITTING AWAY FROM THE BEAK, TRY CARVING TOWARD YOU. REMOVE A SMALL 45° ANGLE PIECE FROM THE TOP OF THE HEAD, CONTINUING DOWN TO THE END OF THE BEAK. YOUR BEAK SHOULD HAVE AN OCTAGONAL SHAPE AT ITS EXTREME END.

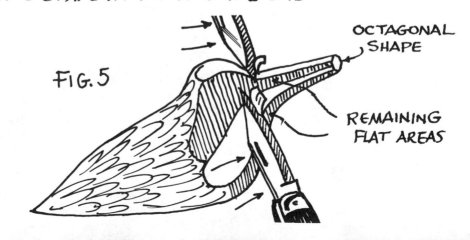

FIG. 5

OCTAGONAL SHAPE

REMAINING FLAT AREAS

STEP 4. ROUNDING HEAD & NECK CONCLUDED

BY CARVING AWAY, ROUND NECK INTO BREAST (FIG. 6). BY CARVING TOWARD YOU, ROUND THE TOP OF THE HEAD, DOWN THE NECK, ONTO THE BACK. DO NOT WORK ON THE BEAK AREA YET. THE BODY, NECK & BREAST SHOULD BE EVENLY ROUNDED & READY FOR SANDING. IF YOU WISH TO CARVE THE MORE DIFFICULT DECORATIVE BIRD, SANDING WILL NOT BE NECESSARY.

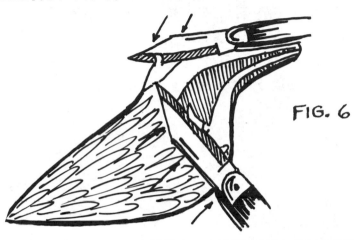

FIG. 6

STEP 5. ACCENTING THE SHOULDERS

IN THE AREA WHERE THE NECK COMES INTO THE BODY, ON BOTH SIDES CARVE A CONCAVE DEPRESSION WHICH NARROWS THE NECK & ACCENTS WHERE THE FOLDED WINGS WOULD BE ON THE BODY. CONTINUE AROUND THE BACK OF THE NECK CARVING SHALLOWER THAN THE SIDE CUTS (FIG. 7). YOUR NECK SHAPING SHOULD LOOK LIKE FIG. 8.

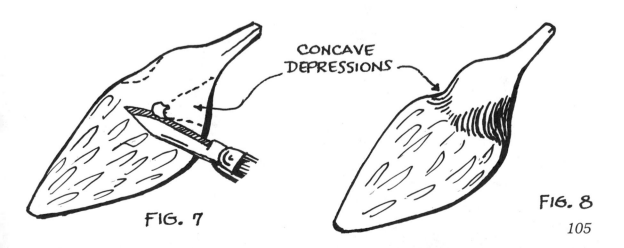

CONCAVE DEPRESSIONS

FIG. 7

FIG. 8

105

STEP 6. SHAPING THE BACK

USING A SMALL HALF-ROUND GOUGE (FIG. 9) CARVE A GROOVE AT THE BASE OF BOTH SIDES OF THE NECK (FIG. 10). CARVE A SIMILAR GROOVE DOWN THE MIDDLE OF THE BACK MAKING THE DEPTH LESS AS YOU NEAR THE TAIL. THIS CUT DOES NOT GO ALL THE WAY TO THE TIP OF THE TAIL. ROUND OVER ALL EDGES FORMED BY YOUR GOUGE EVENLY WITH YOUR JACKKNIFE. AT THE BASE OF THE NECK THERE IS A LITTLE HOLLOW AREA. CARVE DOWN THE BACK OF THE NECK (FIG. 11) REMOVING THE BULK OF THE WOOD FORMED BY YOUR HALF ROUND AT THE INTERSECTING 'Y.' THIS ROUNDING WILL ACCENT THE BULK OF THE BIRD'S WINGS.

FIG. 9

USE ANY SIZE HALF ROUND BETWEEN 2 SIZES SHOWN ABOVE

REFER TO TEXT ON PROCEDURE OF HOW TO HOLD & USE YOUR GOUGE SAFELY

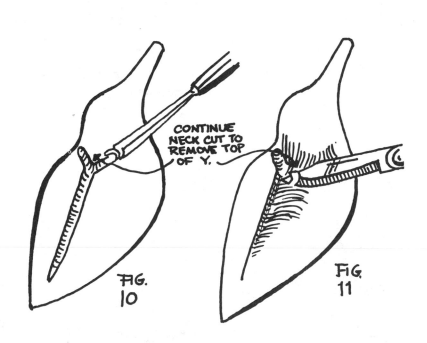

CONTINUE NECK CUT TO REMOVE TOP OF Y.

FIG. 10

FIG. 11

STEP 7. MAKING THE EYE POCKETS

CARVING WITH YOUR JACKKNIFE, MAKE A DEPRESSION ON BOTH SIDES OF THE HEAD (FIG.12 & 13). THIS DEPRESSION SHOULD BE SLIGHTLY CONCAVE (FRONT VIEW FIG.13). YOU MAY HAVE TO USE MORE OF THE KNIFE POINT TO MAKE THIS CUT. IF YOU USE TOO MUCH OF THE WIDER PART OF THE BLADE YOU WILL BE UNABLE TO TURN THE KNIFE TO ACHIEVE THIS DEPRESSION. ROUND OVER THE TOP OF THE HEAD & CHEEKS INTO THIS DEPRESSION ELIMINATING ANY SHARP EDGES.

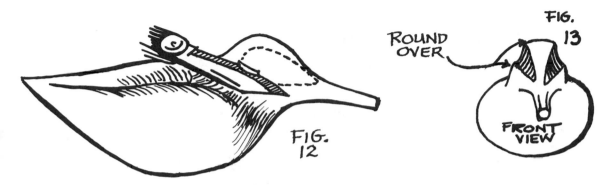

FIG. 12

ROUND OVER

FIG. 13

FRONT VIEW

STEP 8. SHAPING THE NECK & BEAK

CARVE DOWN THE BACK OF THE NECK (FIG.14A) FROM THE TOP OF THE HEAD & SHAPE INTO THE SHOULDER AREA, SLIGHTLY CONCAVE AROUND THE BASE OF THE NECK. THIS SHAPING WILL SLIGHTLY NARROW THE NECK FROM THE BODY. CARVE FROM THE FORWARD END OF THE EYE DEPRESSION DOWN THE BEAK AT AN ANGLE (FIG.14B) SO WHEN BOTH SIDES ARE DONE THE TOP OF THE BEAK WILL COME TO A SHARP EDGE (FIG.15). DO THE SAME TO THE UNDERSIDE OF THE BEAK. FIG. 16 WILL SHOW THE END VIEW OF THE BEAK. THIS DIAMOND SHAPE CONTINUES TO THE HEAD.

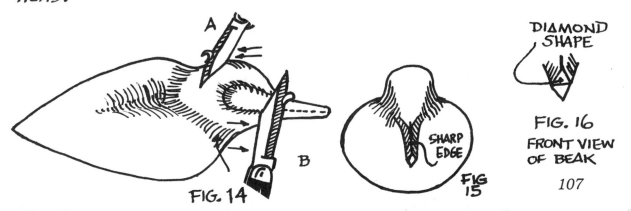

A

B

FIG. 14

SHARP EDGE

FIG 15

DIAMOND SHAPE

FIG. 16 FRONT VIEW OF BEAK

107

STEP 9. FINISHING THE BEAK & EYES

WE ARE NEARING COMPLETION OF THE DECOY CARVING. IF YOU WISH TO CONTINUE TO CARVE THE MORE LIFELIKE DECORATIVE BIRD, MOVE TO PAGE 111. THE DECORATIVE CARVING WILL HAVE GLASS EYES, AN ORNAMENTAL BASE, CARVED LEGS & FEET & INDIVIDUALLY CARVED FEATHERS.

ROUND OVER THE END OF THE BEAK (FIG. 17) & BRING THE TIP OF THE BEAK TO A POINT. FROM THE TOP VIEW BRING THE BEAK TO A POINT (FIG. 18). MARK IN THE LOCATION OF THE NOSTRILS BY USING FIG. 17 & 18 AS A GUIDE. TO CARVE THESE NOSTRILS GO TO PAGE 118. SAND THE BEAK, USING YOUR SANDPAPER TO HELP SHAPE THE RAISED EDGES SO THEY ARE STRAIGHT.

WE WILL ONLY MAKE AN IMPRESSION FOR EYES FOR THE DECOY. IF YOU WISH TO INSERT GLASS EYES IN YOUR DECOY GO TO STEP 15 PAGE 119. TO LOCATE WHERE TO MAKE EYES, USE FIG. 17 & DRAW A LINE TO FOLLOW NOSTRIL LINE ALONG THE SIDES OF THE HEAD. DRAW A LINE UP THE HEAD FROM THE CORNER OF THE UPPER & LOWER BEAK JOINT. YOUR EYES ARE LOCATED IN THE MIDDLE OF THE NOSTRIL & BEHIND THE BEAK LINES. TO MAKE THE EYE DEPRESSIONS USE A PIECE OF 3/16-INCH HOLLOW TUBING & PUSH HARD IN EYE LOCATION & IT WILL DEPRESS A ROUND GROOVE, FORMING THE CIRCUMFERENCE OF THE EYE.

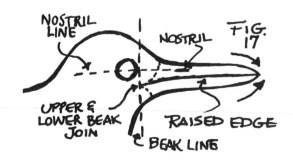

NOSTRIL LINE — NOSTRIL — FIG. 17

UPPER & LOWER BEAK JOIN — RAISED EDGE — BEAK LINE

RAISED EDGE — TOP VIEW FIG. 18

STEP 10. SANDING

TO COMPLETE THE DECOY, THE ENTIRE PIECE MUST BE SANDED. FOLD YOUR SANDPAPER IN THIRDS (FIG. 19) TO FIT THE DIFFERENT SHAPES & CONTOURS OF THE BODY (**FIG. 19A**). THIS METHOD WILL ENABLE YOU TO REMOVE RIDGES & DEPRESSIONS SMOOTHLY. EACH CARVING YOU DO MAY REQUIRE SANDING & PROPER SANDING WILL HELP YOU AS A FINISH-SHAPING TOOL. THIS DECOY SHOULD BE SMOOTH WITH NO CARVING MARKS LEFT ON IT.

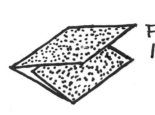

FIG. 19

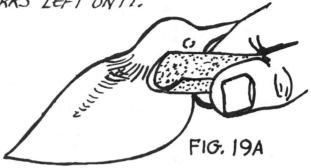

FIG. 19A

STEP 11. MOUNTING

THERE ARE MANY WAYS TO MOUNT A DECOY. IN THIS CASE WE ARE USING A CROSS SECTION OF NATURAL WOOD 3 INCHES IN DIAMETER, ABOUT 3/4 INCHES **THICK**. DRILL A 1/4-INCH HOLE IN THE CENTER OF THE BOTTOM OF THE BODY ABOUT 1/2-INCH DEEP. THE ANGLE DRILLED WILL DETERMINE THE ATTITUDE OF THE DECOY. BE SURE WHEN DRILLING THAT THE HOLE ISN'T CROOKED SIDE TO SIDE. DRILL A 1/4-INCH HOLE IN THE CENTER OF YOUR BASE. CUT 3 INCHES OF 1/4-INCH DOWEL & GLUE BIRD TO BASE.

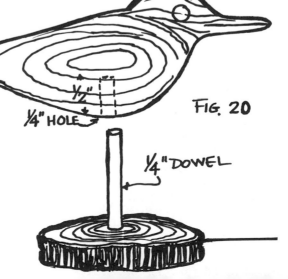

1/2"

1/4" HOLE

FIG. 20

1/4" DOWEL

STEP. 12. STAINING & FINISH

NOW THAT YOUR SANDPIPER IS MOUNTED, IT'S TIME TO DECIDE ON ITS COLORS. TRADITIONALLY DECOYS WERE GIVEN A COAT OF STAIN & THATS ALL. THERE ARE MORE INTERESTING STAIN COMBINATIONS THAT CAN BE USED. PICKING AN OILSTAIN SUCH AS WALNUT OR MAPLE WILL DEPEND ON WHERE YOUR DECOY WILL FINALLY REST.

YOU CAN STAIN THE ENTIRE PIECE ONE COLOR, OR STAIN THE BIRD & DOWEL ONE COLOR & THE BASE ANOTHER, OR LEAVE THE BASE OR BIRD NATURAL. AFTER STAINING, WIPE WITH A CLOTH TO REMOVE EXCESS STAIN. ALLOW TO DRY OVERNIGHT. THERE SHOULD BE A FEW COATS OF FINISH SEALER APPLIED OVER THE STAIN TO MAKE THE CARVING EASIER TO CLEAN & DUST. TRY A SATIN OR GLOSS POLYURETHANE & APPLY AT LEAST 3 COATS TO THE ENTIRE PIECE, SANDING LIGHTLY WITH FINE SANDPAPER BETWEEN COATS. BECAUSE OF THE SHAPE OF THIS PIECE YOU MAY HAVE RUNS OR DRIPS IN YOUR FINISH. BE A LITTLE EXTRA CAREFUL WHEN APPLYING YOUR POLYURETHANE BY NOT BRUSHING ON TOO HEAVILY YOUR COATS.

THE DECORATIVE SANDPIPER (MORE ADVANCED & DIFFICULT) continued from Step 9, page 108.

TO DO A GOOD JOB ON ANY DECORATIVE CARVING KNOWING YOUR SUBJECT IS MOST IMPORTANT. IT WOULD BE HELPFUL TO RESEARCH THE BIRD YOU ARE DOING. A MOUNTED BIRD OR ITS SKIN IS GREAT BUT HARD TO FIND. ACTUAL PHOTOS ARE EXCELLENT, BUT ONLY SHOW ONE VIEW OF THE BIRD, SO A COMBINATION OF DIFFERENT VIEWS ARE NEEDED. BOOKS & MAGAZINES CAN BE HELPFUL IN FILLING IN THOSE VIEWS THAT YOU MAY NEED.

STEP 1. EXPOSING THE WINGS

DRAW LINES ON BOTH SIDES OF THE BODY TO DESIGNATE WHERE THE WINGS ARE (USE FIG. 1 for reference). MAKE SURE THE LINES ARE SIMILAR & BALANCED. MAKE A STOP CUT ALONG THIS WING LINE WITH THE POINT OF YOUR JACKKNIFE. REMOVE WOOD FROM BODY ABOUT 1/8 INCH DEEP ALONG WING LINE. THIS WILL LEAVE THE WINGS RELIEVED FROM THE BODY & WILL LEAVE FLAT AREAS ON THE SIDES OF THE BODY WHICH ARE RE-ROUNDED (FIG. 2).

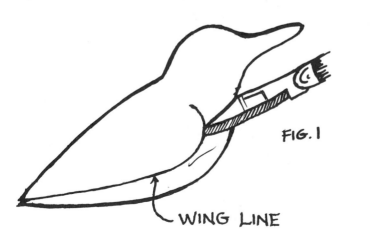

FIG. 1

WING LINE

FIG. 2

STEP 2. FEATHERING

FOLLOW THE FEATHER PATTERN ON FIG. 3 & 4. DRAW IN ALL
FEATHERS ILLUSTRATED. NOTICE THE DISTINCT LINES OF
FEATHERS. DOTTED LINES A TO B REPRESENT THE WING COVERTS
DOTTED LINE C IS THE SECONDARY COVERTS. LINE D IS
THE SECONDARY FEATHERS. THE END GROUP OF FEATHERS
ARE THE PRIMARIES.

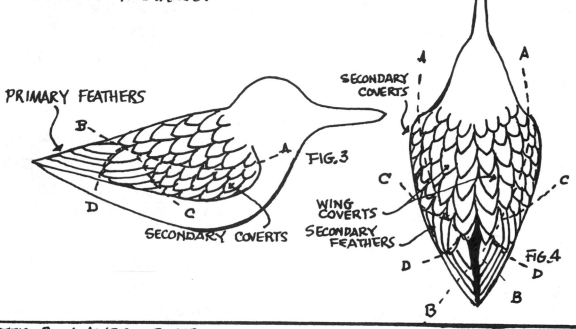

STEP 3. LAYERING FEATHERS

FOLLOW YOUR PENCILED-IN FEATHERS WITH THE POINT OF YOUR
PEN BLADE. GO AROUND ALL FEATHERS WORKING FROM THE
NECK TOWARD THE TAIL (FIG. 5A). REMOVE 1/16 INCH FROM
BEHIND EACH FEATHER, GIVING THE FEATHERS A SHINGLED
LOOK (FIG. 5B).

FIG. 5

STEP 4. SHAPING THE WING COVERT FEATHERS

THESE FEATHERS ARE SHAPED WITH YOUR JACKKNIFE (FIG. 6) BY LOWERING EACH FEATHER'S EDGE TO A FEATHER THICKNESS, LEAVING THE CENTER OF EACH FEATHER RAISED, FORMING A SLIGHT DOME. **FIGS.** 7 & 8 SHOW CLOSE UP OF RESULTS OF SHAPING THESE FEATHERS.

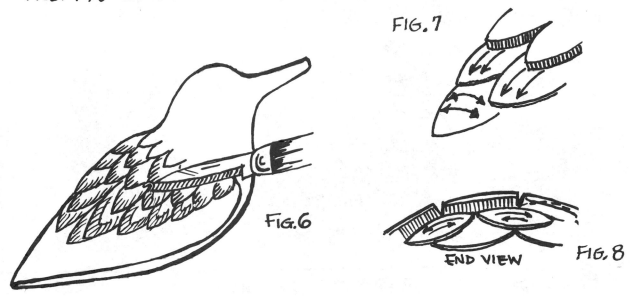

FIG. 7

FIG. 6

END VIEW   FIG. 8

STEP 5. SHAPING THE SECONDARY COVERTS

SHAPE THIS GROUP OF FEATHERS AS YOU DID FOR THE WING COVERTS (FIG. 6) EXCEPT THE DOMED EFFECT HERE IS LESS PRONOUNCED (A LITTLE FLATTER). THE FIRST FEW COURSES OF THESE FEATHERS NEAR THE FRONT EDGE OF THE WING ARE SMALL & MORE ROUNDED & AS YOU GO BACK TOWARD THE TAIL BECOME MORE POINTED (FIG. 9).

FIG. 9

113

STEP 6. SHAPING THE SECONDARY FEATHERS

THESE FEATHERS ARE LAYERED ON ONE SIDE ONLY. FROM THE BACK, LAYER EACH FEATHER LOWER THAN THE PRECEDING ONE, AS IF WALKING DOWN STEPS (FIG. 10 & 11). THIS LAYERING IS A LITTLE DEEPER THAN THE COVERT FEATHERS. THESE FEATHERS ARE FLAT WITHOUT A DOME.

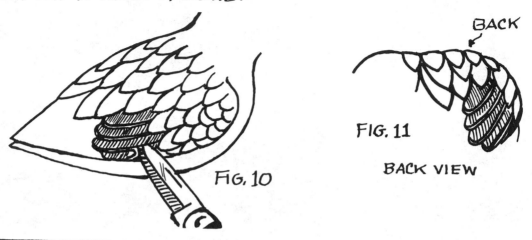

FIG. 10

BACK

FIG. 11

BACK VIEW

STEP 7. SHAPING THE PRIMARY FEATHERS

LAYER THESE FEATHERS AS YOU DID THE SECONDARY FEATHERS. CARVE FROM THE BACK, LAYERING DOWN TO THE WING EDGE. MAKE THIS LAYERING BARELY DEFINED AS THESE ARE THE LARGE WING FEATHERS & LAY VERY CLOSE TO EACH OTHER (FIG. 12 FOR RESULTS).

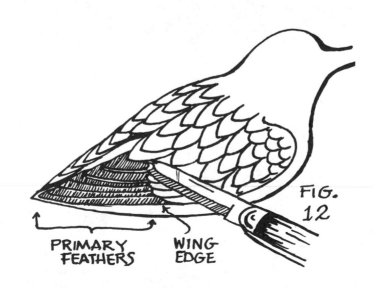

FIG. 12

PRIMARY FEATHERS

WING EDGE

114

STEP 8. FINISHING PRIMARY ENDS

THERE IS A SPACE BETWEEN THE 2 SETS OF PRIMARY FEATHERS THAT WILL BE REMOVED TO THE DEPTH OF THE BODY. DRAW THE INSIDE SHAPE OF THE PRIMARIES REFERRING TO FIG. 13. CARVE STRAIGHT DOWN ALONG THE INSIDE EDGES (FIG. 13 A) & REMOVE SMALL PIECES OF WOOD AT AN ANGLE ON BOTH SIDES OF INNER EDGES OF PRIMARIES UNTIL YOU HAVE A DEPRESSED SPACE BETWEEN PRIMARIES. TO MAKE THESE INSIDE EDGES LOOK THIN, REMOVE A SMALL PIECE OF WOOD ALONG THESE EDGES BY UNDERCUTTING TO THE THICKNESS OF A FEATHER. DO NOT CUT DEEP INTO THE BODY SECTION. REMOVE THIS WOOD TO FOLLOW THE CONTOUR OF THE BODY (FIG. 14).

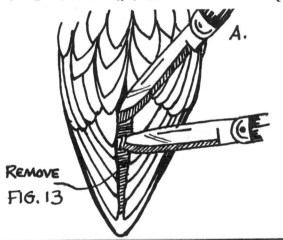

A.

REMOVE
FIG. 13

BODY CONTOUR LINE
FIG. 14

STEP 9. TIPS OF PRIMARIES & TAIL

CUT ALONG EDGE OF PRIMARIES (FIG. 15) TO STRAIGHTEN & SEPARATE FROM BODY & TAIL. REMOVE A SMALL PIECE OF WOOD FROM BENEATH PRIMARY EDGE. AS YOU NEAR THE TAIL, YOU SEPARATE THE TAIL FROM THE TIPS OF THE PRIMARIES. AFTER THE PRIMARIES HAVE BEEN ELEVATED FROM THE TAIL, THIN THE TAIL FROM THE BOTTOM.

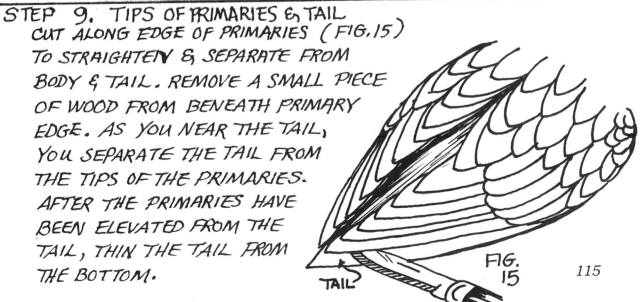

TAIL

FIG. 15

115

STEP 10. SHAPING THE BEAK

WE HAVE ALREADY PRE-SHAPED THE BEAK WHILE CARVING THE DECOY. NOW YOU CAN REFINE THIS CARVING, BUT STILL ALLOW ROOM FOR FINE SANDING. CARVING THE BEAK IS A CRITICAL & IMPORTANT PART OF BIRD CARVING. IF THE BIRD'S BEAK IS NOT WELL DONE, IT COULD RUIN THE OVERALL REALISM OF THE BIRD. FROM THE ORIGINAL DECOY SHAPE, SKETCH THE ACTUAL BEAK STRUCTURE USING FIG. 16 & 17 AS A GUIDE. REMOVE THE WOOD TO THESE LINES. NOTICE THE TIP OF THE BEAK IS HOOKED DOWN SLIGHTLY & IS NOT SHARPLY POINTED, BUT IS SLIGHTLY BLUNT. A MISTAKE THAT IS OFTEN MADE IS GETTING THE BEAK OUT OF ALIGNMENT FROM THE HEAD & BODY, ESPECIALLY FROM THE TOP VIEW. A CENTER LINE DRAWN DOWN THE MIDDLE OF THE HEAD CAN HELP KEEP EVERYTHING LINED UP.

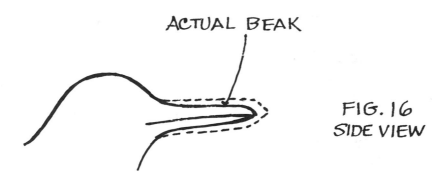

ACTUAL BEAK

FIG. 16
SIDE VIEW

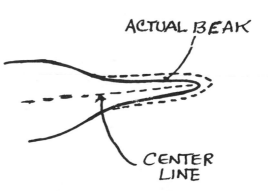

FIG. 17
TOP VIEW

ACTUAL BEAK

CENTER LINE

STEP 11. DETAILING THE BEAK

DRAW A LINE DOWN THE LENGTH OF THE BEAK ON ITS SIDES A LITTLE LOWER THAN THE CENTER (FIG. 18). USING THE POINT OF YOUR JACKKNIFE, CUT A CRISP "V" ALONG THIS LINE TO SEPARATE THE UPPER & LOWER BEAK. MATCH THIS CUT EXACTLY ON THE OTHER SIDE BY DRAWING THE LINE FIRST & EYEING IT UP BY LOOKING STRAIGHT AT THE END OF THE BEAK & ADJUST YOUR LINE SO IT BALANCES PERFECTLY WITH THE OPPOSITE SIDE BEFORE CARVING IT. SKETCH IN WHERE THE BEAK MEETS THE HEAD EXACTLY, USING FIG. 18·19 & 20 AS YOUR REFERENCE. USING THE POINT OF YOUR KNIFE, MAKE A STRAIGHT STOP CUT INTO THESE LINES & LOWER THE BEAK VERY SLIGHTLY FROM THE HEAD (FIG. 20A). RE-SHAPE THE HEAD BACK INTO THE BEAK BY SLIGHTLY ROUNDING BACK INTO THE BEAK (FIG. 20B). FIG. 19 SHOWS THE AMOUNT OF DEPRESSION THE BEAK IS RELIEVED FROM THE HEAD.

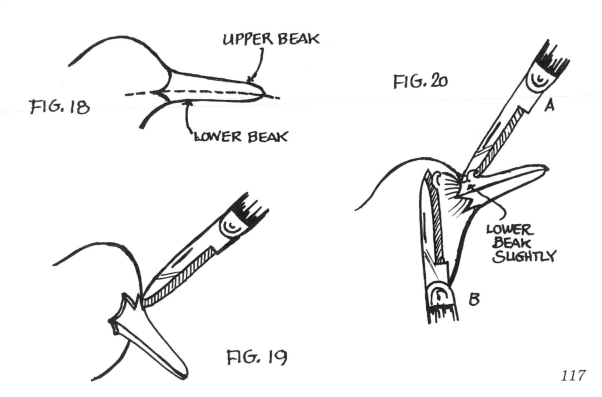

UPPER BEAK

FIG. 18

LOWER BEAK

FIG. 20

A

LOWER BEAK SLIGHTLY

B

FIG. 19

STEP 12. FINISHING BEAK & NOSTRIL

AFTER YOU HAVE SHAPED THE HEAD INTO THE BEAK, CARVE THE TOP OF THE BEAK BY FLATTENING A SMALL TRIANGULAR AREA NEAREST THE HEAD (FIG. 21). FLATTEN ON BOTH SIDES OF THE BEAK NEAR CHEEKS. AS YOU FLATTEN DOWN THE SIDES OF THE BEAK, START ROUNDING THE BEAK OVER AFTER YOU HAVE GONE PAST THE TRIANGULAR AREA (FIG. 22). THE BOTTOM OF THE BEAK IS FLATTENED & ITS EDGES ROUNDED. CHECK YOUR CARVING BY LOOKING FOR EQUAL BALANCE FROM ALL VIEWS. LIGHTLY SAND ENTIRE BEAK WITH 220-GRIT PAPER TO ROUND ALL SHARP EDGES.

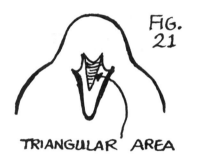

FIG. 21

TRIANGULAR AREA

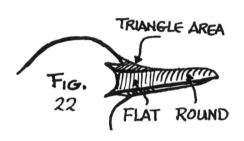

TRIANGLE AREA

FIG. 22

FLAT   ROUND

STEP 13. MAKING THE NOSTRILS

LOCATE & SKETCH IN BOTH NOSTRILS USING FIG. 23 AS A REFERENCE MAKING SURE YOUR PENCIL MARKS ARE BALANCED. USING THE POINT OF YOUR JACKKNIFE CARVE OPPOSITE **ELLIPTICAL** CUTS TO REMOVE WOOD FROM THE NOSTRIL HOLES. START BY REMOVING A VERY SMALL SLIVER & GRADUALLY WIDEN THIS HOLE TO ITS PROPER SIZE (SEE FIG. 24).

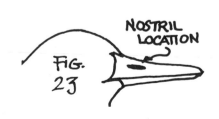

NOSTRIL LOCATION

FIG. 23

FIG. 24

STEP 14. LOCATING THE EYES

THIS METHOD OF LOCATING THE EYES CAN BE USED ON MOST BIRDS. USING YOUR NOSTRILS AS A GUIDE, SKETCH IN A STRAIGHT LINE FOLLOWING THE DIRECTION OF THE NOSTRILS ONTO BOTH SIDES OF THE HEAD (FIG. 25). SKETCH IN VERTICAL LINES ON BOTH SIDES OF THE HEAD FROM THE CORNER OF THE UPPER & LOWER BEAK. THE EYES ARE LOCATED ON THE NOSTRIL LINES & BEHIND THE VERTICAL LINES (FIG. 25 & 26). SKETCH IN A 6 MM CIRCLE ON BOTH SIDES OF THE HEAD WHERE THE EYES ARE LOCATED (FIG 25).

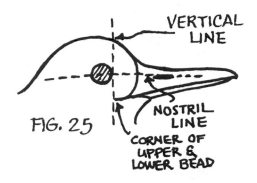

VERTICAL LINE

FIG. 25

NOSTRIL LINE

CORNER OF UPPER & LOWER BEAD

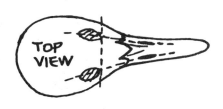

TOP VIEW

FIG. 26

STEP 15. SETTING GLASS EYES

THIS BIRD REQUIRES 6 MM BROWN EYES. THE SOCKET MUST BE CARVED A LITTLE LARGER THAN 6 MM TO ALLOW THEM TO FIT. USE A SMALL HALF-ROUND GOUGE & CUT STRAIGHT IN ON YOUR PENCIL LINES (FIG. 27), TURNING THE GOUGE IN A ROTATING MOTION UNTIL THE SOCKET WOOD IS REMOVED. KEEP INSERTING THE EYE BACKWARDS UNTIL NO PART OF THE EYE SHOWS (THIS WILL ESTABLISH YOUR DEPTH BEFORE CUTTING AWAY WIRES ON EYES). YOU CAN USE A DRILL, BUT IT HAS A TENDENCY TO TEAR THE WOOD AROUND THE SOCKETS.

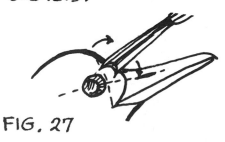

FIG. 28

6MM GLASS EYE ON WIRE (BROWN)

FIG. 27

INSERT BACKWARDS NO EYE PART SHOWS

STEP 16. INSERTING EYES

TRIM ATTACHED WIRES OFF EYES, FILL EACH SOCKET WITH PLASTIC WOOD & PRESS EYES INTO SOCKETS, ALLOWING PLASTIC WOOD TO OOZE OUT (FIG. 29A). KEEP WIPING AWAY EXCESS PLASTIC WOOD TO ENABLE YOU TO SEE HOW THE EYES ARE SEATED. PRESS EYES IN UNTIL THE EDGE OF THE CORNEA IS WITHIN THE SOCKET WHILE THE DOME OF THE CORNEA PROTRUDES A LITTLE FROM THE SIDE OF THE HEAD (FIG. 29B). AFTER BOTH EYES ARE PRESSED IN PLACE THEY HAVE TO BE ADJUSTED. BIRD EYES WILL LOOK A LITTLE FORWARD. BECAUSE YOU HAVE MADE THE SOCKETS A LITTLE LARGER THAN THE EYES, THEY CAN BE ROLLED. ROLL THE EYES WITH YOUR FINGERTIPS SO THE PUPILS LOOK A LITTLE FORWARD EVENLY.

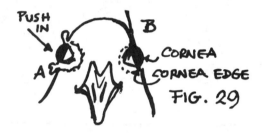

FIG. 29

STEP 17. PACKING LIDS

TO AID IN HOLDING EYES IN PLACE & TO START CONSTRUCTION OF THE LIDS AROUND EYES, TAKE PLASTIC WOOD & PACK AROUND THE EYES SO IT COVERS THEIR CIRCUMFERENCE (FIG. 30). MAKE SURE YOU HAVE APPLIED ENOUGH PLASTIC WOOD AROUND THE EYES TO SHAPE LIDS (NEXT STEP). PLASTIC WOOD WILL SHRINK A BIT, SO KEEP THIS IN MIND.

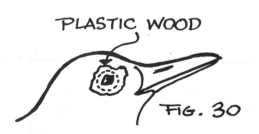

PLASTIC WOOD

FIG. 30

STEP 18. CARVING THE LIDS

ALLOW YOUR PLASTIC WOOD TO DRY HARD. DRAW A LINE FOLLOWING YOUR NOSTRIL LINE ALONG THE SIDES OF THE HEAD THROUGH THE EYES. THIS WILL ESTABLISH WHERE THE CORNERS OF THE EYES ARE. LOCATE THE DARK PUPILS OF THE EYES BY REMOVING A LITTLE PLASTIC WOOD. AFTER YOU CAN PLAINLY SEE THE PUPILS, SLOWLY ENLARGE AROUND THE EYES, FOLLOWING THE PUPILS. ENLARGE THE EYE OPENING EVENLY, KEEPING THE PUPIL IN THE CENTER. AS YOU DO THIS, DO NOT GO STRAIGHT IN. INSTEAD, CARVE AT A SLIGHT ANGLE AWAY FROM THE EYE (FIG. 31 A). DO THE TOP & BOTTOM LIDS SO EYES LOOK LIKE FIG. 32. AFTER YOU ARE SATISFIED WITH THE SHAPE OF YOUR EYES & LIDS, CARVE AWAY FROM THE EYES, REMOVING THE EXCESS PLASTIC WOOD AS MUCH AS POSSIBLE WITHOUT CARVING AWAY THE LIDS (FIG. 31B).

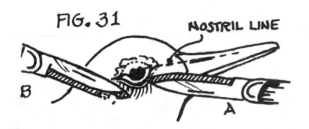

FIG. 31

NOSTRIL LINE

B

A

FIG. 32

STEP 19. SANDING

FOLD A SMALL PIECE OF SANDPAPER IN THIRDS & START SANDING AROUND THE HEAD. SAND VERY CAREFULLY AROUND THE EYES, AVOIDING THE GLASS (IF YOU HIT THE EYES WITH THE PAPER YOU WILL SCRATCH THEM). CAREFUL SANDING IS HELPFUL IN YOUR FINAL SHAPING TO REMOVE BUMPS, HIGH SPOTS OR LOW SPOTS. SAND THE HEAD, NECK & UNDERBODY SMOOTH. THE FEATHERS SHOULD NOT BE SANDED INDIVIDUALLY BUT AS A GROUP. THE ENDS OF THE FEATHERS SHOULD BE SANDED SO THEY ARE SNUG TO THE BODY BUT STILL DEFINED.

STEP 20. WOOD FOR BASE & LEGS

FIG. 33 & 34 ARE ILLUSTRATED TO SHOW PERSPECTIVE OF THE LEG & BASE PATTERNS. MANY TYPES OF WOOD CAN BE USED FOR THESE PATTERNS. OUR OBJECTIVE IS TO CARVE THE LEGS FROM A HARDER TYPE OF WOOD FOR STRENGTH & DETAIL. ON BIRDS WITH SKINNY LEGS, BLACK WALNUT OR MAPLE CAN BE USED. FROM THE BASE WE WILL BE CARVING THE FEET & AN ORNAMENTAL SHELL. THE WOOD USED ON THE BASE DOESN'T HAVE TO BE AS STRONG AS THE LEG WOOD, BUT HAS TO HAVE GRAIN CLOSE ENOUGH FOR CARVING THE FEET WITHOUT BREAKING THEM AWAY.

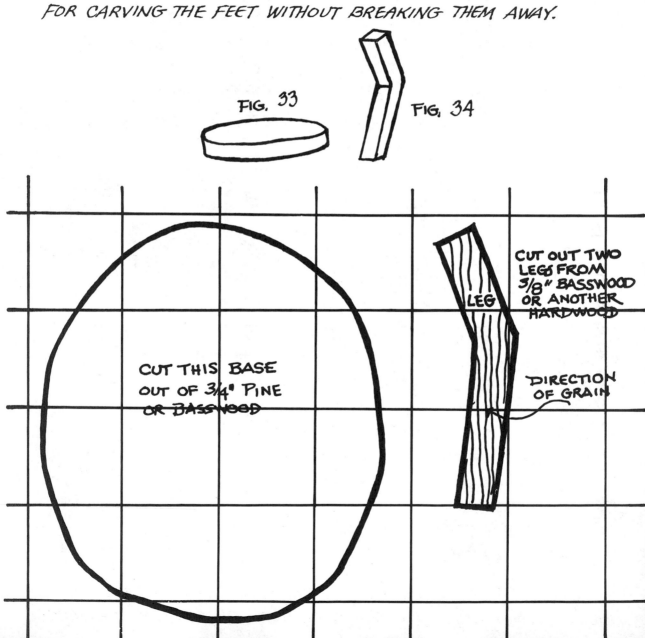

FIG. 33

FIG. 34

CUT OUT TWO LEGS FROM 3/8" BASSWOOD OR ANOTHER HARDWOOD

LEG

CUT THIS BASE OUT OF 3/4" PINE OR BASSWOOD

DIRECTION OF GRAIN

STEP 21. FITTING THE LEGS TO THE BASE

YOU WILL BE SECURING THE LEGS TO THE BODY & BASE BY CARVING BOTH ENDS OF EACH LEG ROUND TO FIT ¼ INCH DRILLED HOLES (FIG. 35). TO ENSURE A TIGHT FIT, CARVE EACH END TAPERED SO THE END CAN FIT INTO A ¼-INCH HOLE. DRILL A ¼-INCH DEEP HOLE INTO A PIECE OF SCRAP HARDWOOD. THE SCRAP WOOD YOU CHOOSE SHOULD BE HARDER THAN THE WOOD THE LEGS ARE MADE OF. PUSH EACH LEG END IN HOLE & TWIST UNTIL THE CARVED END BECOMES ROUND & SMOOTH & ALL CARVING MARKS HAVE DISAPPEARED.

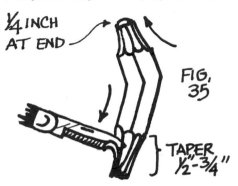

¼ INCH AT END

FIG. 35

TAPER ½"-¾"

STEP 22. POSITION & FITTING LEGS TO THE BODY (FIG. ON NEXT PAGE)

TO LOCATE THE PROPER AREA TO DRILL YOUR ¼-INCH DIAMETER HOLES IN THE BODY SEE BOTTOM VIEW FIG. 36. DRAW 2 X'S JUST BEHIND THE MIDWAY POINT OF THE BODY FROM THE BODY ROUNDNESS TO THE TAIL & MIDWAY BETWEEN THE CENTER LINE & THE EDGE OF THE BODY. BEFORE DRILLING ANY HOLES, THE LEGS HAVE TO BE IN SOME KIND OF ALIGNMENT WITH THE FRONT & SIDE. FRONT VIEW FIG. 37 SHOWS 2 SETS OF LEGS, THE DOTTED LINES BEING IN- CORRECT. BIRDS LEGS DO NOT SPLAY OUTWARD, THEY ARE MORE PERPENDICULAR. ON A LESS CRITICAL AREA IS THE SIDE VIEW. THE LEGS HERE SHOULD NOT SEEM STRAIGHT UP & DOWN. HERE (FIG. 38) WE HAVE POSITIONED THE LEGS AS IF WALKING. THIS WILL GIVE YOUR BIRD MORE **CHARACTER** & SEEM LESS RIGID. NOW YOU ARE READY TO DRILL YOUR HOLES. TO KEEP ALL THIS PROPERLY ALIGNED, THE BEST WAY IS TO DO IT BY EYE BY LAYING YOUR BIRD ON ITS SIDE ON A BENCH & DRILLING SIDEWAYS USING THE BENCH AS A PARALLEL GUIDE TO MAKE SURE YOU ARE GOING STRAIGHT. DRILL YOUR HOLES ABOUT ½ INCH DEEP & PUSH THE LEGS INTO THE HOLES.

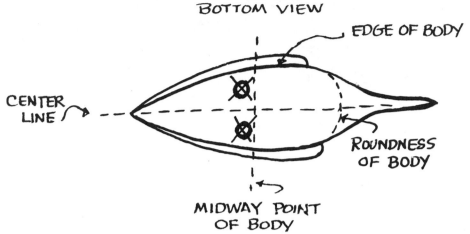

FIG. 36
BOTTOM VIEW

EDGE OF BODY

CENTER LINE

ROUNDNESS OF BODY

MIDWAY POINT OF BODY

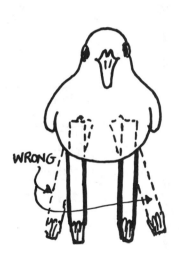

WRONG

FIG. 37
FRONT VIEW

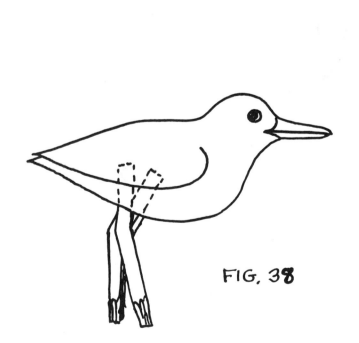

FIG. 38

124

STEP 23. MOUNTING THE BIRD TO ITS BASE

POSITION YOUR BIRD ON THE BASE SO IT IS OFF TO A SIDE (FIG. 39). WE HAVE TO LEAVE AMPLE ROOM FOR THE FEET & THE SHELL WHICH WILL BE CARVED FROM THE BASE. HOLD YOUR BIRD IN POSITION & WITH A SHARP PENCIL DRAW AROUND LEG ENDS FOR EXACT POSITION OF LEGS ON BASE (FIG. 40). DRILL 1/4-INCH HOLES ABOUT 1/2 INCH DEEP. WHEN DRILLING REMEMBER THE ANGLE OF THE LEGS GOING INTO THE BASE. TO OBTAIN CORRECT ANGLE, MOVE THE BIRD AWAY FROM THE BASE, BUT HOLD HIM UPRIGHT TO THE PROPER ATTITUDE IN LINE WITH THE BASE. USE THE BIRD AS A MODEL FOR THE DIRECTION OF THE DRILL. INSERT LEGS INTO FEET HOLES & PRESS FIRMLY IN PLACE. IF EVERYTHING LINES UP PROPERLY, GLUE ONLY THE LEGS INTO THE BASE. WE WILL BE REMOVING THE BIRD TO CARVE THE LEGS & FEET.

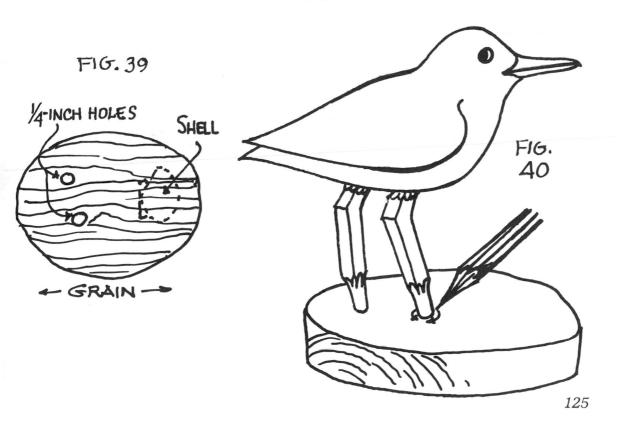

FIG. 39

1/4-INCH HOLES

SHELL

← GRAIN →

FIG. 40

125

STEP 24. BASE PATTERN

AFTER THE GLUE HAS DRIED ON THE LEGS IN THE BASE, REMOVE THE BIRD & PUT IT ASIDE. SKETCH IN FREEHAND THE FEET & SHELL AS IN FIG. 41. THIS SKETCH IS LARGER THAN YOU NEED FOR THE SHELL & FEET, LEAVING AMPLE WOOD FOR CARVING THEM LATER.

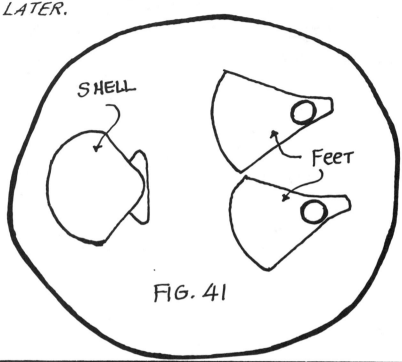

SHELL

FEET

FIG. 41

STEP 25. RELIEVING THE FEET & SHELL

USING A SMALL HALF-ROUND (FIG. 42 FOR SIZE), CARVE A GROOVE AROUND THE SHELL & FEET TO A DEPTH OF 1/4 INCH TO YOUR PENCIL LINES (FIG. 43).

USE ANY HALF-ROUND
BETWEEN THESE SIZES

FIG. 43

U u
HALF-ROUND
SIZE
FIG. 42

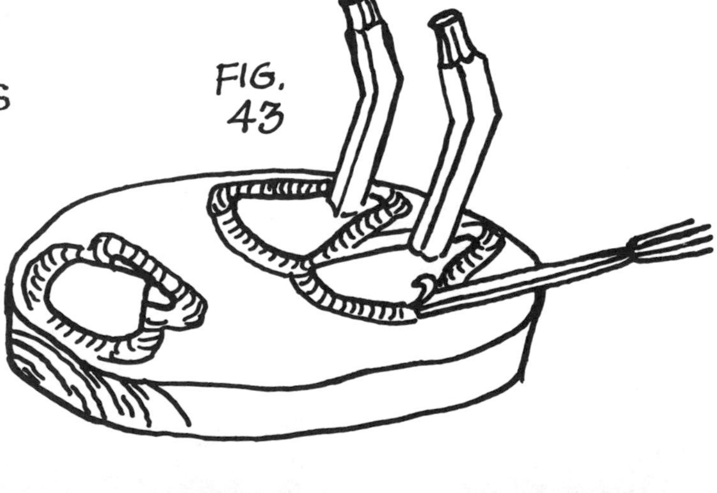

STEP 26. SHAPING THE BASE

AFTER YOU HAVE GROOVED AROUND THE FEET & SHELL, USE THE FISHTAIL GOUGE TO REMOVE ALL EXCESS WOOD (FIG. 44) FROM THE BASE. AS YOU CARVE AWAY THIS WOOD, START SHAPING THE BASE SO IT HAS A SLIGHT DOME TO IT. THIS WILL RELIEVE PORTIONS OF THE FEET & SHELL MORE THAN THE ORIGINAL 1/4 INCH, BUT THAT'S O.K. SEE FIG. 45 FOR DOME SHAPE & THE DIFFERENCE IN DEPTH AROUND THE FEET & SHELL. DO NOTHING TO THE FEET & SHELL EXCEPT GO AROUND THEM. WE ARE INTERESTED IN SHAPING THE BASE TO WITHIN 1/8 INCH OF REMAINING FLAT EDGE AROUND ITS CIRCUMFERENCE.

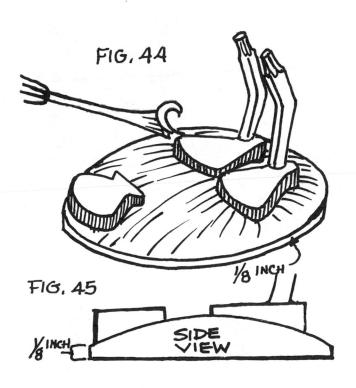

FIG. 44

FIG. 45

1/8 INCH

1/8 INCH

SIDE VIEW

STEP 27.   SHAPING THE LEGS, FEET & SHELL

WITH YOUR JACKKNIFE, CARVE YOUR LEGS ROUND,   LEAVING A SLIGHT BULGE WHERE THE LEG IS BENT AT THE JOINT OF THE UPPER & LOWER LEG. CAREFULLY WATCHING THE DIRECTION OF THE GRAIN ROUND OUT THE LEGS SO THEY ARE SLENDER (FIG. 46). WHEN YOU NEAR THE FEET, TWIST THE KNIFE SHARPLY AT THE ANKLES TO ROUND INTO THE FEET WITHOUT NOTCHING. CARVE INTO THIS AREA IN ONE CARVED MOTION, BRINGING THE FEET & LEGS TO A THICKNESS SHOWN IN FIG. 47. DROP THE FEET DOWN SO THEY CONFORM TO THE CONTOUR OF THE BASE. THE SHELL IS SHAPED TO THE BASE WITH A SLIGHT DOME TO IT (FIG. 47).

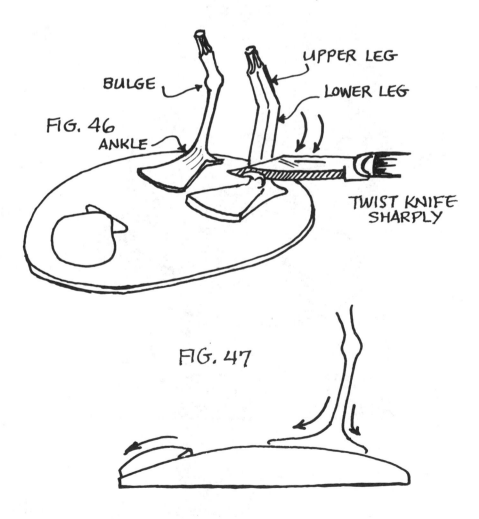

UPPER LEG

LOWER LEG

BULGE

FIG. 46

ANKLE

TWIST KNIFE SHARPLY

FIG. 47

STEP 28. CARVING THE FEET & SHELL

AFTER YOU HAVE DROPPED THE BASE AWAY FROM THE SHELL & FEET, SKETCH IN THE EXACT SHAPE OF THE FEET & SHELL USING FIG. 48 AS A GUIDE. USING THE POINT OF YOUR JACKKNIFE, CUT STRAIGHT DOWN ALONG SKETCHED LINES & REMOVE EXCESS WOOD (FIG. 49) FROM AROUND FEET & SHELL. ROUND OVER EACH EACH TOE SEPARATELY AFTER DROPPING THEM DOWN SO ONLY 1/8 INCH IS ABOVE THE BASE. THE SHELL SHOULD BE ROUNDED OVER FROM ITS MIDDLE (FIG. 49). THE SHELL TABS SHOULD BE A LITTLE LOWER THAN THE SHELL ITSELF, BUT FLAT TO THE BASE AS IF RESTING ON IT. AT THE JUNCTION OF THE FEET & LEGS, CONCENTRATE ON KEEPING THE FEET LOW TO THE BASE SO THEY ARE NOT SHOWING A LOT OF BULK IN THE CREVICES OF THE TOES. BACKCUT A SMALL TRIANGULAR PIECE OF WOOD FROM BENEATH THE FEET AT THE BASE OF THE LEGS. EACH TOE SHOULD BE POINTED FOR THE TOENAILS.

FIG. 48

FIG. 49

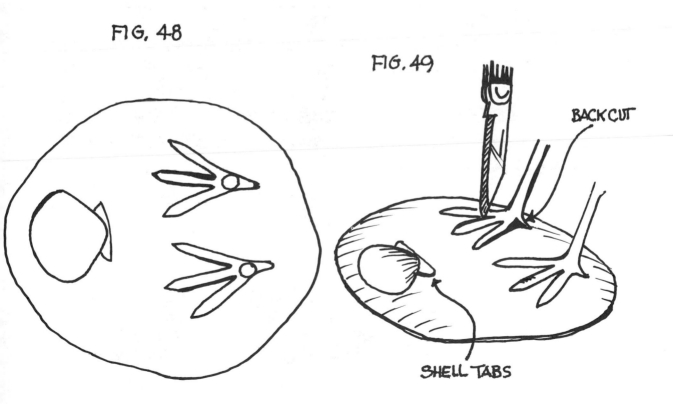

BACK CUT

SHELL TABS

STEP 29. CARVING THE SHELL

SKETCH IN FAN-SHAPED LINES ABOUT ⅛ INCH APART AT THE SHELL EDGE, COMING TO A POINT NEAR THE TAB. CARVE WITH A PARTING TOOL (FIG. 50) FROM THE TAB TOWARD THE SHELL EDGE, SKIPPING EVERY OTHER LINE STARTING ON THE SECOND STRIPE FROM THE OUTER EDGE. MAKE SURE THE STRIPES COME OUT EVEN SO BOTH OUTER STRIPES ARE RAISED. CREASE YOUR SAND PAPER & SAND ALL RECESSED & RAISED STRIPES.

FIG. 50

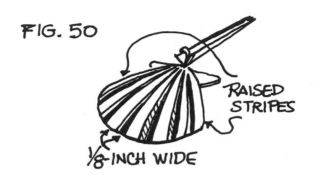

RAISED STRIPES

⅛-INCH WIDE

STEP 30. SHAPING THE SHELL TO THE BASE

AFTER ALL THE FAN GROOVES HAVE BEEN CARVED & SANDED, USE THE TIP OF YOUR JACKKNIFE & CUT ALONG THE EDGES OF THE SHELL (FIG. 51) & REMOVE WOOD TO THE CONTOUR OF THE FLUTES (FAN GROOVES) TO GIVE THE ILLUSION OF A THIN SHELL, DO THIS AROUND THE WHOLE SHELL, SLIGHTLY RELIEVING THE SHELL FROM THE BASE.

FIG. 51

FLUTES (FAN GROOVES)

STEP 31. DETAIL BURNING (LEGS & FEET)

MANY OF THE DECORATIVE BIRD CARVERS ARE ACHIEVING TREMENDOUS ACCURACY IN FINISHING THEIR BIRDS BY USING THE ELECTRIC BURNING PEN. THERE ARE MANY BURNING PENS AVAILABLE ON THE MARKET & ALL ARE EASY TO USE.

WITH YOUR BURNER, BURN A LINE DOWN BOTH SIDES OF THE LEGS TO THE FEET (FIG. 52). FILL IN THE ENTIRE BACKS OF THE LEGS WITH STRAIGHT PARALLEL LINES TO YOUR SIDE LINES ABOUT 1/16 INCH APART. CROSS HATCH THESE PARALLEL LINES 1/16 INCH APART, FORMING MANY SMALL SQUARES ON THE BACK OF THE LEGS.

ON THE FRONT OF THE LEGS (FIG. 52), BURN ACROSS FROM SIDE LINES 1/8 INCH WIDE BANDS TO FORM THE LEG SCALES. CONTINUE THIS DOWN THE LEGS ONTO THE FEET TO THE TOES. AGAIN, THE BACK OF THE LEGS & SOME OF THE SIDE OF THE TOES WILL BE CROSS-HATCHED INTO SMALL SQUARES. ACCENT THE TOENAILS WITH YOUR BURNER & RUN THE BURNER ALONG THE EDGE OF THE FEET AT THE BASE TO BURN AWAY ANY SPLINTERS OR LOOSE WOOD. YOUR FEET, LEGS & TOES SHOULD LOOK LIKE FIG. 52.

GLUE YOUR BIRD TO ITS LEGS & FILL ANY SPACES WHERE THE BODY & LEGS MEET WITH WOODFILLER OR PLASTIC WOOD. SHAPE THE BODY INTO LEGS WITH THE POINT OF YOUR JACKKNIFE & LIGHTLY SAND, BLENDING BODY TO LEGS.

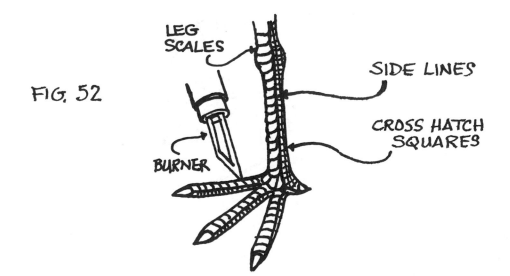

FIG. 52

LEG SCALES

SIDE LINES

CROSS HATCH SQUARES

BURNER

STEP 32. PAINTING YOUR BIRD

IN THIS PROCESS WE WILL USE A NEW METHOD THAT WAS ACCIDENTALLY REACHED IN THE USE OF UNIVERSAL TINTING COLORS. YOU WILL NEED A FINE ARTIST SABLE BRUSH, TURPENTINE, A RAG, A PALETTE, FLAT WHITE OIL BASE PAINT (INTERIOR PRIMER) & UNIVERSAL TINTING COLORS IN THESE COLORS: ① RAW UMBER ② BURNT UMBER ③ RAW SIENNA ④ BURNT SIENNA. SQUIRT A DIME-SIZE BLOB OF EACH COLOR ONTO YOUR PALETTE (A SHINY-PAGED MAGAZINE WORKS NICELY AS A PALETTE). BY USING TURPENTINE AS A THINNING AGENT, YOU WILL ACTUALLY BE MAKING A STAIN WHEN MIXED ON YOUR PALETTE WITH THE TINTING COLORS.

WITH YOUR FINE BRUSH, MIX ½ WHITE INTO ½ RAW SIENNA & THIN TO A WATERY STAIN WITH TURPENTINE. THIS WILL GIVE YOU A LIGHT GOLD COLOR TO BE PAINTED AROUND ALL THE EDGES OF ALL CARVED FEATHERS EXCEPT THE PRIMARIES (FIG. 53). A CLOSE-UP (FIG. 54) SHOWS HOW MUCH OF THE EDGE THAT IS PAINTED. AFTER FEATHER EDGES ARE DONE, PAINT THIS COLOR SOLID FROM UNDER THE BEAK TO DOTTED, SHADED LINES (FIG. 53) ONTO BREAST, UP BEHIND NECK, LEAVING THE TOP OF THE HEAD ALONE. WITH THIS COLOR, DO THE LEGS & FEET. WITH A RAG, WIPE ALL COLORED AREAS HARD. THIS WILL SOFTEN ANY DEFINITE LINES.

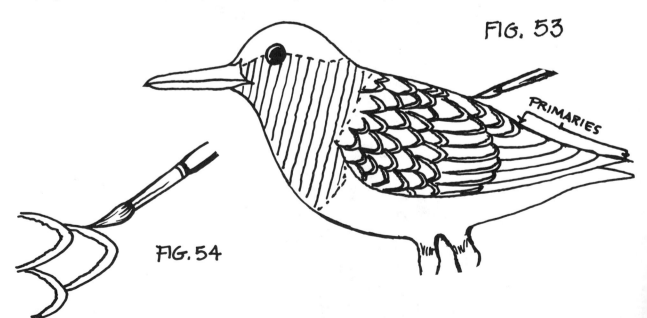

FIG. 53

PRIMARIES

FIG. 54

STEP 33.   APPLYING BURNT SIENNA

USING STRAIGHT BURNT SIENNA & THINNING WITH TURPENTINE, PAINT THE LOWER EDGES OF ALL BACK & UPPER WING FEATHERS (FIG. 55). DO NOT PAINT OVER YOUR RAW SIENNA, BUT PAINT CLEANLY FROM MIDWAY OF EACH FEATHER (CENTER), DOING ONLY LOWER SIDE OF EACH FEATHER. PAINT FROM THE TOP OF THE BEAK UP THE TOP OF THE HEAD FOLLOWING THE CONTOUR OF THE EYES. LEAVE A SPACE BETWEEN YOUR BURNT SIENNA & EYES. PAINT DOWN THE NECK, BUT NOT ALL THE WAY TO THE BACK FEATHERS. RUB THE HEAD AREA WITH A RAG UNTIL THE BURNT SIENNA IS BLENDED INTO YOUR PREVIOUSLY PAINTED RAW SIENNA.

FOLLOWING THE CONTOUR OF THE HEAD & NECK, PAINT BURNT SIENNA AS DOTTED PARALLEL LINES DOWN THE BACK OF THE HEAD ONTO THE BODY & ON THE SIDES OF THE HEAD (FIG. 55) SO THEY ARE LARGER ON THE SIDE OF THE HEAD & BECOME SMALLER & SHORTER AS YOU GO UNDER THE CHIN. TRY TO KEEP THESE DOTTED LINES AS A VERY WATERY STAIN SO YOU AVOID BRIGHT DOTS. IF THE BURNT SIENNA STAIN IS THIN ENOUGH, THEN THE DOTS WILL AUTOMATICALLY BLEND INTO YOUR PREVIOUS RAW SIENNA. STAIN BETWEEN THE WING TIPS OF THE BACK & ONTO THE TAIL TOP.

FIG. 55

DARK AREAS
ARE BURNT SIENNA

STEP 34. APPLYING BURNT UMBER (FIG. 56)

STAIN ALL AREAS THAT HAVE DIAGONAL LINES (SHADING) WITH BURNT UMBER. STAIN THE TOP OF THE HEAD WHERE YOU HAVE ALREADY DONE WITH BURNT SIENNA (FIG. 55) & RUB HARD WITH A RAG, BLENDING COLORS TOGETHER. THIS OVER-STAINING ADDS DEPTH TO YOUR ORIGINAL SOLID COLOR. WHEN STAINING WITH A DARKER COLOR OVER A LIGHTER COLOR, THE DARKER COLOR WILL NOT ABSORB & STAIN AS DARK AS IT WOULD ON UNSTAINED WOOD. THIS IS BECAUSE THE LIGHTER COLOR HAS ALREADY SATURATED THE WOOD GRAIN, LEAVING THE AMOUNT OF PENETRATION OF A DARKER COLOR AT A MINIMUM. STAIN THE REMAINING PORTION OF EACH FEATHER ON THE BACK & UPPER WINGS. STAIN THE SECONDARY FEATHERS, NOT COVERING YOUR ORIGINAL RAW SIENNA EDGING. OVERSTAIN BETWEEN WING FEATHERS DOWN TO THE TIP OF THE TAIL. STAIN A STRIPE THROUGH EACH EYE (FIG. 56) & RUB WITH A RAG. STAIN DOTS ON THE BREAST AROUND TO THE BACK OF THE HEAD, USING YOUR ORIGINAL DOTTED BURNT SIENNA DOTS. DO NOT PLACE YOUR DOTS DIRECTLY ON TOP OF EACH OTHER.

STEP 35. APPLYING RAW UMBER (CROSS-HATCHED LINES)

STAIN THE BEAK & PRIMARY FEATHERS WITH SOLID, THINNED RAW UMBER. OVERSTAIN LIGHTLY THE HEAD & EYE STRIPE & DOTTED LINES. REMEMBER TO STAIN UNDER PRIMARY FEATHERS. STAIN TOE NAILS. THE REMAINING COLOR WE WILL USE IS FLAT WHITE, SLIGHTLY TINTED WITH BURNT UMBER. PAINT WITH THIS SLIGHTLY OFF-WHITE THE BREAST TO THE TAIL, GOING A LITTLE DOWN ON THE LEGS (FIG. 56). PAINT THE AREA BETWEEN THE EYE STRIPE & THE TOP OF THE HEAD WITH A STRIPE OF YOUR OFF-WHITE. PAINT OFF-WHITE UNDER THE BEAK. WIPE ALL THESE PLACES HARD WITH A RAG TO REMOVE ALL EXCESS PAINT. ALL THESE AREAS SHOULD BLEND INTO EACH OTHER WITH NO HARD LINES. AFTER WE HAVE BURNED THE BIRD (STEP 36.), WE WILL GO BACK OVER THE WHITE AREAS ONLY.

ILLUSTRATION FOR STEPS 34 + 35

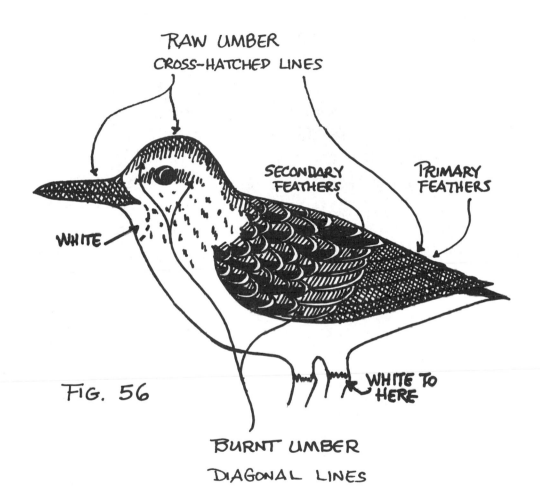

RAW UMBER
CROSS-HATCHED LINES

SECONDARY
FEATHERS

PRIMARY
FEATHERS

WHITE

FIG. 56

WHITE TO
HERE

BURNT UMBER
DIAGONAL LINES

STEP 36. BURNING THE HEAD & BREAST DETAILS

USING THE TIP OF THE BURNER, ACCENT AROUND THE BEAK WITH SHORT
TIGHT-TOGETHER STROKES, WORKING AWAY FROM THE BEAK ONTO THE
HEAD. MAKE THE BEAK-TO-HEAD LINE AS CLEAN & DEFINITE AS
POSSIBLE. AFTER YOU HAVE WELL DEFINED THE BEAK, BURN IN A
LITTLE LONGER STROKE & MAKE IT LONGER AS YOU GO ONTO THE
BREAST & SIDES OF THE HEAD. BURN A SERIES OF DIRECTIONAL LINES.
DO NOT BURN THEM PERFECTLY STRAIGHT, BURN THEM SQUIGGLY &
OVERLAPPING. THE ENTIRE AREA WILL BE BURNT WITH LINES AS
CLOSE TOGETHER AS YOU CAN GET THEM. THERE SHOULD BE NO FLAT
AREAS OR RAW WOOD SHOWING. THESE ORIGINAL DIRECTIONAL LINES
(FIG. 57) ARE NOT CLOSE TOGETHER, THEY ARE MADE QUICKLY TO
GIVE YOU FREEDOM FOR DIRECTION. THESE WILL ALL BE FILLED IN
SOLID WITH ADJACENT LINES. CONTINUE THIS BURNING OVER THE
BREAST TO THE TAIL & DOWN THE BACK OF THE NECK UNTIL YOU
REACH THE FIRST BACK FEATHERS. BE CAREFUL AROUND THE EYES
NOT TO BURN INTO THE LIDS. ACCENT THE LIDS EVENLY, FORMING A
CLEAN THIN LID.

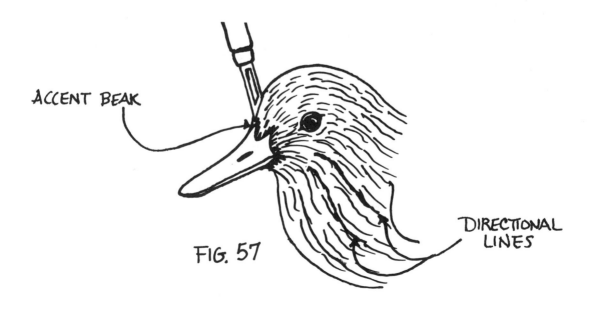

ACCENT BEAK

DIRECTIONAL
LINES

FIG. 57

STEP 37. BURNING IN THE BODY FEATHERS & WING FEATHERS

EACH OF THE INDIVIDUAL FEATHERS ON THE BACK & BODY WILL BE BURNT PRIMARILY THE SAME WAY. START WITH THE QUILL LINE IN THE DIRECT CENTER OF EACH FEATHER. THE QUILL LINE SHOULD BE 2 LINES PARALLEL TO EACH OTHER TAPERING TO A POINT AT ITS TIP. BURN THESE PARALLEL QUILL LINES ON ALL FEATHERS EXCEPT THE VERY SMALL FEATHERS NEAR THE BASE OF THE NECK. HERE YOU CAN GET BY WITH ONE LINE. BURN 2 OR 3 MAIN DIRECTIONAL FEATHER LINES ON EACH SIDE OF THE QUILL (FIG. 58). DO NOT BURN THESE LINES PERFECTLY STRAIGHT, GIVE THEM A LITTLE ARC. IN FIG. 58, THE UPPER FEATHER SHOWS A COMPLETELY FILLED-IN FEATHER. THE FEATHER BELOW (FIG. 58) SHOWS THE QUILL & DIRECTIONAL LINES. ON YOUR PRIMARY & SECONDARY FEATHERS, MORE OFTEN YOU WILL BURN ONLY ONE SIDE OF THE FEATHER BECAUSE YOU DO NOT SEE THE OPPOSITE SIDE OF THE FEATHER DUE TO THEM OVERLAPPING EACH OTHER. TRY NOT TO MAKE YOUR BURNING PERFECT. BURN SOME OF THE CUTS IN THE FEATHERS A LITTLE DARKER TO BREAK UP THE EVEN LOOK OF THE FEATHER PATTERN. BURN IN STRAIGHT LINES AS YOU DID ON THE HEAD & BREAST, THE SPACE BETWEEN THE WINGS ONTO THE TAIL. YOUR BIRD SHOULD NOW BE COMPLETELY BURNED. FIG. 59 SHOWS THE DIRECTION OF BURNING ON FEATHERS, BUT IS NOT COMPLETELY FILLED IN.

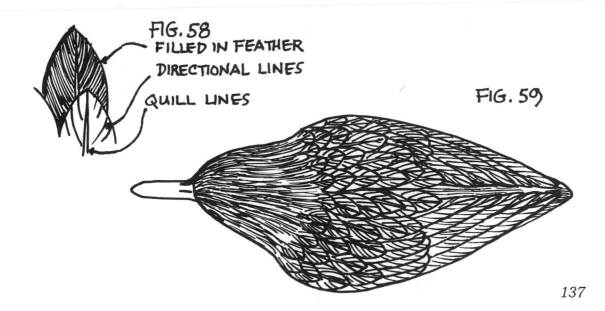

FIG. 58
FILLED IN FEATHER
DIRECTIONAL LINES
QUILL LINES

FIG. 59

STEP 38. FINISHING TOUCHES

USING YOUR ARTIST BRUSH, GO TO THE FLAT WHITE PAINT & PAINT THE WHITE STRIPE ABOVE THE EYES (FIG. 60) & BLEND THE EDGES BY DABBING WITH THE CORNER OF A RAG. ACCENT VERY LIGHTLY, USING AN ALMOST DRY BRUSH, WITH WHITE ALONG THE LOWER EDGES OF THE BACK & WING FEATHERS & BLEND INTO THE FEATHERS BY RUBBING LIGHTLY WITH YOUR FINGERTIPS. PAINT THE UNDER BELLY UP TO THE JAGGED LINE (FIG. 60) DOWN & INCLUDE THE TAIL WITH WHITE. BLEND AT THE JAGGED LINE BY RUBBING WITH A RAG. FINISH THE BEAK, LEGS & TOENAILS BY APPLYING 2 OR 3 COATS OF SATIN FINISH POLYURETHANE TO GIVE THEM A SLIGHT SHEEN. PAINT BRIGHT WHITE IN AREA BENEATH THE BEAK (FIG. 60) & BLEND INTO BREAST.

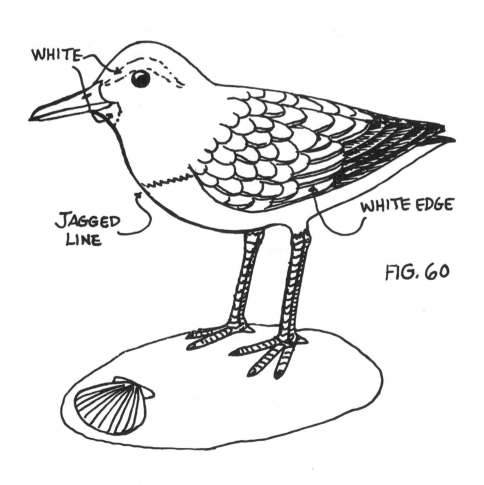

WHITE

JAGGED LINE

WHITE EDGE

FIG. 60

STEP 39. FINISHING THE BASE

PAINT YOUR SHELL WITH OFF-WHITE & LET IT DRY. AFTER IT HAS COMPLETELY DRIED, MIX BURNT UMBER WITH THE WHITE TO GET A MEDIUM BEIGE COLOR. PAINT THIS BEIGE IN THE CREVICES OF THE SHELL & WIPE LIGHTLY WITH A RAG, ALLOWING THE WHITE UNDERCOAT TO SHOW THROUGH. WIPE THE SHELL SIDEWAYS. IF YOU WIPE ALONG THE CREVICES, YOU WILL WIPE AWAY ALL THE BEIGE COLOR.   OBTAIN SOME BEACH SAND OR ANY WHITE SAND & PAINT THE ENTIRE BASE EXCEPT THE SHELL & FEET WITH YOUR WHITE PAINT. SPRINKLE THE SAND DIRECTLY ON THE WET WHITE PAINT. MAKE SURE YOU COMPLETELY COVER ALL THE WET PAINT WITH THE SAND. WHEN THE PAINT DRIES, IT WILL ACT LIKE A GLUE & WILL HOLD THE SAND ON THE BASE. CLEAN AWAY ANY SAND THAT MAY STICK TO THE FEET OR SHELL. IF DONE PROPERLY, THE BIRD & THE SHELL WILL LOOK AS IF THEY ARE ON A SANDY BEACH.

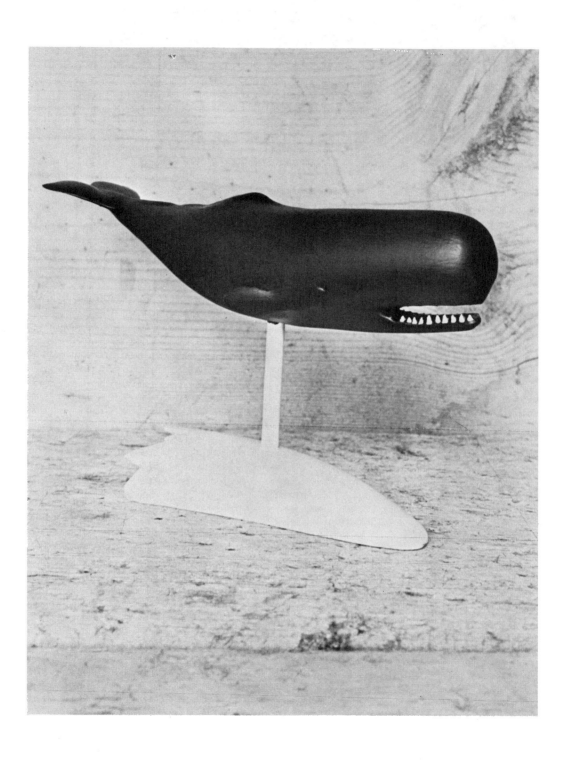

Carving the
SPERM WHALE

Project No. 3

TOOLS NEEDED
JACKKNIFE
HALF-ROUND GOUGE (FIG.12)
CARVER'S CHISEL

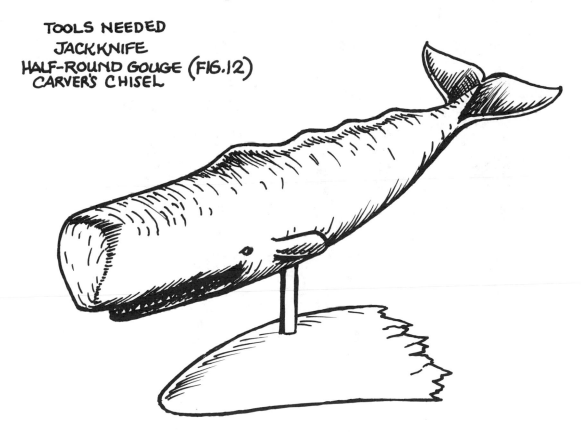

This project will make an 8-inch full round carving of the Sperm Whale, mounted on a carved replica of a Sperm Whale tooth. This is an Ideal carving to be displayed on a mantle or a knick-knack shelf.

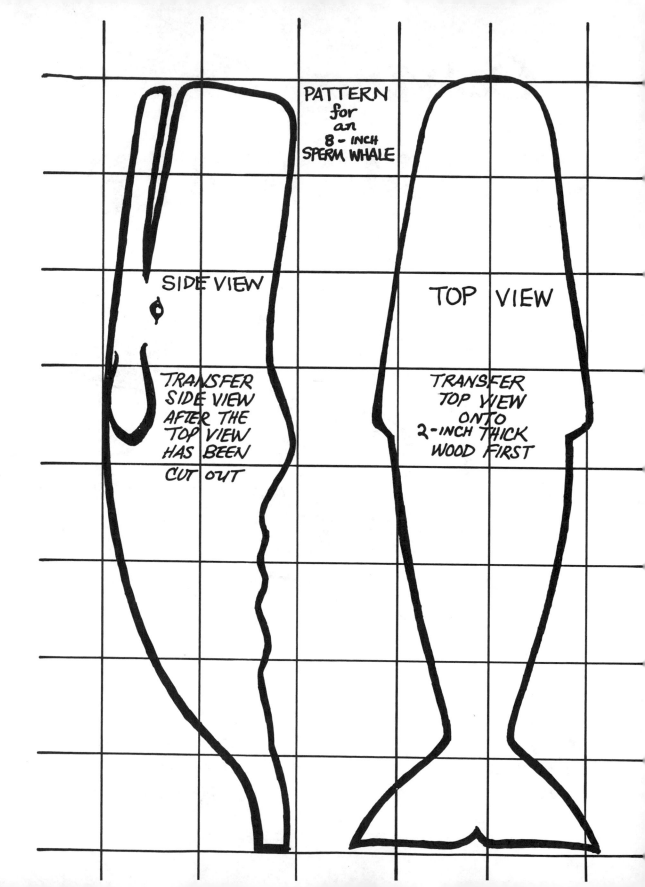

PATTERN
for
an
8 - INCH
SPERM WHALE

SIDE VIEW

TOP VIEW

TRANSFER
SIDE VIEW
AFTER THE
TOP VIEW
HAS BEEN
CUT OUT

TRANSFER
TOP VIEW
ONTO
2-INCH THICK
WOOD FIRST

STEP 1. CUTTING OUT & USING THE PATTERNS

HERE'S A WAY MANY CABINETMAKERS & WOODCARVERS MAKE & USE PATTERNS & TEMPLATES. TRANSFER THE PATTERN ONTO SOME 1/8-INCH MASONITE OR SOME THIN PLYWOOD, ALTHOUGH CARDBOARD OR OAKTAG IS GOOD. TRACE AROUND THE TOP VIEW TEMPLATE (FIG. 1), USING A SHARP, SOFT LEAD PENCIL. BANDSAW THE OUTLINE & SAVE THE SIDE PIECES (FIG. 2). TACK THEM BACK TO THE CUTOUT WITH SMALL NAILS (FIG. 3). THIS IS DONE TO MAINTAIN A FLAT SURFACE WHEN THE BLOCK IS AGAIN PUSHED INTO THE BANDSAW BLADE. TAKE YOUR SIDE VIEW TEMPLATE & DRAW AROUND IT. WHEN THIS VIEW IS SAWN, THE TACKED-ON WOOD WILL FALL AWAY.

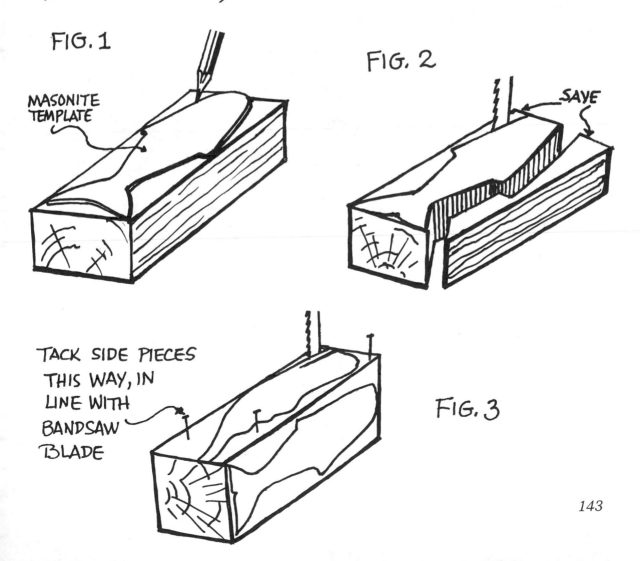

FIG. 1

MASONITE TEMPLATE

FIG. 2

SAVE

TACK SIDE PIECES THIS WAY, IN LINE WITH BANDSAW BLADE

FIG. 3

STEP 2. ROUNDING THE BODY

HOLD YOUR WHALE CUTOUT & CARVE AWAY, WITH YOUR JACK-KNIFE PEN BLADE, FROM THE FIRST BUMP ON THE WHALE'S BACK TOWARD THE HEAD (FIG. 4). CONTINUE TO ROUND UNTIL THIS FORWARD PORTION OF THE BODY LOOKS LIKE FIG. 5. IN MANY CASES YOU MAY BE CARVING WITH THE GRAIN IN ONE STROKE & AGAINST IT IN THE NEXT. IF YOU START SPLITTING AWAY THE WOOD, CARVE IN THE OPPOSITE DIRECTION.

FIG. 4

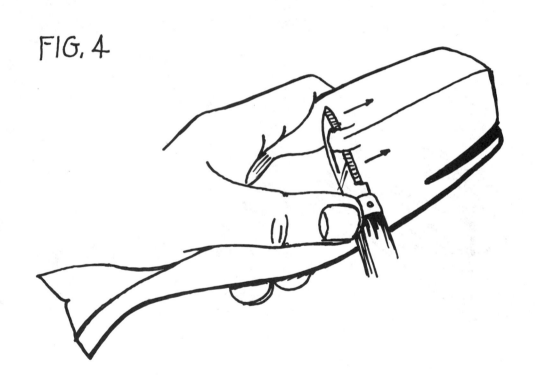

FIG. 5

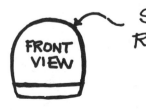

FRONT VIEW

SHAPE OF ROUNDNESS

STEP 3. ROUNDING THE BODY (Cont'd)

TURN YOUR WHALE AROUND & CARVE AT AN ANGLE DOWN BOTH SIDES OF THE BACK TOWARD THE TAIL BUT NOT ONTO THE TAIL (FIG. 6). THIS AREA WILL HAVE A RIDGE DOWN THE MIDDLE OF THE BACK. BRING THE TWO SIDES TOGETHER WITHIN ¼ INCH, USING THE CENTER LINE AS A GUIDE (FIG. 7).

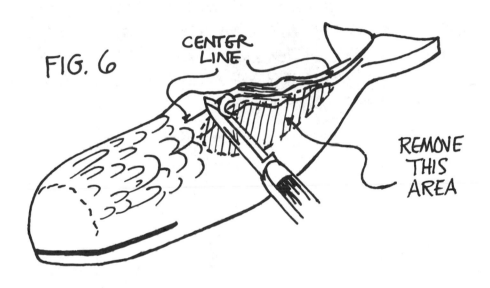

FIG. 6

CENTER LINE

REMOVE THIS AREA

LEAVE ¼-INCH RIDGE

REMOVE

ANGLE OF WOOD TO BE REMOVED

FIG. 7

STEP 4. CARVING THE FINS & MORE BODY SHAPING

SPERM WHALES HAVE FINS ON BOTH SIDES OF THEIR BODY BEHIND THE MOUTH OPENING. REFER TO THE PATTERN FOR THE PROPER LOCATION & SHAPE. CARVE STRAIGHT IN AROUND BOTH FINS WITH YOUR PEN BLADE (FIG. 8) & DROP THE BELLY BACK BY ROUNDING IT OVER, STARTING AT THE FINS BACK TO THE TAIL, DON'T SHAPE THE FINS YET, JUST TAKE OUT WOOD AROUND THEM. CONCENTRATE ON SHAPING THE BODY. WHEN ROUNDING THE BODY, CONTINUE ROUNDING BOTH SIDES EVENLY UNTIL YOU HAVE REMOVED ALL THE BAND SAW MARKS AT THE CENTER OF THE BELLY. THIS WILL MEAN YOUR UNDERBODY HAS TO BE ROUNDED. TO TEST YOUR ROUNDNESS, EYE IT UP BY LOOKING AT YOUR WHALE TAIL FIRST (END VIEW).

FIG. 8

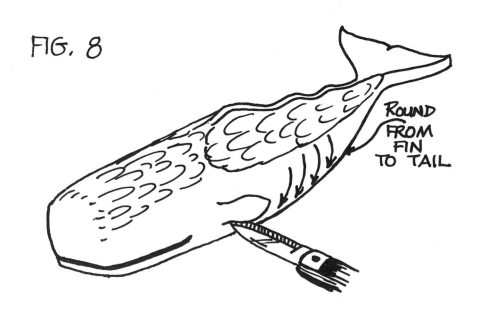

ROUND FROM FIN TO TAIL

STEP 5. CARVING THE FINS & BODY SHAPING (Cont'd)

CONTINUE RELIEVING THE TWO FINS BY ROUNDING FROM BELOW THEM & UP THE BOTTOM OF THE HEAD (FIG. 9). AS YOU ROUND IN THIS HEAD AREA, THE FINS WILL PROJECT EVEN MORE. AGAIN, DO NOT SHAPE THE FINS, LEAVE THEM AS RAISED BLOCKS. AS YOU REMOVE WOOD FROM AROUND THE FINS, YOU WILL NEED TO MAKE STRAIGHT-IN CUTS OFTEN AS EACH LAYER OF WOOD IS REMOVED. TRY TO KEEP THE STRAIGHT-IN CUT STRAIGHT. IN MANY CASES YOU MAY HAVE A TENDENCY TO CHANGE THE ANGLE SOMEWHAT. IF YOU DO NOT CUT YOUR STRAIGHT-IN CUTS CONFORMING WITH THE ACTUAL SHAPE OF THE FINS, YOUR FINS WILL BE TOO BIG OR TOO SMALL WHEN FINALLY COMPLETED.

FIG. 9

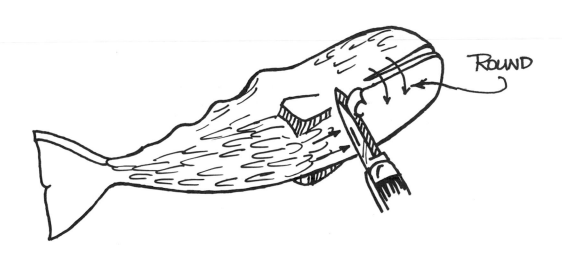

ROUND

STEP 6. CARVING THE LOWER JAW & HEAD

THE LOWER JAW OF A SPERM WHALE IS QUITE NARROW & WILL BE CARVED TO A WIDTH OF ¼ INCH (FIG.10 BOTTOM VIEW). THE LOWER SIDES OF THE HEAD WILL BE CARVED TO THE CONTOURS OF FIG.11 FRONT VIEW. USING A HALF-ROUND GOUGE (FIG.12 for size) CARVE DOWN BOTH SIDES OF THE LOWER JAW (FIG.13) & REMOVE ALL WOOD SHOWN IN FIG.11 & FIG.13 (dotted Lines). YOU CAN USE A JACKKNIFE TO SHAPE IN FLAT AREAS AFTER YOU HAVE CUT YOUR IN-DENTATION WITH YOUR HALF-ROUND AT THE BASE OF THE LOWER JAW.

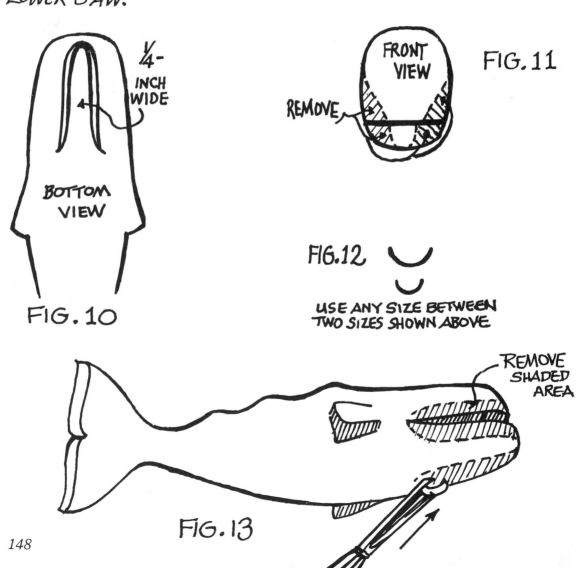

¼-INCH WIDE

BOTTOM VIEW

FIG.10

FRONT VIEW

REMOVE

FIG.11

FIG.12

USE ANY SIZE BETWEEN TWO SIZES SHOWN ABOVE

REMOVE SHADED AREA

FIG.13

STEP 7. SHAPING THE FINS

USING YOUR JACKKNIFE, MAKE THE AREA WHERE THE FINS JOIN THE BODY SLIGHTLY CONCAVE (FIG. 14 A & FIG. 15). TO KEEP THE BODY STREAMLINED, CONTINUE DOWN OFF THE FINS ONTO THE SIDES OF THE HEAD & ROUND OVER THE FRONT OF THE HEAD (FIG. 15). REMOVE A SMALL 'V' OF WOOD FROM BEHIND THE TOP & BOTTOM OF EACH FIN (FIG. 15). REMOVE THIS 'V' BY CARVING WITH THE POINT OF YOUR JACKKNIFE GOING TOWARD THE TAIL. IF YOU TRY CARVING AWAY THIS 'V' BY GOING TOWARD THE HEAD, YOU MAY BREAK AWAY THE FIN. AFTER YOU HAVE REMOVED THIS 'V', BRING THE END OF EACH FIN TO A POINT, LEAVING A BULK OF WOOD IN THE MIDDLE (FIG. 15). IMAGINE THE SHAPE OF A CLAM -- SHARP EDGES WITH A FAT MIDDLE.

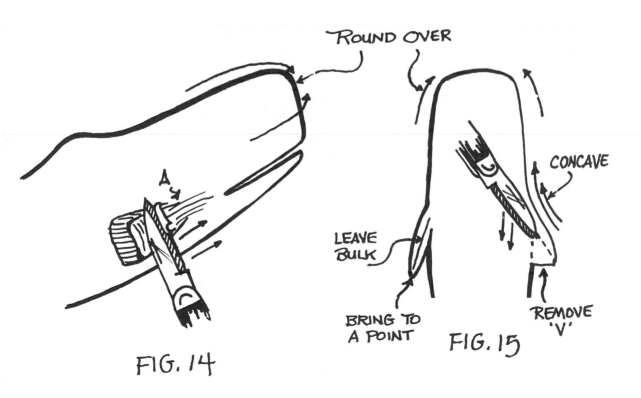

ROUND OVER

A

LEAVE BULK

CONCAVE

BRING TO A POINT

REMOVE 'V'

FIG. 14

FIG. 15

STEP 8. SHAPING THE HEAD & UPPER JAW

ADDITIONAL SHAPING IS NECESSARY TO COMPLETE THE UPPER JAW. IT IS NECESSARY TO COMPLETE STEP 7, SHAPING THE FINS INTO THE SIDES OF THE HEAD BEFORE THIS FINAL SHAPING OF THE UPPER JAW.

USING A HALF-ROUND, RUN A GROOVE DOWN BOTH SIDES OF THE HEAD NEXT TO THE UPPER JAW (FIG. 16A). THIS GROOVE NARROWS THE UPPER JAW TO MAKE IT ANATOMICALLY CORRECT TO ENABLE THE TWO JAWS TO FIT TOGETHER. ROUND ANY ANGLES OR RIDGES FORMED BY YOUR HALF-ROUND WITH THE TIP OF YOUR PEN BLADE (FIG. 16B). WHEN YOU'RE FINISHED, THE FRONT VIEW SHOULD LOOK LIKE FIG. 17.

FIG. 16

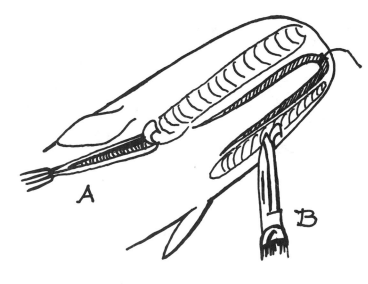

A

B

FLATTENED AREA (UPPER JAW) REMAINS A LITTLE LARGER THAN LOWER JAW

FRONT VIEW

STEP 9. FINISHING THE UPPER & LOWER JAW

USING YOUR JACKKNIFE, CARVE AWAY ALL SAW MARKS FROM INSIDE UPPER & LOWER JAWS. DRAW A LINE (FIG 18 DOTTED LINE) FROM THE FRONT OF THE LOWER JAW TO THE REAR OF THE MOUTH, ENDING WITH AN UPSWING AS IF THE WHALE HAS A SMILE. STARTING AT THE UPSWING, USE THE POINT OF YOUR PEN BLADE & MAKE A STRAIGHT-DOWN CUT (1/8 INCH DEEP) ALL THE WAY TO THE END OF LOWER JAW (FIG. 18 A). AT THE UPSWING, REMOVE WOOD TO COINCIDE WITH THE SHAPE OF THE UPPER JAW (FIG. 18 B). THIS WILL LEAVE THE UPSWING SLIGHTLY RELIEVED FROM THE UPPER JAW. THE DOTTED LINE THAT YOU HAVE CUT WILL BE THE TEETH & THIS NARROW STRIP HAS TO BE DROPPED BACK FROM THE LOWER JAW 1/8 INCH ON BOTH SIDES (FIG 18 & 19).

FIG. 18

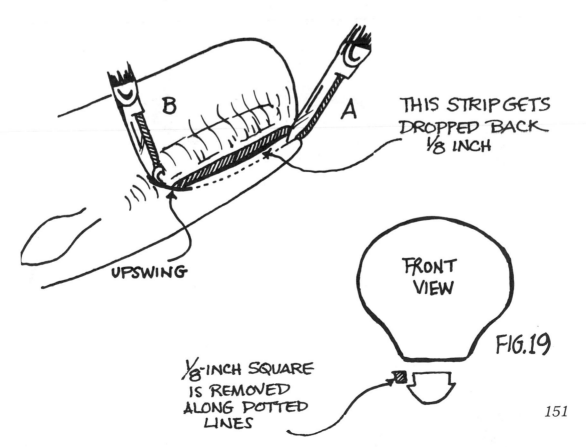

THIS STRIP GETS DROPPED BACK 1/8 INCH

UPSWING

FRONT VIEW

FIG. 19

1/8-INCH SQUARE IS REMOVED ALONG DOTTED LINES

151

STEP 10. CARVING THE TEETH

SKETCH IN THE TEETH USING FIG. 20 AS A REFERENCE. NOTICE THE TEETH ARE NOT PERFECT PYRAMID SHAPES, BUT ARE A LITTLE BACK INTO THE MOUTH. THE SPERM WHALE HAS TEETH ONLY IN THE LOWER JAW & IN A REAL WHALE THESE LOWER TEETH WOULD FIT INTO SOCKETS IN THE UPPER JAW WHEN THE MOUTH IS CLOSED. USING THE TIP OF YOUR PEN BLADE, CAREFULLY CARVE AWAY THE NOTCHES BETWEEN THE TEETH. ON A SMALL WHALE LIKE THIS PROJECT, IT IS NOT NECESSARY TO REMOVE WOOD FROM BEHIND THE TEETH. MAKE YOUR NOTCHES SHARP ENOUGH SO THE OUTER TOOTH SHAPE IS DEFINITE.

FIG. 20

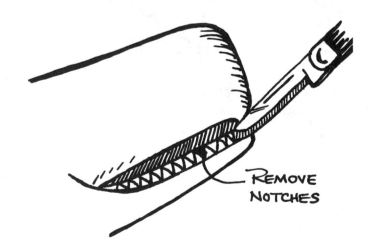

REMOVE NOTCHES

STEP 11.   SHAPING THE BACK

FROM THE POINT WHERE THE FIRST BUMP ON THE BACK
STARTS, DOWN THE BACK, THE BODY IS NO LONGER ROUND
ON THE BACK. THIS BUMPY AREA IS REALLY A RIDGE
WITH CONCAVE SIDES. LEAVE AN 1/8-INCH CENTER LINE
DOWN THE MIDDLE OF THE BACK & CARVE WITH YOUR
HALF-ROUND GOUGE DOWN BOTH SIDES OF THIS CENTER
LINE TOWARD THE TAIL (FIG. 21A). WITH YOUR PEN
BLADE, RE-ROUND THE BODY INTO THE GROOVE AREA (FIG. 21B).
BY THIS TIME ALL OF YOUR WHALE HAS BEEN CARVED, WITH
THE EXCEPTION OF THE TAIL.

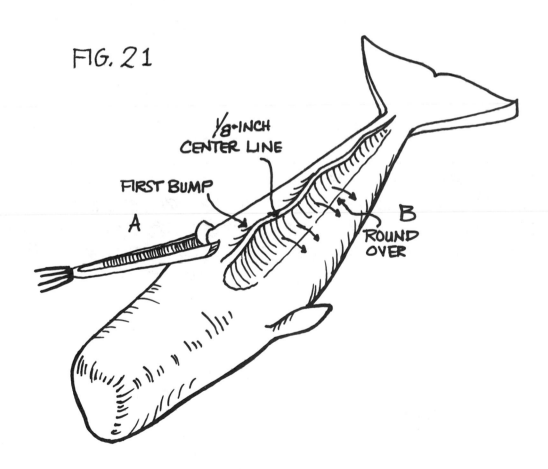

FIG. 21

1/8-INCH
CENTER LINE

FIRST BUMP

A

B

ROUND
OVER

STEP 12. CARVING THE TAIL

USING YOUR HALF-ROUND, CUT TWO GROOVES, FOLLOWING THE CONTOUR OF THE BODY WHERE THE TAIL IS CONNECTED TO THE BODY (FIG. 22 A). SKETCH IN LINES (DOTTED LINES FIG. 22) ON THE END OF THE TAIL. MAKE THEM ABOUT ⅛ INCH APART. WITH YOUR JACK KNIFE, CARVE AWAY WOOD TO THE SHAPE OF THOSE LINES, WORKING IN TOWARD YOUR GROOVES (FIG. 22B). DO THE TOP OF THE TAIL FIRST & THEN THE BOTTOM.

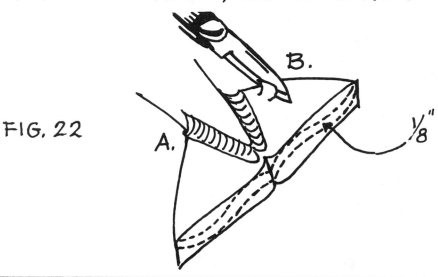

FIG. 22

STEP 13. FINISHING THE TAIL

YOUR TAIL SHOULD LOOK LIKE FIG. 23. TO GET THE STREAM-LINED LOOK OF THE TAIL, CARVE ALL EDGES TO A POINT, LEAVING A BULK OF WOOD IN THE CENTER. FINISH ROUNDING BODY INTO THE TAIL. SAND YOUR ENTIRE PIECE SMOOTH.

FIG. 23

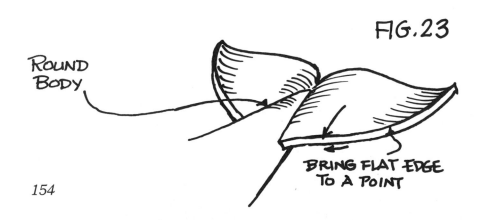

ROUND BODY

BRING FLAT EDGE TO A POINT

STEP 14. CUTTING OUT & HOLDING TOOTH (BASE)
THE SPERM WHALE TOOTH CAN EASILY BE SAWN TO SHAPE ON
A BAND SAW. TO HOLD IT DOWN WHILE CARVING, TAKE A
PIECE OF SCRAP WOOD LARGER THAN THE TOOTH & DRIVE TWO
NAILS THROUGH THE BACK OF THE SCRAP SO 1/4 INCH OF THE
POINTED END OF THE NAIL PROTRUDES. PRESS THE TOOTH
CUTOUT FIRMLY ONTO THE NAILS (FIG. 24).

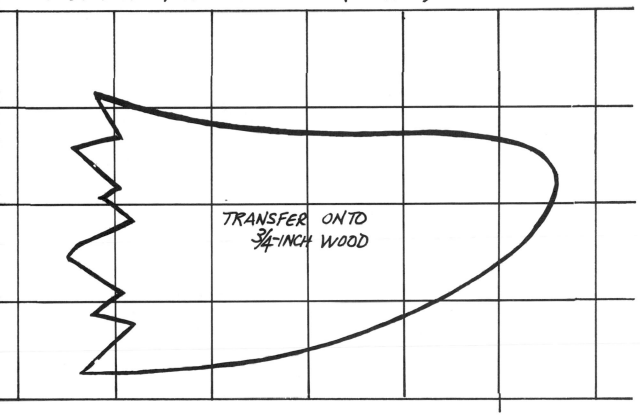

TRANSFER ONTO
3/4-INCH WOOD

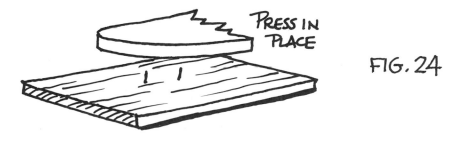

PRESS IN
PLACE

FIG. 24

STEP 15. SHAPING THE TOOTH

THIS TOOTH WILL BE USED AS AN ORNAMENTAL BASE FOR YOUR WHALE. THEREFORE WE WILL BE CARVING ONLY ½ A TOOTH, LEAVING THE BOTTOM FLAT. WITH A CARVER'S CHISEL, CARVE FROM THE NOTCHED END TOWARD THE TIP OF THE TOOTH (FIG. 25). CARVE BOTH SIDES AT AN ANGLE SHOWN IN FIG. 26. REMOVE THE WOOD RIGHT TO THE EDGE. TAKING AN EQUAL AMOUNT OF WOOD OFF BOTH SIDES WILL ALLOW EVEN ROUNDING IN THE NEXT STEP.

FIG. 25

NOTCHED END

REMOVE

END VIEW

FIG. 26

STEP 16. ROUNDING THE TOOTH
WITH YOUR CARVER'S CHISEL, ROUND-OVER ALL ANGLES. WORK TOWARD THE TIP & ROUND IT OVER SHARPLY (FIG. 27).

ROUND SHARPLY

FIG. 27

STEP 17. HOLLOWING THE BACK OF THE TOOTH
REMOVE THE TOOTH FROM YOUR NAILED BACK BOARD & HOLD IT FIRMLY IN YOUR PALM WITH THE FLAT SIDE UP. USING A HALF-ROUND, REMOVE WOOD FROM NOTCHED END (FIG. 28). BRING THE EDGE OF THE NOTCHES TO A THICKNESS OF 1/8 INCH. THIS WILL GIVE THE ILLUSION OF A HOLLOW TOOTH WHEN LAYING FLAT. FIG. 29 SHOWS THE AMOUNT OF WOOD TO BE REMOVED. SAND THE TOOTH 'TIL SMOOTH.

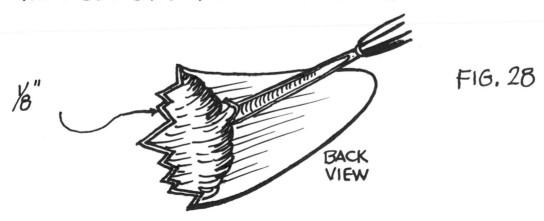

1/8"

FIG. 28

BACK VIEW

REMOVE

SIDE VIEW

FIG. 29

157

STEP 18. MAKING THE WHALE EYES

TO LOCATE THE WHALE EYES, DRAW LINE A (FIG. 30) UP THE SIDE OF THE HEAD, JUST BEHIND THE END OF THE "SMILE" OF THE LOWER JAW & ANOTHER LINE B ALONG THE SIDE OF THE HEAD JUST ABOVE THE FIN. WHERE THESE TWO LINES CROSS IS THE LOCATION OF THE EYE. FOR THIS SIZE WHALE, USE AN 1/8-INCH NAIL SET & PRESS IT FIRMLY ON THE POINT WHERE THE LINES CROSS. AS YOU PRESS, SLOWLY TURN THE NAIL SET TO ACHIEVE A CLEAN IMPRESSION OF THE END OF THE NAIL SET.

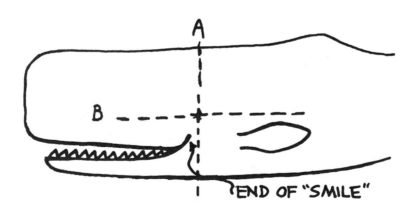

FIG. 30

STEP 19. MOUNTING THE WHALE

YOUR WHALE & BASE SHOULD BE COMPLETELY SANDED & READY FOR PAINTING. PAINTING IS DONE AFTER YOUR WHALE IS ATTACHED TO THE BASE FOR EASIER HANDLING. USE A 1/4 INCH DRILL BIT & DRILL A HOLE 1/2 INCH DEEP IN THE CENTER OF THE WHALE'S UNDERSIDE (FIG. 31). DO THE SAME FOR THE TOOTH BASE, BUT MAKE THAT HOLE ONLY 1/4 INCH DEEP. APPLY A LITTLE GLUE TO BOTH ENDS OF A 1/4 INCH DOWEL ABOUT 2 1/2 INCHES LONG & ASSEMBLE THE 3 PIECES (FIG. 31). YOU CAN LINE UP THE WHALE ON THE TOOTH ANY WAY THAT YOU LIKE.

FIG. 31

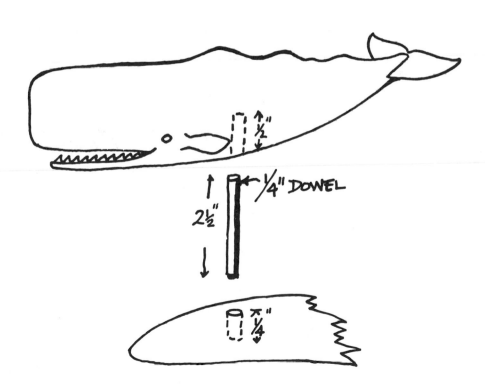

STEP 20. FINISHING THE WHALE

STAINING • USE ANY COLOR STAINS THAT WILL BLEND WELL WHERE YOU PLAN ON PLACING THE WHALE. A GOOD CHOICE IS USING STRAIGHT BLACK PAINT & RUBBING HARD WITH A RAG TO GET AN EBONY STAIN. FINISH WITH 3 COATS OF POLYURETHANE.

PAINTING • APPLY A PRIMER. PAINT THE BACK WITH A DULL BLACK OR FLAT ENAMEL MIXED WITH A LITTLE BLUE ENAMEL SO THE COLOR ISN'T PURE BLACK. BRUSH THIS BLUE-BLACK MIXTURE ON THE AREAS INDICATED IN FIG. 32. IMMEDIATELY PAINT A SOLID WHITE ON THE REMAINING AREA. WHERE THE TWO COLORS MEET, BLEND THEM TOGETHER WITH A DRY BRUSH (USE YOUR FINGER TIPS). PAINT THE TOOTH & DOWEL WHITE & APPLY A COAT OF SATIN POLYURETHANE. THIS WILL YELLOW THE TOOTH A LITTLE, MAKING IT LOOK AGED. THE WHALE'S TEETH SHOULD BE INDIVIDUALLY PAINTED WHITE. A DROP OF FINGERNAIL POLISH CAN BE APPLIED TO THE EYES FOR GLOSSINESS.

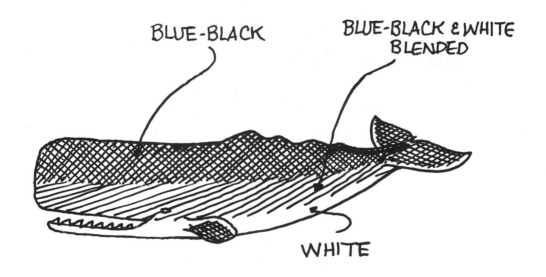

BLUE-BLACK

BLUE-BLACK & WHITE BLENDED

WHITE

FIG. 32

The Shell Doorknocker
Project No. 4

TOOLS NEEDED
HALF-ROUND GOUGE (Pg.165)
CARVER'S CHISEL

Besides using this project as a door knocker, it also makes an attractive wall hanging.

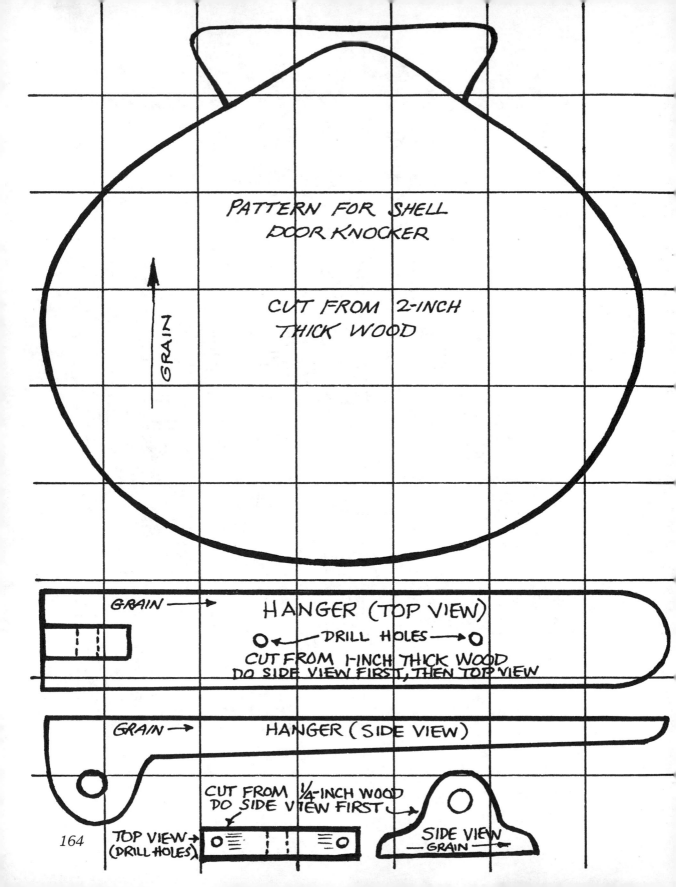

PATTERN FOR SHELL
DOOR KNOCKER

GRAIN

CUT FROM 2-INCH
THICK WOOD

GRAIN → HANGER (TOP VIEW)

O ← DRILL HOLES → O

CUT FROM 1-INCH THICK WOOD
DO SIDE VIEW FIRST, THEN TOP VIEW

GRAIN → HANGER (SIDE VIEW)

CUT FROM ¼-INCH WOOD
DO SIDE VIEW FIRST

164

TOP VIEW →
(DRILL HOLES)

SIDE VIEW
— GRAIN →

STEP 1.

SECURE YOUR SHELL TO A BACKBOARD BY USING SCREWS OR
TWO NAILS THROUGH THE BOARD & PRESS SHELL ONTO THEM
(PROCEDURE FOR THE NAILS THROUGH THE BOARD COVERED IN
SPERM WHALE PROJECT). SOMETIMES IT IS EASIER TO USE THE
NAILS BECAUSE IT MAKES IT SIMPLE TO LIFT THE SHELL OFF
& PRESS IT BACK ON ANY TIME YOU WISH.

USING A HALF-ROUND GOUGE, FOLLOW THE PATTERN OUT-
LINE OF THE HINGED AREA & CARVE THE HINGED AREA DOWN
(FIG. 1) UNTIL IT IS ONLY ¼ INCH THICK. REMOVE THIS WOOD
FLAT & EVEN, BEING CAREFUL NOT TO LOSE YOUR SHELL SHAPE
BY REDUCING THE SIZE OF THE HINGED AREA AS YOU CARVE
IT DOWN. TRY TO MAKE YOUR CUTS PERPENDICULAR SO
AS THE HINGED AREA IS RECESSED, THE SHELL WALL IS
STRAIGHT (FIG. 2). THE SMALLER THE HALF-ROUND YOU
USE, THE TIGHTER & CLEANER THIS AREA WILL BE WHERE
THE SHELL MEETS THE HINGED AREA.

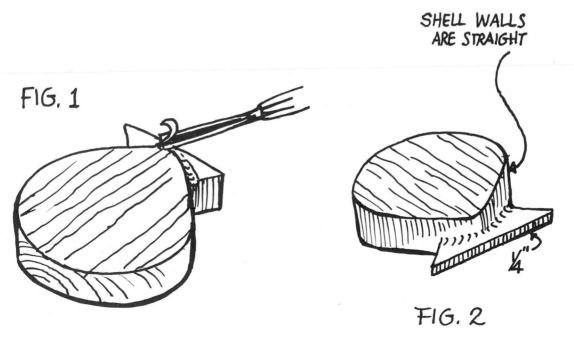

FIG. 1

SHELL WALLS
ARE STRAIGHT

¼"

FIG. 2

STEP 2. ROUNDING THE SHELL

USING A CARVER'S CHISEL, CARVE FROM THE SIDES TOWARD THE CENTER ALONG DOTTED LINES (FIG. 3) & REMOVE WOOD FLAT ACROSS THE SHELL, FROM THE HIGH POINT ROUND OFF THE SHELL TO WITHIN ¼ INCH OF THE EDGE (FIG. 4). USE THESE DOTTED LINES TO KEEP YOUR ROUNDING EVEN. AFTER THE MAJORITY OF THE WOOD HAS BEEN REMOVED, CARVE TO A MORE ROUNDED SHAPE AS FIG. 4 SIDE VIEW.

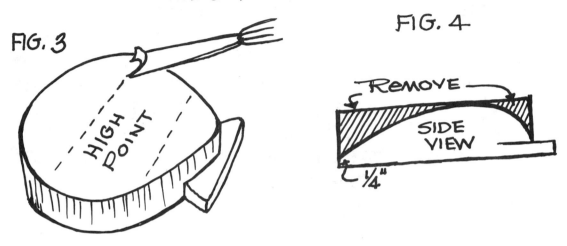

FIG. 3

HIGH POINT

FIG. 4

REMOVE

SIDE VIEW

¼"

STEP 3. ROUNDING THE SHELL (concluded)

USING THE CARVER'S CHISEL, ROUND THE SHELL SIDE TO SIDE, STARTING ON THE OUTSIDE EDGES WORKING TOWARD THE CENTER (FIG. 5), WORK BOTH SIDES AT THE SAME TIME FOR MORE EVEN ROUNDING. SEE TOP VIEW (FIG. 6) FOR FINISHED SHAPE.

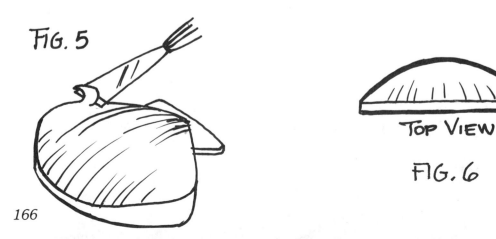

FIG. 5

TOP VIEW

FIG. 6

STEP 4. CARVING THE CONTOUR GROOVES

AFTER YOUR ROUNDING IS COMPLETED, SAND THE ENTIRE SHELL SMOOTH. DRAW IN 3 OR 4 LINES FOLLOWING THE CONTOUR OF THE CIRCUMFERENCE OF THE SHELL (FIG. 7) & CARVE GROOVES ALONG THESE LINES WITH A SMALL HALF-ROUND. CARVE THESE GROOVES ABOUT 1/8 INCH DEEP & WITH YOUR FOLDED SANDPAPER SAND THESE GROOVES SMOOTH, BLENDING THEM INTO THE SURFACE OF THE SHELL.

CONTOUR GROOVES

FIG. 7

STEP 5. CARVING THE SHELL EDGE

TURN YOUR SHELL OVER & WITH A HALF-ROUND GOUGE, CARVE ALONG THE OUTER EDGE OF THE SHELL. REMOVE WOOD FROM THE REMAINING 1/4-INCH EDGE UNTIL YOU BRING THE SHELL EDGE TO 1/16 INCH. THE HALF-ROUND WILL MAKE A CONCAVE GROOVE WHICH WILL MAKE THE SHELL LOOK THIN. (FIG. 8). FIG. 9 WILL SHOW THE RECESS YOU NEED.

FIG. 8

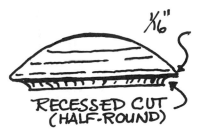

1/16"

RECESSED CUT (HALF-ROUND)

FIG. 9

STEP 6. ASSEMBLING YOUR DOOR KNOCKER
AFTER COMPLETELY SANDING ALL PARTS INCLUDING THE
HANGERS, SCREW & GLUE THE SHELL HANGER TO THE SHELL
WITH 2 1/4-3/8-INCH SCREWS (FIG. 10 A). NOTICE THESE
SCREWS ARE NOT STRAIGHT IN BUT AT A LITTLE ANGLE.
THIS IS BECAUSE THE HANGER IS SAWN AT A LITTLE ANGLE,
& IF THE SCREW IS PUT IN STRAIGHT, IT WILL SPLIT THE
HANGER. NEXT, PRESS IN PLACE TWO UPHOLSTERY TACKS
(FIG. 10 B) ONTO BACK OF THE SHELL AT ITS BOTTOM & ONTO
THE DOOR HANGER AT ITS BOTTOM. MAKE SURE THESE TACKS
STRIKE EACH OTHER WHEN THE DOOR HANGER & THE SHELL
ARE PUT TOGETHER WITH A 1/4-INCH DOWEL (FIG. 10 C). THE
1/4-INCH SECURING DOWEL SHOULD BE SLIGHTLY TAPERED
& THE SHELL HANGER LOOSE FITTED SO THE KNOCKER CAN
BE RAISED & LOWERED WITH EASE. SECURE THE WHOLE
UNIT TO YOUR DOOR WITH TWO 1/2-INCH SCREWS THROUGH
THE DOOR HANGER (FIG. 10 D).

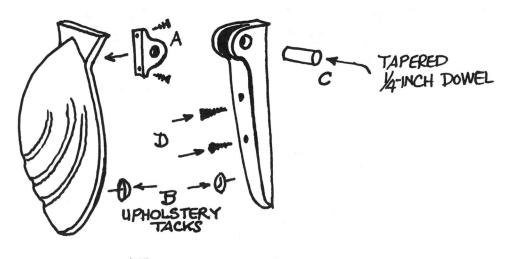

A

C   TAPERED
     1/4-INCH DOWEL

D

B
UPHOLSTERY
TACKS

FIG. 10

STEP 7.   FINISHING YOUR SHELL KNOCKER

ALL THE PARTS OF YOUR SHELL KNOCKER SHOULD BE SEALED, BUT DO NOT SEAL THEM WHEN TOGETHER. TAKE THE SHELL WITH ITS HANGER (**THESE** ARE GLUED TOGETHER) & SEAL IT BY ITSELF. SEAL THE DOOR HANGER SEPARATELY. THE DOWEL ONLY GETS SEALED ON ITS ENDS TO PREVENT ABSORPTION OF MOISTURE THROUGH THE END GRAIN. AFTER YOUR SEALING IS COMPLETED, ADJUST THE FIT OF THE DOWEL TO THE HANGERS. DURING THE SEALING PROCESS WITH POLYURETHANE, YOU CAN EXPECT A BUILD-UP OF POLYURETHANE ON YOUR HANGERS, MAKING THE DOWEL FIT TOO TIGHTLY ON THE SHELL HANGER. IT IS IMPORTANT THE SHELL HANGER IS MOVEABLE ON THE DOWEL AFTER ASSEMBLY.   IF YOU CHOOSE TO USE A STAIN COLOR ON THE SURFACE OF THE SHELL, DO THE STAINING PRIOR TO ANY SEALING.   IF YOU CHOOSE TO GOLD LEAF YOUR SHELL, SEAL FIRST & GOLD LEAF LAST.   ALL THESE PARTS SHOULD GET AT LEAST 3 COATS OF SEALER.

The Gold Panner

Project No. 5

A figurine Sculpture of an Old West Gold Panner perfect for your mantle.

TOOLS NEEDED

JACKKNIFE

HALF-ROUND
GOUGE (SMALL)

FISH TAIL
GOUGE (FIG. 14)

PARTING
TOOL (SMALL)

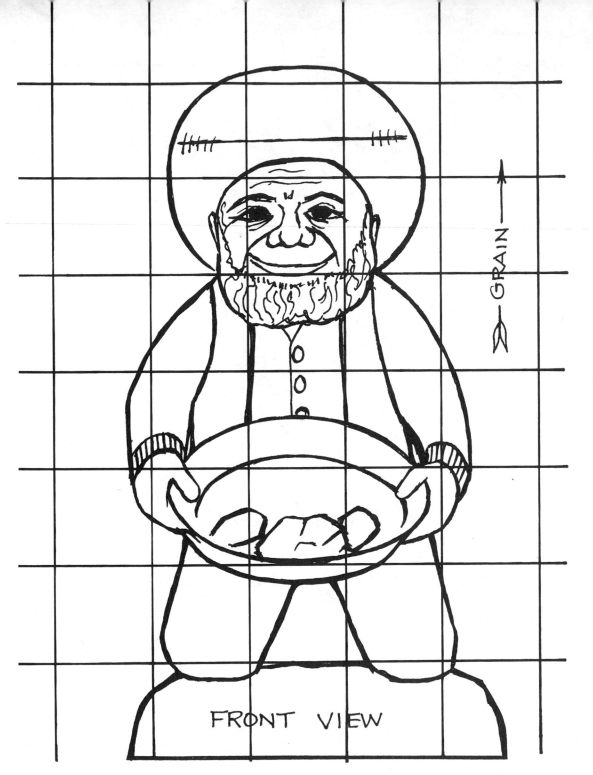

FRONT VIEW

USE THIS PATTERN FOR REFERENCE

GRAIN

GRAIN

SIDE VIEW

CUT TWO SIDE VIEWS OUT OF 2-INCH
THICK WOOD & GLUE THEM TOGETHER
SIDE TO SIDE.

STEP 1. BLOCKING OUT

IN DOING 3-D SCULPTING, THE DIFFICULT PART IS KNOWING
WHERE TO START. WE GENERALLY EVALUATE THE PIECE & SELECT
AREAS WE KNOW WHERE THE WOOD HAS TO BE REMOVED. THE
BEST PROC E DURE IS TO ELIMINATE THESE AREAS PRIOR TO ANY
ROUNDING OR SHAPING. THIS IS CALLED BLOCKING OUT. INSTEAD
OF CUTTING OUT THE FRONT VIEW ON THE BAND SAW, WE WILL
DO ALL THE BLOCKING OUT BY CARVING. THE REASON IS THAT
THERE IS LITTLE TO SAW OUT FOR SHAPE & YOU STAND A CHANCE
OF SAWING AT THE WRONG ANGLE.

USING YOUR PATTERNS AS A GUIDE, SKETCH IN THE ROUNDED
SHAPE OF THE TOP VIEW OF THE HAT (FIG. 1). CARVE FROM THE
SHOULDERS UPWARD & REMOVE WOOD FROM BOTH SIDES TO THE
BRIM EDGE (FIG. 1). USE YOUR CLIP BLADE BECAUSE OF ITS LENGTH
& REACH.

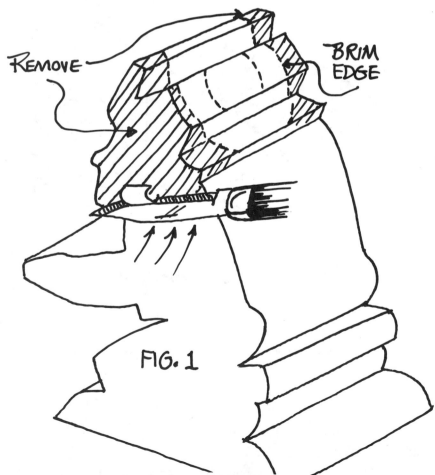

REMOVE

BRIM
EDGE

FIG. 1

STEP 2. BLOCKING OUT THE FACE - LAYOUT

DRAW A LINE USING SIDE VIEW FIG. 2 ALONG THE BRIM OF THE HAT ON BOTH SIDES. DO THE SAME FOR THE SHOULDER LINE. GO TO FIG. 3 & DRAW LINES TO ESTABLISH WHERE THE FACE WILL BE. USE YOUR PATTERNS FOR A GUIDE FOR THE SIZE & SHAPE OF THE HEAD. SKETCH IN YOUR LINES A WEE BIT LARGER THAN YOU EXPECT TO CARVE AWAY. THIS AREA, FROM THE FRONT VIEW FACE LINES BACK TO THE HAT & BRIM LINES & SHOULDER LINES, WILL BE REMOVED, EXPOSING THE BLOCKED-OUT FACE.

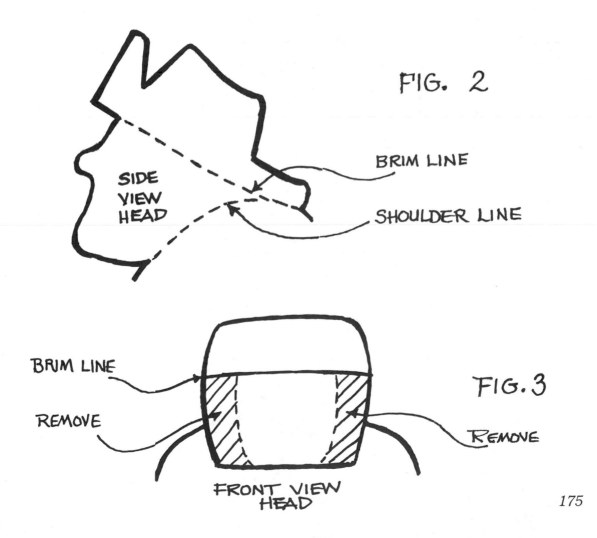

FIG. 2

BRIM LINE

SIDE VIEW HEAD

SHOULDER LINE

BRIM LINE

FIG. 3

REMOVE

REMOVE

FRONT VIEW HEAD

STEP 3. BLOCKING OUT THE FACE

USING YOUR JACKKNIFE, CAREFULLY CUT STRAIGHT IN ON THE BRIM LINE (FIG. 4A) & REMOVE WOOD A LITTLE AT A TIME IN EVEN LAYERS WITH AN UP-CUT ON THE SIDES OF THE FACE (FIG. 4B). AS YOU CARVE THE FACE NARROWER, CUT WITH STRAIGHT CUTS INTO THE SHOULDERS (FIG. 4C). CONTINUE TO DO THIS SEQUENCE UNTIL YOU HAVE RECESSED THE HEAD FROM THE BRIM ACCORDING TO YOUR LAYOUT LINES. IF YOUR CUTS ARE PERFECTLY STRAIGHT IN, THE FACE WILL NOT WIDEN AS IT GOES BACK TOWARD THE NECK. IN FIG. 4B YOU WILL NOTE THAT THE ARROWS GO IN BOTH DIRECTIONS. THIS IS BECAUSE IN THIS AREA YOU ARE CARVING DIRECTLY PARALLEL WITH THE GRAIN &, WHEN CARVING THIS CLOSE TO PARALLEL, THE GRAIN DIRECTION WILL OFTEN CHANGE. IF YOU NOTICE YOU ARE BREAKING & TEARING THE WOOD IN ONE DIRECTION, TRY THE OTHER WAY. CONTINUE THIS UP & DOWN CARVING, BEING SURE TO CLIP CLEAN ON THE BRIM & SHOULDER STROKES.

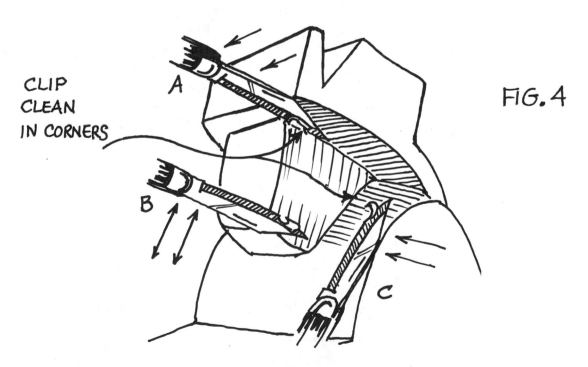

CLIP CLEAN IN CORNERS

A

B

C

FIG. 4

STEP 4. SHAPING THE HAT & BRIM

SKETCH IN LINES FOR THE TOP OF THE HAT & BRIM LINES (FIG. 5 & 6). USING YOUR JACKKNIFE POINT, INCISE ALONG THE BRIM LINE & REMOVE EXCESS WOOD FROM THE SIDES OF THE HAT WITH GRADUAL DOWNSTROKES INTO, BUT NOT GOING BEYOND, THE INCISED BRIM CUT (FIG. 6). MAKE SURE YOUR INCISED BRIM CUT IS ALWAY DEEPER THAN WHAT YOU ARE CARVING AWAY ON YOUR DOWNSTROKE OR ELSE YOU COULD EASILY SNAP OFF OR BREAK A PIECE OF THE BRIM AWAY. THE TOP SECTION OF THE HAT HAS TO COINCIDE WITH THE SHAPE OF THE HEAD. A GENERAL MISTAKE IN CARVING HATS ON HEADS IS YOU MAY HAVE A TENDENCY TO CARVE THE HAT TO MAKE IT LOOK 4 SIZES TOO SMALL FOR THE HEAD, THUS EITHER MAKING THE HAT SIT WAY UP ON THE HEAD OR SQUASHING THE HEAD.

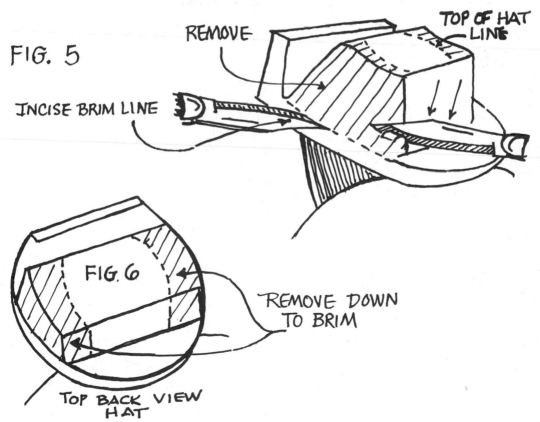

FIG. 5

REMOVE

TOP OF HAT LINE

INCISE BRIM LINE

FIG. 6

REMOVE DOWN TO BRIM

TOP BACK VIEW HAT

STEP 5. BLOCKING OUT THE GOLD PAN

USING YOUR FRONT VIEW PATTERN AS A REFERENCE, SKETCH IN LINES ROUNDING THE TOP OF THE FRONT OF THE UPTURNED BRIM, AND ROUNDING ON THE TOPS OF THE SHOULDERS. DRAW A CIRCLE WHERE THE GOLD PAN IS LOCATED BY DIVIDING THE AREA FROM THE END OF THE GOLD PAN & THE ELBOW CREASE & DIVIDING THE AREA SIDE TO SIDE. WHERE THESE LINES INTERSECT, USE A COMPASS & DRAW THE WIDEST CIRCLE THAT WILL FIT. SKETCH IN WHERE HANDS GRASP PAN & ARC INTO THE ARMS (FIG. 7). CARVE AWAY ALL SHADED CORNERS WITH YOUR JACKKNIFE. WHEN CARVING AWAY THESE CORNER AREAS, TRY NOT TO RE-MOVE TOO MUCH AT A TIME SINCE THESE AREAS BREAK AWAY EASILY.

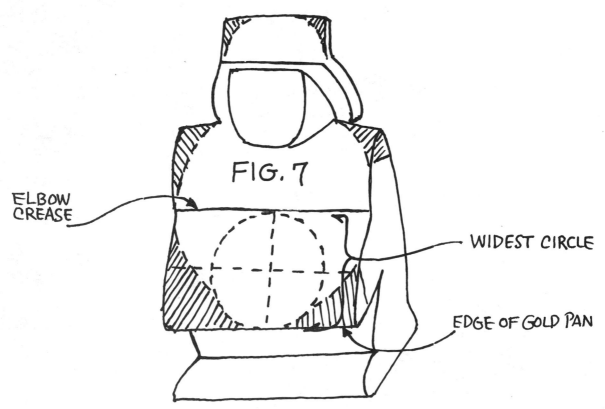

REMOVE ALL SHADED AREAS

FIG. 7

ELBOW CREASE

WIDEST CIRCLE

EDGE OF GOLD PAN

STEP 6. BLOCKING OUT THE ARMS

USE YOUR REFERENCE PATTERNS TO SKETCH IN WHERE THE ARMS ARE LOCATED. NOTICE THE CENTER OF THE ARMS FORMS THE CENTER OF THE SHOULDERS (FIG. 8). DO NOT HAVE YOUR SHOULDERS TOO FAR FORWARD. REMOVE WOOD FROM SIDES OF THE BODY TO EXPOSE ARMS (FIG.8 & 9) & ALLOW FOR ROUNDING OF THE ARMS.

REMOVE
SEE FRONT
VIEW
PATTERN

REMOVE
SEE BACK
VIEW

SIDE VIEW

FIG. 8

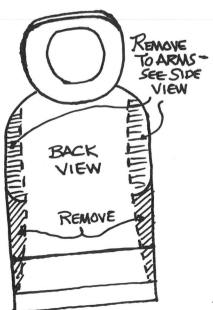

REMOVE
TO ARMS—
SEE SIDE
VIEW

BACK VIEW

REMOVE

FIG. 9

STEP 7. BLOCKING TORSO & UPPER ARMS
USING A SMALL HALF-ROUND GOUGE, CARVE A CONCAVE
GROOVE FROM THE FRONT OF THE ARM TO THE BODY. THIS IS
DONE TO ACCENT WHERE THE UPPER ARM IS LOCATED PRIOR
TO ROUNDING (FIG. 10). REMOVE ONLY AS MUCH WOOD AS
NEEDED TO SHOW THE THICKNESS OF THE ARMS & THE SHAPE
OF THE TORSO.

FIG. 10

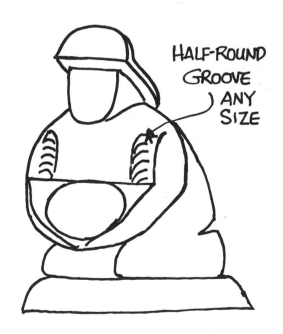

HALF-ROUND
GROOVE
ANY
SIZE

STEP 8. SHAPING THE BACK

CARVE FROM THE BUTTOCKS UP THE BACK ON BOTH SIDES (FIG. 11). ROUND OVER ALL SHARP CORNERS. FOLLOW THE DOTTED LINES IN THE AREA OF THE FEET & REMOVE EXCESS WOOD. CUT A DEEP 'V' WHERE THE UPPER & LOWER LEGS ARE CREASED. ROUND THE UPPER & LOWER LEGS INTO THIS 'V' FOLLOWING ARROWS (FIG.11). TO ROUND THE LOWER LEG INTO THE BASE, YOU WILL HAVE TO MAKE A STRAIGHT-IN CUT AT THE BASE & ROUND THE LEG INTO THIS CUT.

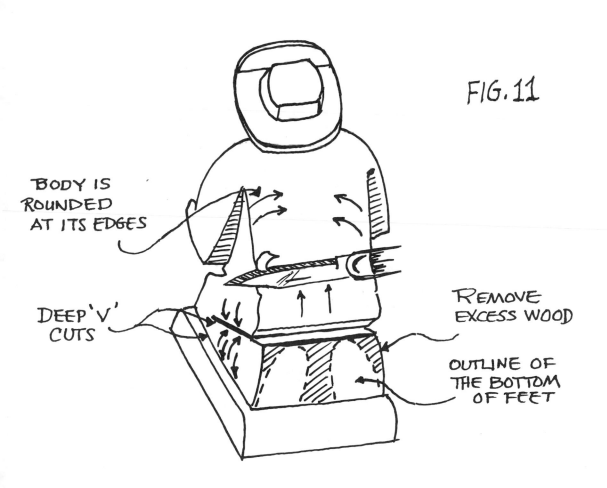

FIG. 11

BODY IS ROUNDED AT ITS EDGES

DEEP 'V' CUTS

REMOVE EXCESS WOOD

OUTLINE OF THE BOTTOM OF FEET

STEP 9. ROUNDING THE ARMS & BLOCKING OUT THE FACE

ROUND OVER THE OUTSIDE EDGES OF BOTH ARMS DOWN TO THE AREA WHERE THE HANDS WILL BE (FIG. 12). THIS OUTSIDE ROUNDING WILL ENABLE US TO ESTABLISH WHERE THE INSIDE ROUNDING & SEPARATION OF THE ARMS ARE FROM THE GOLD PAN & THE BODY. REMOVE WOOD FROM THE **SIDES** OF THE FACE, LEAVING AN UN- CARVED STRIPE DOWN THE CENTER OF THE FACE THE WIDTH OF THE NOSE, (SEE PATTERN FOR REFERENCE & SIZE) ABOUT 1/4 INCH WIDE.

FIG. 12

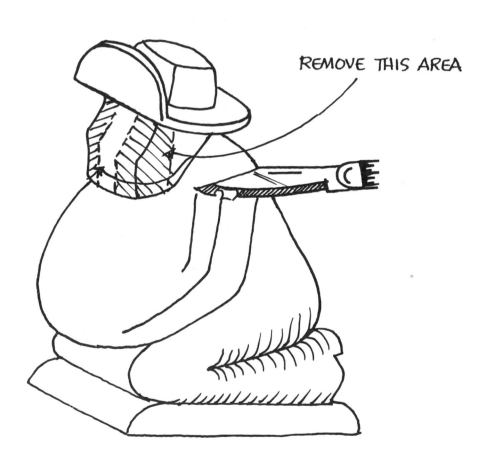

REMOVE THIS AREA

STEP 10. LAYOUT OF THE GOLD PAN & SHAPING (FIG. 13)

WE NOW HAVE TO LOCATE THE POSITION OF THE HANDS & THUMBS ON THE PAN. ON THE REMAINING FLAT AREA OF THE FORE-ARMS & PAN, DRAW A CIRCLE SLIGHTLY SMALLER (1/8 INCH) THAN YOUR ORIGINAL CIRCLE DONE IN STEP 5, WHICH WILL FORM THE LIP OF THE GOLD PAN. DRAW ANOTHER CIRCLE ABOUT 1/2 INCH IN FROM THE LARGEST CIRCLE TO FORM THE BOTTOM OF THE PAN. SKETCH IN 3 ROCKS IN THE LOWER BOTTOM OF THE PAN. SKETCH IN THUMBS' LOCATION BY USING THE PATTERN AS A GUIDE. SKETCH IN INSIDE OF ARMS.

USE YOUR JACKKNIFE POINT & REMOVE AREA BETWEEN THE PAN & THE ARMS WITH A DEEP CREVICE (FIG. 13). THE BOTTOM OF THE PAN HAS TO BE RECESSED & THE WALLS OF THE PAN HAVE TO BE SLOPED FROM THE PAN LIP TO THE PAN BOTTOM. USING A SHALLOW FISH TAIL GOUGE (FIG. 13A), REMOVE WOOD A LITTLE AT A TIME FROM INSIDE THE PAN, LEAVING THE ROCKS ALONE. CLEAN THE SLOPED EDGES STRAIGHT WITH A JACK-KNIFE.

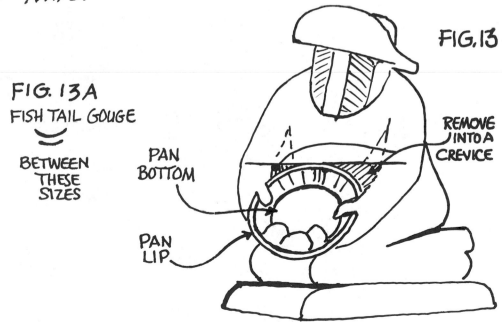

FIG. 13

FIG. 13A
FISH TAIL GOUGE

BETWEEN THESE SIZES

PAN BOTTOM

REMOVE INTO A CREVICE

PAN LIP

STEP 11. BLOCKING OUT EYES

MOST OF OUR BLOCKING OUT & SHAPING IS COMPLETED & WE ARE NOW READY TO START FINISHING THE GOLD PANNER. THE BEST PLACE TO START IS THE FACE & HEAD. ONCE THE HEAD IS CARVED, WE WILL HAVE A PROPORTIONAL SIZE TO GO BY FOR **THE RE-MAINDER** OF THE FIGURE. USING A SMALL HALF-ROUND GOUGE, CARVE A DEEP GROOVE ALONG THE EYE BROW LINE & ANOTHER GROOVE UP THE SIDES OF THE NOSE (FIG.14). NOTICE THE NOSE GROOVES LEAVE THE NOSE WIDER AT ITS END & NARROW IT TOWARD THE BRIDGE OF THE NOSE. WHERE THE BROW LINE & THE NOSE LINE COME TOGETHER, IT WILL BE THE DEEPEST, FORMING THE INSIDE CORNERS OF THE EYES. FLATTEN THE AREA OF THE EYE & CHEEK SO THE NOSE IS WELL EXPOSED.

FIG. 14

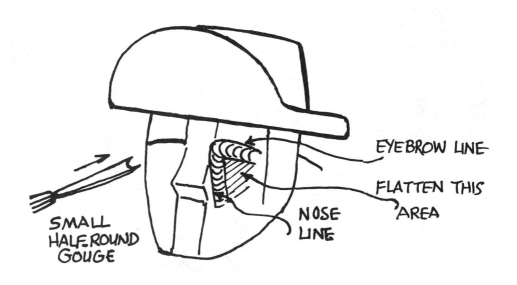

SMALL HALF-ROUND GOUGE

NOSE LINE

EYEBROW LINE

FLATTEN THIS AREA

STEP 12. SHAPING NOSE & MOUTH FEATURES

SHAPE THE FOREHEAD WITH YOUR JACKKNIFE BY REMOVING ALL FLAT AREAS. THE FOREHEAD HAS A NICE EVEN ROUNDING FROM SIDE TO SIDE (FIG. 15). DO THE SAME TO THE UPTURNED BRIM. CARVE THE NOSE SO IT HAS A TRIANGULAR SHAPE LOOKING AT IT FROM ITS END. SKETCH IN YOUR MOUTH LINE & CHEEK LINES. YOUR CHEEK LINES START AT THE EDGE OF THE **NOSE & GO** A LITTLE PAST THE END OF THE MOUTH (FIG. 15). USING THE POINT OF YOUR JACKKNIFE, CARVE CRISP V-CUTS ALONG THESE LINES.

FIG. 15

ROUND BRIM (DOTTED LINE)

ROUND FOREHEAD (DOTTED LINE)

CHEEK LINE 'V' CUT

MOUTH LINE 'V' CUT

STEP 13. CARVING THE FACE (FIG. 16)

ROUND OVER THE FRONT EDGE OF THE UPTURNED HAT BRIM. USING A HALF-ROUND, CARVE A GROOVE UNDER THE LOWER LIP, FOLLOWING THE SLIGHT ARC IN FIG. 16. WITH YOUR HALF-ROUND, CARVE A SHORT GROOVE IN THE MIDDLE OF THE UPPER LIP UP TO THE NOSE (SEPTUM). WITH A JACKKNIFE, CARVE FROM YOUR SEPTUM GROOVE TOWARD THE SIDES OF THE FACE INTO THE CHEEK CUTS. ROUND OUT YOUR NOSE UP TO THE BRIDGE. THE END OF THE NOSE IS QUITE ROUND & ROUNDS DOWN ONTO THE SIDES OF THE NOSTRILS. USE THE POINT OF YOUR JACKKNIFE & MAKE CRISP 'V' CUTS FOR THE EYES, UPPER & LOWER LIDS, & CROW'S-FEET AT THE OUTSIDE CORNERS OF THE EYES. USE FIG. 16 FOR LOCATION OF THESE 'V' CUTS. SKETCH IN THE BEARD & DROP THE FACE BACK FROM THE BEARD SLIGHTLY. ROUND BEARD INTO THE FACE. ROUND CHEEKS INTO UPPER LIP. SAND THE FACE CAREFULLY.

FIG. 16

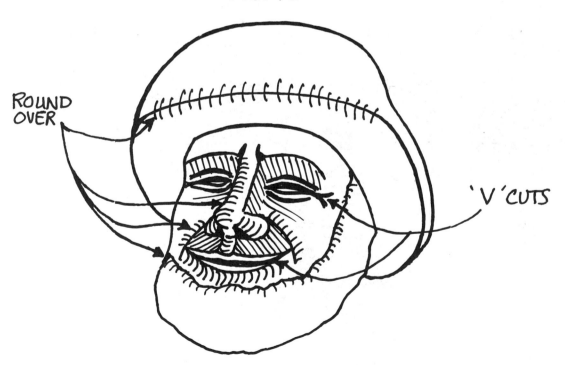

ROUND OVER

'V' CUTS

STEP 14. CARVING THE BEARD

YOU HAVE SHAPED THE BEARD INTO THE FACE. NOW YOU
HAVE TO CARVE THE BEARD INTO THE NECK & SHOULDERS.
USE YOUR JACKKNIFE & GIVE YOUR BEARD A TRIM. SHAPE
THE BEARD TO THE FACE & IN DOING THIS PROPERLY, YOU
WILL HAVE ACCENTED THE SHOULDERS, ENABLING YOU
TO START SHAPING THE SHOULDER ROUNDNESS.
TO CARVE THE BEARD, USE A PARTING TOOL & CARVE IRREG-
ULAR GROOVES INTO THE BEARD, FOLLOWING FIG. 17. SKIP
BY THE AREA OF THE EARS WHICH WE CARVE LATER.
CUT SMALL GROOVES INTO THE UPPER LIP (FIG. 17) TO MAKE
YOUR GOLD PANNER LOOK OLD. ALSO CUT A FEW EXTRA
LINES UNDER THE EYES.

FIG. 17

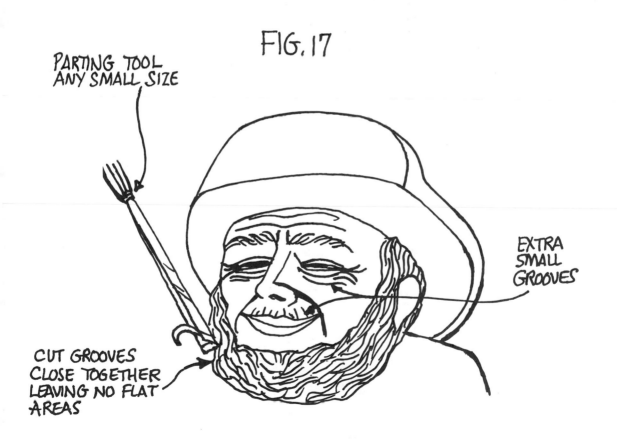

PARTING TOOL
ANY SMALL SIZE

EXTRA
SMALL
GROOVES

CUT GROOVES
CLOSE TOGETHER
LEAVING NO FLAT
AREAS

STEP 15. TOP OF THE HAT

NOW THE BEARD & FACE HAVE BEEN SHAPED. GO TO THE TOP OF THE HAT & SHAPE IT SO IT CONFORMS TO THE HEAD. BE CAREFUL NOT TO MAKE THE HAT SMALLER THAN THE SIZE OF THE HEAD. THE HAT FITS ON THE HEAD. MAKE IT LOOK THAT WAY. YOU CAN SHAPE THE HAT TO ANY SHAPE YOU WANT. THIS GOLD PANNER IS RUGGED SO HIS HAT SHOULD NOT LOOK LIKE A NEW HAT. WITH YOUR JACKKNIFE, CARVE AROUND THE TOP OF HAT BY CARVING DOWN ITS SIDES INTO THE BRIM. AT THE SAME TIME CARVE ALONG THE BRIM, THINING IT INTO THE TOP (FIG. 18). AS YOU CARVE DOWN THE SIDE, YOU CAN CHANGE THE SHAPE OF THE TOP (IN FIG. 18 WE HAVE A SQUARER, MORE BEATEN LOOK). THIN THE UPPER BRIM TO CONFORM TO THE LOWER BRIM. TRY TO BRING THE EDGES OF THE BRIM TO 1/8 INCH. USING A HALF-ROUND, CARVE A GROOVE INTO TOP OF THE HAT (FIG. 18 as a guide) TO FORM A DEPRESSION FOLLOWING THE CONTOUR OF THE TOP OF THE HAT. USE THE POINT OF YOUR JACKKNIFE TO SCORE THE HAT BAND & CARVE AWAY A SMALL AMOUNT OF WOOD TO EXPOSE THE BAND FROM THE TOP OF THE HAT.

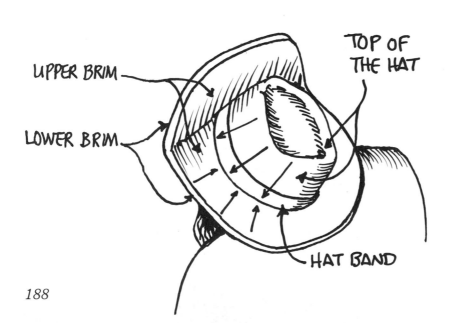

UPPER BRIM

LOWER BRIM

TOP OF THE HAT

FIG. 18

HAT BAND

STEP 16.

CHECK THE HAT BRIM FOR EVEN THICKNESS & SAND THE HAT, BRIM & BAND SMOOTH. USE FIG. 19 AS A GUIDE & SKETCH IN THE EAR SHAPE. WITH THE POINT OF YOUR JACKKNIFE, CARVE A SLIGHT ARC ON THE FORWARD PART OF THE EAR, STRAIGHT IN. LAY YOUR BLADE FLAT AGAINST THE EAR & REMOVE WOOD FROM THE EDGE OF THE EAR INTO THE ARC CUT (FIG. 19A). WITH A LITTLE ROUNDING OVER OF THE EAR EDGE & A LITTLE SANDING, YOUR EARS ARE DONE. THIS GOLD PANNER'S KERCHIEF (AROUND HIS NECK) HAS TO BE RELIEVED FROM THE SHOULDERS & BACK. TO DO THIS, CARVE UP THE SHOULDERS INTO THE NECK AREA & LOWER THE SHOULDERS 1/8 INCH. CARVE UP TO THE NECK, LEAVING 1/8 INCH AT THE BASE OF THE NECK (FIG. 19B). CONTINUE UP & OVER THE SHOULDERS ONTO THE BACK, LEAVING THIS 1/8 INCH SQUARE BUNDLE AROUND THE NECK. ON THE BACK, SKETCH IN THE FLUFFED END OF THE KERCHIEF (DOTTED LINES FIG. 20). WITH THE POINT OF YOUR JACKKNIFE, CARVE STRAIGHT IN ALONG THE DOTTED LINE & CARVE WOOD FROM THE BACK, RELIEVING THE KERCHIEF END. WHEN DROPPING BACK THE BACK, DO THE ENTIRE BACK & RE-ROUND THE SIDES.

FIG. 19

B.

A.

1/8 INCH THICKNESS

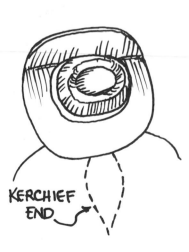

KERCHIEF END

FIG. 20

189

STEP 17. THE BACK & VEST

SHAPE THE KERCHIEF END BY ROUNDING WITH YOUR JACKKNIFE & USING A PARTING TOOL, CARVE UP THE KERCHIEF INTO THE HAT BRIM WITH A NUMBER OF CLOSE-TOGETHER, IRREGULAR CUTS (FIG. 21 A). USING THE POINT OF YOUR JACKKNIFE CARVE A STRAIGHT-IN CUT TO OUTLINE THE ARMHOLES & BOTTOM OF THE VEST (SEE FIG. 21 FOR THEIR LOCATION). DROP THE ARMS BACK FROM THE VEST ARM HOLES 1/8 INCH. DROP THE TROUSERS BACK FROM THE BOTTOM OF THE VEST A LITTLE MORE THAN 1/8 INCH. NOTICE WE HAVE LEFT A BULGE FOR THE FLASK IN HIS LEFT REAR POCKET. AFTER YOU HAVE OUTLINED THE VEST YOU MAY HAVE TO RE-SHAPE THE BACK BECAUSE IT MAY LOOK TOO LARGE. ALSO THE SHOULDERS & OUTSIDE UPPER ARMS ARE RE-SHAPED BY FLATTENING EQUALLY. WE WILL CONTINUE THE VEST SHAPING IN THE NEXT STEP FOR THE FRONT.

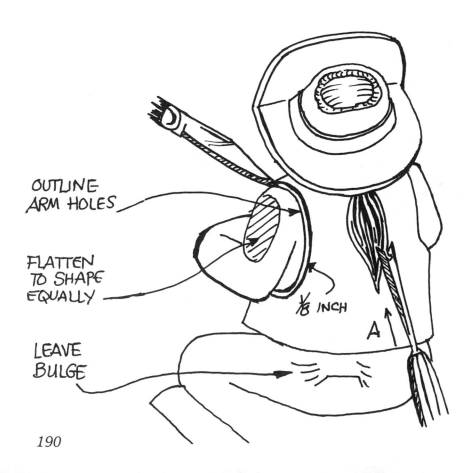

FIG. 21

OUTLINE ARM HOLES

FLATTEN TO SHAPE EQUALLY

LEAVE BULGE

1/8 INCH

A

STEP 18. FRONT OF BODY & ARMS

SKETCH IN THE FRONT ELLIPSE OF THE VEST ARM HOLES. USE THE POINT OF YOUR JACKKNIFE & RECESS THE SHOULDERS & BODY FROM THE ARM HOLE. MAKE SURE YOU HAVE CARVED THESE ARM HOLES SO THEY WOULD MATCH FRONT TO BACK (FIG. 22 DOTTED LINE). YOU MAY NOT BE ABLE TO CARVE THE RECESS AT THE ARM PIT, BUT THE FRONT & THE BACK OF THE ARM HOLE SHOULD LINE UP. ESTABLISH THE ACTUAL SIDE VIEW OF THE ARM (FIG. 22) & SHAPE TO ITS PROPER SIZE. THE ARMS CAN NOW BE ROUNDED INTO THE SHOULDERS & THE BODY. MAKE A DEFINITE 'V' CUT AT THE TOP OF THE ELBOW FOR A SHARP CREASE IN YOUR GOLD PANNER'S LONG UNDERWEAR SHIRT TO ESTABLISH WHERE THE ELBOW JOINT IS. CUT 'V' GROOVES ON BOTH SIDES OF YOUR ELBOW CUT & WITH FOLDED SANDPAPER, SAND 'TIL ALL THESE GROOVES HAVE ROUNDED INTO EACH OTHER (FIG. 22). CONTINUE YOUR ARM-ROUNDING ON THE INSIDE OF THE ARMS NEXT TO THE BODY BY FOLLOWING THE ROUNDING YOU HAVE ALREADY DONE TO THE OUTSIDE OF THE ARMS. ON THIS INSIDE ARM ROUNDING, YOU WILL PROBABLY HAVE TO RESHAPE THE BODY TO FIT THE ARMS & SHOULDERS. KEEP A CAREFUL EYE OUT FOR YOUR BODY SHAPE. DO NOT MAKE THE BODY TOO BIG BY NOT ALLOWING ENOUGH ROOM FOR YOUR ARMS. TO CONTINUE YOUR ROUNDING OF YOUR FOREARMS YOU WILL HAVE TO CARVE THROUGH THE AREA BETWEEN THE FOREARM, BODY & GOLD PAN (FIG. 22A) FOLLOWING THE CONTOUR OF THE VEST WHICH IS ALSO ROUNDED FROM ITS BOTTOM INTO THE ARMS & UPPER BODY (FIG. 22B). THIS AREA IS VERY DIFFICULT TO CARVE BECAUSE ALL YOU CAN USE IS THE POINT OF YOUR JACKKNIFE TO REMOVE A SMALL BIT OF WOOD AT A TIME. ONCE YOU HAVE OPENED THIS AREA SO YOU CAN SEE, MAKE 'V' CUTS TO SHOW THE LAPEL EDGE OF THE VEST & 'V' CUTS TO SHOW BUTTONED EDGE

STEP 18. FRONT OF BODY & ARMS (Con't)

OF THE LONG UNDERWEAR SHIRT (SEE PATTERN FOR LOCATION).
FOR THE BUTTONS, ALL WE NEED IS A DEPRESSION TO SHOW
THEIR LOCATION. CARVE THIS AREA AS **SMOOTHLY** AS POSSIBLE
BECAUSE SANDING HERE IS VERY DIFFICULT.
CONTINUE ROUNDING DOWN THE FOREARMS LEAVING A
BLOCK FOR THE THUMB ONLY ON THE GOLD PAN. THE REMAINDER
OF THE HAND IS ROUNDED INTO THE BOTTOM OF THE GOLD
PAN. GO BACK TO THE VEST & SHAPE IT DOWN TO THE
BODY & ARMS SO ITS EDGES SHOWING (ARM HOLES & LAPEL)
ARE ONLY 1/16-INCH THICK. MAKE SURE THE VEST CONFORMS
TO THE CONTOUR OF THE BODY. ROUND OVER THE KER-
CHIEF UNDER THE CHIN.

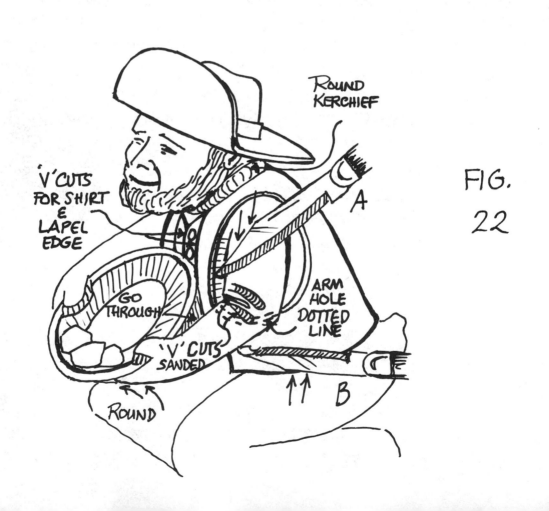

ROUND KERCHIEF

'V' CUTS FOR SHIRT & LAPEL EDGE

GO THROUGH

'V' CUTS SANDED

ROUND

ARM HOLE DOTTED LINE

A

B

FIG. 22

STEP 19. THE GOLD PAN

IT IS ALMOST IMPOSSIBLE TO CARVE THE UNDERSIDE & BACK OF THE GOLD PAN BECAUSE OF LACK OF ROOM TO WORK. TO REACH THIS AREA, YOU MUST DROP BACK THE LEGS FROM THE VEST (FIG. 23) BY SHAVING WOOD OFF THE SIDES OF THE LEGS WITH YOUR JACKKNIFE. AFTER YOU HAVE RECESSED THE LEGS, YOU CAN ROUND OVER THE TOPS OF THEM (FIG. 24) INTO THE VEST AREA. THIS ROUNDING SHOULD GIVE YOU AMPLE ROOM TO SHAPE THE PAN (FIG. 24 DOTTED LINES). TO REACH MUCH OF THIS AREA, USE A SMALL GOUGE (FIG. 25) & YOUR JACKKNIFE TO ACHIEVE AS MUCH OF THE BOTTOM SHAPE OF THE PAN AS POSSIBLE. SKETCH IN THE SHAPE OF THE HANDS & CAREFULLY, WITH THE POINT OF YOUR JACKKNIFE, SCORE AROUND THE HANDS. MAKE SURE WHEN YOU SKETCH YOUR HANDS THAT THEY ARE THE SAME SIZE. THE THUMB IS ON TOP OF THE PAN EDGE. DO NOT TRY TO CARVE THE THUMB YET. YOU ARE MORE INTERESTED IN GETTING THE ROUNDED SHAPE OF THE GOLD PAN FIRST. THE GREATEST HAZARD IN CARVING IN A TIGHT AREA SUCH AS BEHIND & UNDER THE PAN IS SLIPPING & CUTTING INTO THE BODY OR OTHER PLACES THAT HAVE ALREADY BEEN CARVED. THE REASON FOR THIS IS POOR VISIBILITY. AS YOU MAKE YOUR CUTS, BE SURE TO LOOK TO WHERE YOU ARE CARVING. THIS MAY MEAN YOU HAVE TO LOOK AT YOUR PIECE IN ALL DIRECTIONS BY TURNING IT OVER AND OVER. YOU WILL PROBABLY HAVE TO RECARVE THE INSIDE OF THE PAN TO COINCIDE WITH ITS OUTSIDE SINCE THE OUTSIDE IS MORE DIFFICULT TO REACH. IF YOU RE-CARVE THE INSIDE, LEAVE THE THUMB BLOCKS ALONE. CONCENTRATE ON THE GOLD PAN SHAPE ALONE. THE HANDS HAVE TO BE FITTED TO THE PAN, WHICH IS AN ABSOLUTE SHAPE. CARVE THE CUFFS A LITTLE SMALLER THAN THE SHIRT SLEEVES (FIG. 24).

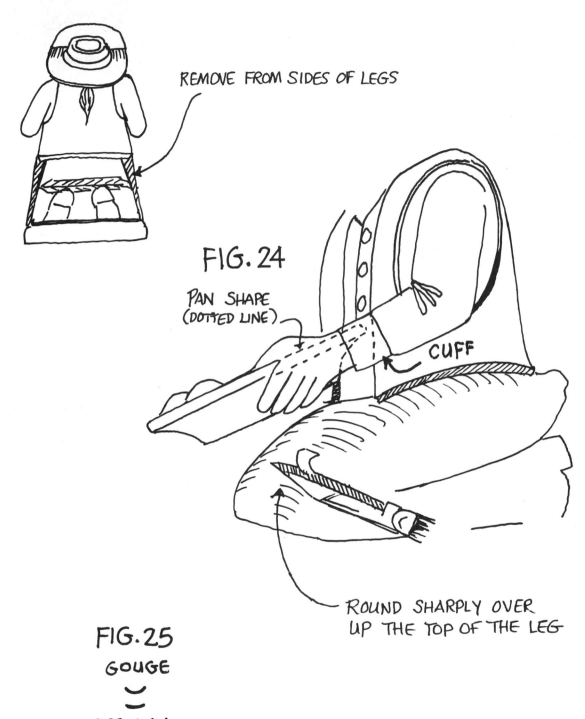

FIG. 23

REMOVE FROM SIDES OF LEGS

FIG. 24

PAN SHAPE
(DOTTED LINE)

CUFF

ROUND SHARPLY OVER
UP THE TOP OF THE LEG

FIG. 25

GOUGE

USE ANY
SIZE
BETWEEN
THESE
SIZES

STEP 20. THE HANDS

SKETCH IN THE THUMBS & HANDS USING FIG. 26 & FIG. 27 AS A
GUIDE. WITH THE POINT OF YOUR JACKKNIFE, CARVE STRAIGHT IN
AROUND THE THUMBS & HANDS & REMOVE WOOD DOWN TO THE
SHAPE OF THE GOLD PAN. SHAPE THE THUMBS BY ROUNDING
THEM OVER, LEAVING THEM FLAT ON THE PAN. YOU WILL HAVE
TO CARVE THE 3 ROCKS TO THEIR IRREGULAR SHAPES (FIG. 26)
& RE CARVE THE WALLS & BOTTOM OF THE PAN. THE FINGERS
(FIG. 27) ARE CARVED FLAT TO THE WALLS OF THE OUTSIDE
OF THE PAN & THE FINGERS ARE MADE BY CARVING THREE
SHALLOW 'V'S' WITH YOUR JACKKNIFE. ROUND EACH FINGER
SLIGHTLY.

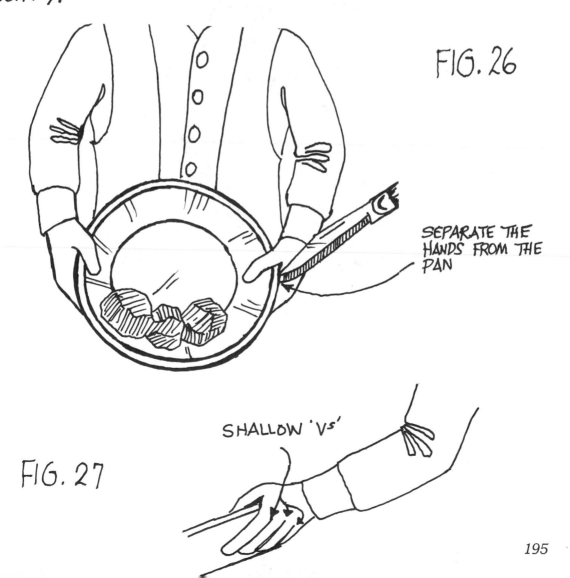

FIG. 26

SEPARATE THE
HANDS FROM THE
PAN

SHALLOW 'V'S'

FIG. 27

195

STEP 21. CARVING THE FLASK

THE BULGE THAT IS IN THE LEFT REAR WILL BE CARVED INTO THE PANNER'S POCKET. SKETCH IN THE SHAPE (FIG. 28) OF THE FLASK & USING A SMALL HALF-ROUND GOUGE (FIG. 29), CARVE AROUND THE FLASK (FIG. 28A), RELIEVING THE FLASK SHAPE FROM THE PANTS. WITH YOUR JACKKNIFE, CARVE THE ENTIRE REAR BACK FROM THE FLASK 1/4 INCH (FIG. 28 B). SHAPE THE FLASK USING FIG. 29A AS A GUIDE. WITH THE POINT OF YOUR JACKKNIFE, SCORE A STRAIGHT LINE ACROSS THE UPPER 1/3RD OF THE FLASK & DROP THIS AREA BACK TO SHOW THE TOP OF THE POCKET.

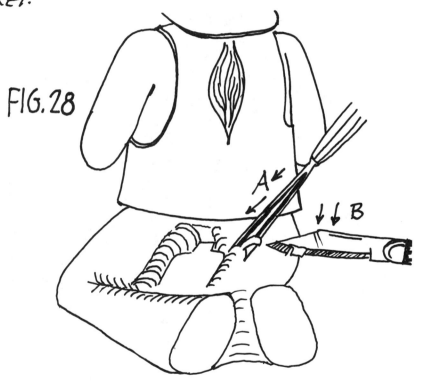

FIG. 28

A

B

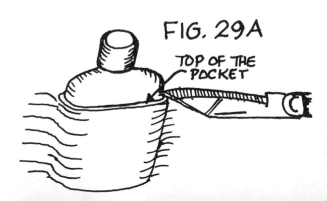

FIG. 29
USE ANY SIZE
BETWEEN THESE
SIZES

FIG. 29A

TOP OF THE
POCKET

STEP 22. CARVING THE SHOES

USING YOUR FISHTAIL GOUGE (FIG. 29), CARVE DOWN THE RUMP INTO A CREVICE BETWEEN THE LEGS (FIG. 30A). AS YOU REMOVE WOOD HERE, SHAPE THE RUMP INTO THE LEGS BY ROUNDING THE RUMP. TO REMOVE WOOD FROM THE CREVICE, CARVE ALONG THE TOP OF THE BASE BETWEEN THE LEGS & SNIP THE WOOD FREE. CARVE THIS CREVICE UNTIL YOU HAVE LEFT TWO BLOCKS (DOTTED LINES FIG. 30) A LITTLE LARGER THAN THE SIZE NEEDED TO CARVE THE SHOES. SKETCH ON THE ENDS OF THESE BLOCKS THE SHAPE OF THE BOTTOM OF THE SHOES (USE FIG. 31 AS A GUIDE). CARVE THE BACK OF THE HEEL WITH YOUR JACKKNIFE INTO A ROUNDED SHAPE. CONTINUE THIS ROUNDING ONTO THE CREASE OF THE LEG, FOLLOWING THE ROUNDED SHAPE OF THE HEEL (FIG. 31). ROUND THE PANTS INTO THE BASE, LEAVING THE TOE OF THE SHOE BLOCKY. IN THIS ILLUSTRATION (FIG. 31) WE HAVE CUT A STRAIGHT CUT FOR THE BOTTOM OF THE CUFF. REMOVE THE WOOD FROM BETWEEN THE CUFF & THE SHOE BY DROPPING IT BACK 1/8 INCH. CUT A HARD 'V' CREASE INTO WHERE THE SHOE WOULD BEND (FIG. 31) & SHAPE INTO THIS AREA BY ROUNDING OVER THE TOE & INTO BOTH SIDES OF THE CREASE. WITH YOUR JACK-KNIFE, CUT A STRAIGHT CUT TO SHOW THE SOLE EDGE. ROUND THE SHOE SLIGHTLY INTO THE SOLE EDGE WHICH WILL RELIEVE THE SOLE EDGE ABOUT 1/16 INCH FROM THE SIDES OF THE SHOE. THE HEEL IS ALSO 1/16 INCH SMALLER THAN THE SOLE EDGE. CARVE AWAY ALL THE SAW MARKS FROM THE BOTTOM OF THE SHOES & CARVE THE SOLE EVENLY SO IT RESTS ON THE BASE. KEEP CHECKING YOUR CARVING BY MAKING SURE EACH SHOE IS THE SAME SHAPE & SIZE & EACH RESTS ON THE BASE AT THE SAME LEVEL.

IF YOU WISH TO HAVE THE BOTTOM OF THE CUFFS RAGGED, CARVE NOTCHES INTO THE EDGE OF THE CUFFS WITH THE POINT OF YOUR JACKKNIFE (Dotted Line FIG. 31).

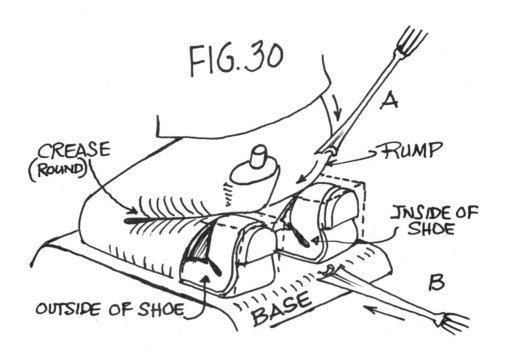

FIG. 30

CREASE (ROUND)

RUMP

INSIDE OF SHOE

OUTSIDE OF SHOE

BASE

A

B

CARVE THE OUTSIDE OF THE SHOES COMPLETELY & CARVE AS MUCH OF THE INSIDE AS YOU CAN REACH. WE WILL CARVE THROUGH BETWEEN THE LEGS IN THE NEXT STEP & FINISH THE INSIDE.

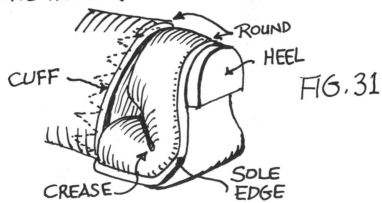

ROUND

HEEL

CUFF

FIG. 31

CREASE

SOLE EDGE

STEP 23. CARVING BETWEEN THE LEGS & THE BASE

WITH YOUR SMALL FISHTAIL GOUGE (FIG. 25), CARVE AWAY WOOD BETWEEN THE KNEES USING THE PATTERN AS A GUIDE FOR THE SHAPE & SIZE OF THE KNEES & LEGS (FIG. 32 A). CARVE INTO THIS AREA GOING THROUGH TO THE BACK OF THE LEGS BY CARVING SIDE TO SIDE & SNIPPING CLEAN AT THE BASE. ONCE YOU HAVE ACHIEVED AN OPENING FROM THE FRONT TO THE BACK YOU WILL BE ABLE TO SEE THE INSIDE SHAPE EASILY. CONTINUE TO OPEN THIS HOLE UNTIL THE SIDES OF THE INSIDE OF THE LEGS ARE STRAIGHT FROM FRONT TO BACK. WITH YOUR JACKKNIFE, ROUND OVER THE KNEES & TOPS OF THE LEGS (FIG. 32 B) THE SAME SIZE ON BOTH LEGS. IT IS VERY DIFFICULT TO REACH IN THIS AREA TO CLEAN SMOOTHLY BUT DO THE BEST YOU CAN. CARVE AWAY THE CORNERS OF THE BASE TO GIVE IT ROUNDED CORNERS (FIG. 32C) & ROUND THE BASE FROM ITS EDGE INTO THE LEGS.

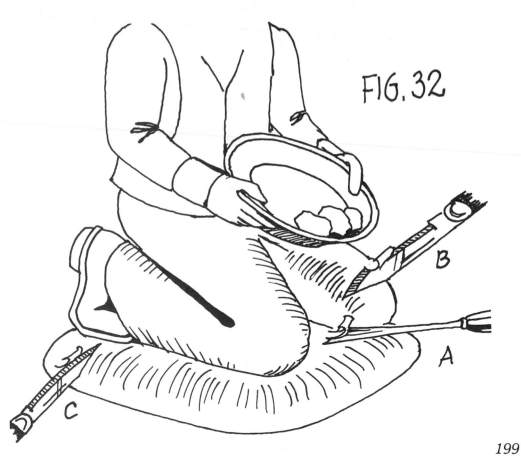

FIG. 32

STEP 24 · FINISHING

YOUR ENTIRE FIGURE MUST BE SANDED EXCEPT FOR THE BASE, WHICH IS LEFT CHIP CARVED. WE WILL USE THE UNIVERSAL TINTING COLORS TO MAKE STAIN BY MIXING WITH TURPENTINE. FIG. 33 WILL SHOW THE COLORS AND AREAS TO BE STAINED. AFTER STAINING, GIVE THE ENTIRE PIECE THREE COATS OF SATIN FINISH POLYURETHANE. GOLD LEAF IS DONE LAST. ALL THESE COLORS USED CAN BE CHANGED TO OTHER COLORS IF YOU WISH. THESE ARE THE COLORS WE USED.

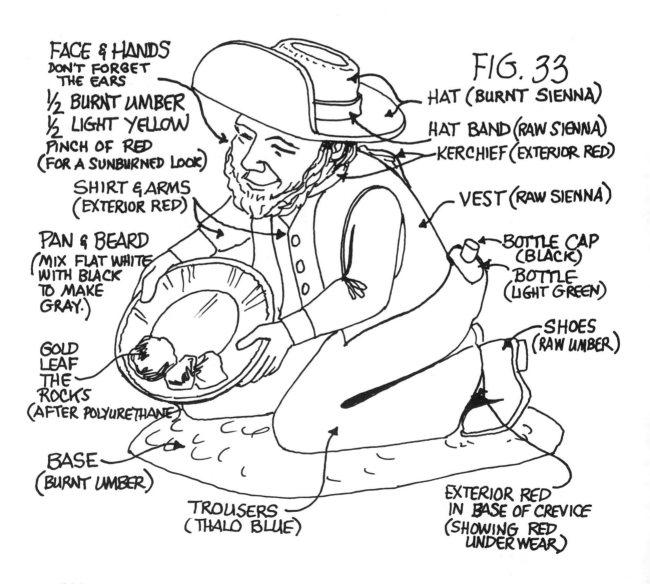

FACE & HANDS
DON'T FORGET
THE EARS
½ BURNT UMBER
½ LIGHT YELLOW
PINCH OF RED
(FOR A SUNBURNED LOOK)

SHIRT & ARMS
(EXTERIOR RED)

PAN & BEARD
(MIX FLAT WHITE
WITH BLACK
TO MAKE
GRAY.)

GOLD
LEAF
THE
ROCKS
(AFTER POLYURETHANE)

BASE
(BURNT UMBER)

FIG. 33
HAT (BURNT SIENNA)
HAT BAND (RAW SIENNA)
KERCHIEF (EXTERIOR RED)

VEST (RAW SIENNA)

BOTTLE CAP
(BLACK)
BOTTLE
(LIGHT GREEN)

SHOES
(RAW UMBER)

TROUSERS
(THALO BLUE)

EXTERIOR RED
IN BASE OF CREVICE
(SHOWING RED
UNDER WEAR)

STEP 25. FINAL TOUCHUPS

AFTER YOU HAVE APPLIED YOUR THREE COATS OF POLYURETHANE, YOUR GOLDPANNER SHOULD BE WELL SEALED. TO CHECK THIS, CAREFULLY LOOK OVER YOUR PIECE WITH A LIGHT ON IT TO MAKE A GLARE ON ITS SURFACE & LOOK FOR FLAT SPOTS (AREAS THAT DO NOT GLARE). IF YOU SEE ANY OF THESE FLAT AREAS, YOU NEED ANOTHER COAT OF POLYURETHANE. WE HAVE SUGGESTED USING A SATIN FINISH POLYURETHANE BECAUSE WE CAN ACCENT PARTS OF THE CARVING WITH A HIGH GLOSS FINISH. PAINT HIGH GLOSS POLYURETHANE ON THE GOLD PAN & THE BOTTLE. THIS WILL MAKE THEM LOOK SHINIER & MORE NATURAL. WITH A FINE ARTIST'S BRUSH, PAINT DULL OR FLAT BLACK TO MAKE THE OUTLINE OF THE PATCHED KNEES, SHOE LACES, CUFF LINES & THIN LINES UP THE SIDES OF THE GOLD PAN (SEE PATTERNS). WITH RAW UMBER, BRUSH COMPLETELY OVER THE FACE & HANDS & WIPE CLEAN WITH A RAG. THIS WILL ANTIQUE THE FIGURE BECAUSE THE UMBER WILL REMAIN IN THE CRACKS & CREVICES SUCH AS THE EYES & NOSTRILS & GIVE THEM MORE DEPTH. A LITTLE OF THE COLOR WILL ALSO REMAIN ON THE SURFACE TO CHANGE THE ORIGINAL FACE COLOR TO MAKE HIM LOOK MORE AGED & BRONZED. YOUR GOLD PANNER SHOULD NOW BE COMPLETED.

For the Kitchen
Project No. 6

A large breadboard (CUTTING BOARD) with a strawberry, leaf & flower design.
A large wooden tasting spoon with a wheat design & a wooden icing knife with a strawberry flower design plus a rack to hold them.

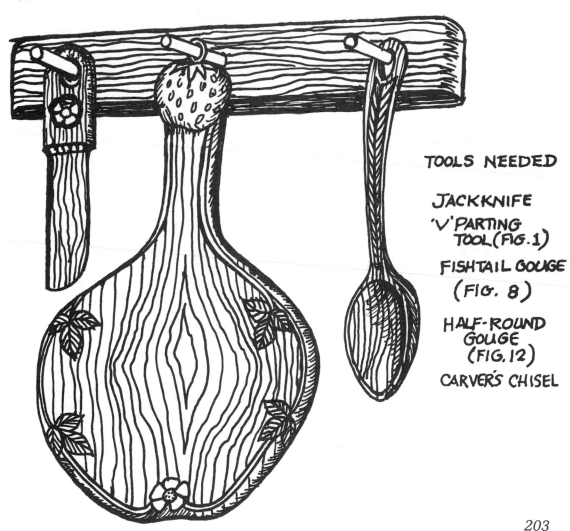

TOOLS NEEDED

JACKKNIFE

'V' PARTING
TOOL (FIG. 1)

FISHTAIL GOUGE
(FIG. 8)

HALF-ROUND
GOUGE
(FIG. 12)

CARVER'S CHISEL

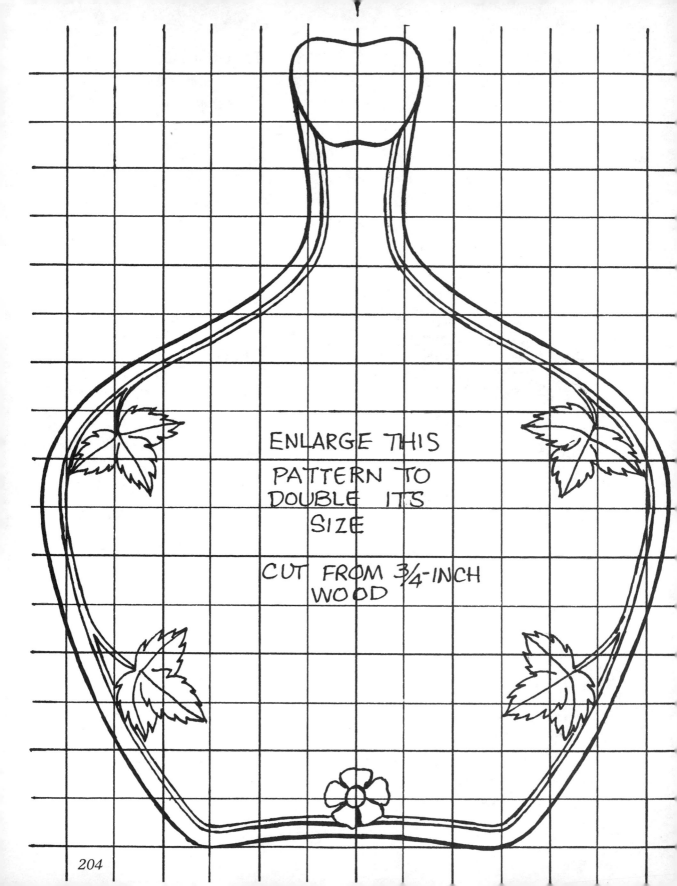

ENLARGE THIS
PATTERN TO
DOUBLE ITS
SIZE

CUT FROM 3/4-INCH
WOOD

STEP 1. TRANSFERRING PATTERNS WITH DESIGNS.

WHEN ENLARGING A PATTERN SUCH AS THIS BREAD BOARD, DRAW YOUR ENLARGED GRID DIRECTLY ONTO SOME HEAVY CARD OR POSTER BOARD & ENLARGE ACCORDING TO THE PATTERN GRID ILLUSTRATED ON THE PATTERN PAGE. WHEN ENLARGING THIS PROJECT, BECAUSE IT IS EVENLY BALANCED ON BOTH SIDES, IT IS EASIER TO DO ONLY ½ OF THE PATTERN. SKETCH IN, USING THE GRID SCALE, ALL THE LEAVES & OTHER DECORATIVE OBJECTS ONTO THIS ½ PATTERN. TO TRANSFER THE OUTER SHAPE TO BE SAWED OUT, CUT YOUR CARD BOARD PATTERN TO ITS OUTER SHAPE WITH A SHARP KNIFE, & AFTER DRAWING A STRAIGHT CENTER LINE ON YOUR WOOD, PUT THE STRAIGHT CENTER LINE EDGE TO THE CENTER LINE OF THE WOOD & TRACE AROUND YOUR PATTERN. FLIP THE PATTERN OVER & TRACE THE OPPOSITE SIDE. SAW THIS OVERALL SHAPE OUT FOR YOUR BLANK. TO TRANSFER THE ORNAMENTATION, USE TRACING PAPER & TRACE THE LEAVES, VINES, etc. FROM YOUR HALF PATTERN. TRACE THESE DESIGNS WITH A SOFT LEAD PENCIL. FLIP THIS HALF TRACING OVER SO THE SOFT PENCIL LINES ARE AGAINST THE WOOD ON THE OPPOSITE SIDE FROM WHERE YOU TRACED. TAPE THIS PATTERN DOWN, & AGAIN USE YOUR SOFT LEAD PENCIL. FOLLOW YOUR TRACED LINES FROM THE BACK OF THE TRACING PAPER. YOU HAVE ACTUALLY MADE A DOUBLE-SIDED CARBON OF YOUR PATTERN. WHEN YOU HAVE COMPLETED YOUR OPPOSITE-SIDE TRACING, FLIP YOUR PATTERN BACK TO THE ORIGINAL SIDE & TAPE ONTO YOUR BLANK. TRACE OVER YOUR LINES AGAIN. THIS PROCEDURE WILL GIVE YOU AN EVENLY BALANCED DESIGN & YOU NOW HAVE A PERMANENT TRACING OF YOUR DESIGN. GO BACK TO YOUR CUT-OUT & DARKEN ALL TRACED LINES. SOMETIMES YOUR TRACED LINES ARE VERY LIGHT & CAN HARDLY BE SEEN, SO WHILE DARKENING THESE LINES, BE CAREFUL NOT TO SMUDGE THEM.

STEP 2. RELIEVING THE LEAVES

USE A SMALL 'V' PARTING TOOL (FIG. 1 for size) & CARVE A GROOVE AROUND EACH OF THE FOUR LEAVES COMPLETELY, INCLUDING THE BASE OF THE LEAF WHERE THE STEM MEETS IT (FIG. 1A).

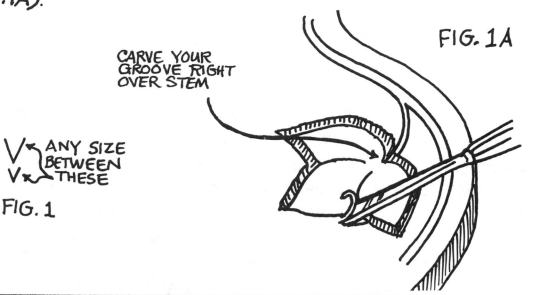

CARVE YOUR GROOVE RIGHT OVER STEM

FIG. 1A

V ANY SIZE BETWEEN V THESE

FIG. 1

STEP 3. SHAPING THE LEAF BACKGROUND

REMOVE ALL WOOD AROUND EACH LEAF BY SHAPING THE BACKGROUND WOOD INTO THE LEAVES WITH A GENTLE SLOPE (FIG. 2). USE A CARVER'S CHISEL IN REMOVING OPEN AREAS (FIG. 2A) & USE THE POINT OF YOUR JACKKNIFE IN REMOVING WOOD IN TIGHT CORNERS & HARD-TO-REACH AREAS (FIG. 2B). GRADUALLY SLOPE WOOD INTO THE BASE OF THE GROOVE MADE BY YOUR 'V' PARTING TOOL. THIS IS A VERY LOW RELIEF CARVING SO TRY NOT TO GO DEEPER THAN 1/8 INCH.

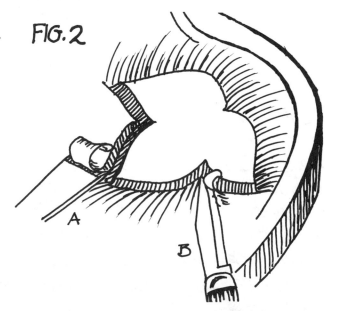

FIG. 2

A

B

STEP 4. SHAPING THE FLOWER & ITS BACKGROUND

THERE IS A SINGLE STRAWBERRY FLOWER AT THE BOTTOM OF YOUR CUTTING BOARD. WHEN TRANSFERRING YOUR HALF PATTERN, YOU CANNOT SKETCH IN THE PETALS PROPERLY BECAUSE THERE ARE 5 PETALS ON A STRAWBERRY FLOWER. THE PATTERN WILL GIVE YOU THE CIRCLE FOR THE OUTER PERIMETER OF THE FLOWER. FROM THIS OUTER CIRCLE, SKETCH A SMALLER CIRCLE (FIG. 3) IN THE CENTER OF THE OUTER CIRCLE. SKETCH IN YOUR 5 PETALS FREEHAND. THEY DON'T HAVE TO BE PERFECT, BUT TRY TO KEEP THEM FAIRLY EQUAL. USING THE SAME PROCEDURE AS IN STEPS 2 & 3, GO AROUND THE OUTER CIRCLE WITH YOUR SMALL 'V' PARTING TOOL. GO AROUND THE SMALLER CIRCLE ALSO. WITH THE PARTING TOOL, CUT SLOTS BETWEEN EACH PETAL. AFTER YOU HAVE ACCENTED THE PETALS & CENTER, SLOPE THE BACK-GROUND AROUND THE FLOWER INTO THE PETALS AS IN STEP 3.

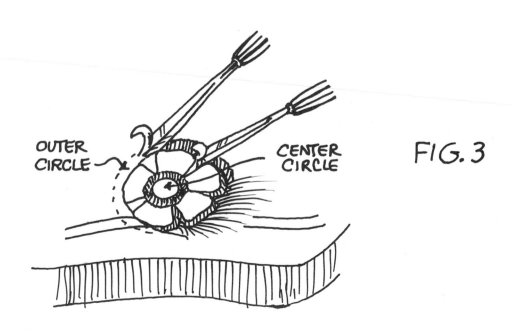

OUTER CIRCLE

CENTER CIRCLE

FIG. 3

STEP 5. ACCENTING EACH STRAWBERRY LEAF
FOLLOWING THE PATTERN, YOU WILL NOTICE THAT
THE 4 LEAVES WILL OVERLAP EACH OTHER. TO ACCENT THESE
OVERLAPS, CUT STRAIGHT DOWN ALONG THE LEAF EDGE (FIG. 4A)
& BY LAYING YOUR JACKKNIFE LOW TO THE BOARD REMOVE
A PIECE OF WOOD (FIG. 4B) UNTIL YOUR CUTS LOOK LIKE FIG. 4C.

FIG. 4

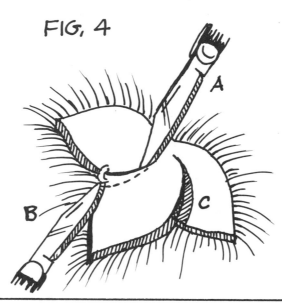

STEP 6. SHAPING THE LEAVES
DRAW CENTER LINES DOWN THE
MIDDLE OF EACH LEAF & SCORE
WITH THE POINT OF YOUR JACKKNIFE
(FIG. 5 A). CARVE AWAY WOOD BY
SLIGHTLY ROUNDING FROM A HIGH
POINT AT THE LEAF EDGE INTO
THE SCORED CENTER LINE (FIG. 5 B)
LEAVING THE CENTER LINE LOWER
THAN THE EDGES. ARROWS (FIG. 5C)
SHOW GRADUAL ROUNDING INTO
THE CENTER LINE. FIG. 5 D SHOWS
FINISHED LEAF SURFACE. SAND
ALL THE LEAF SURFACES.

FIG. 5

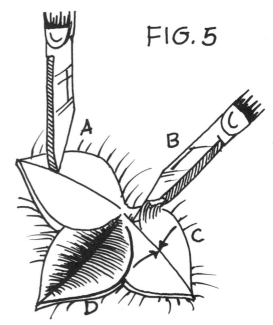

STEP 7. FINISHING THE LEAVES

SKETCH IN THE SERRATIONS ALONG THE EDGES OF ALL THE LEAVES USING THE PATTERN & FIG. 6 AS GUIDES. NOTICE THE SERRATIONS DO NOT CONTINUE ALL THE WAY TO THE STEM CROTCH & THE TIPS ARE ALL POINTING OUT FROM THE LEAF. USE YOUR PARTING TOOL & SNIP OUT THESE SERRATIONS WITH A CLEAN DOWNSTROKE (FIG. 6A). WITH YOUR JACK-KNIFE, FOLLOW THE SLOPE OF THE BACKGROUND INTO THE NOTCHED LEAF EDGES & SHAVE A LITTLE WOOD OFF THE SLOPE TO REMOVE THE PARTING TOOL MARKS MADE AT THE BASE OF THE SERRATIONS (FIG. 6B). USE THE POINT OF THE JACKKNIFE & GO AROUND EACH LEAF TO CLEAN ANY CORNERS THE PARTING TOOL MAY NOT HAVE CUT CLEANLY.

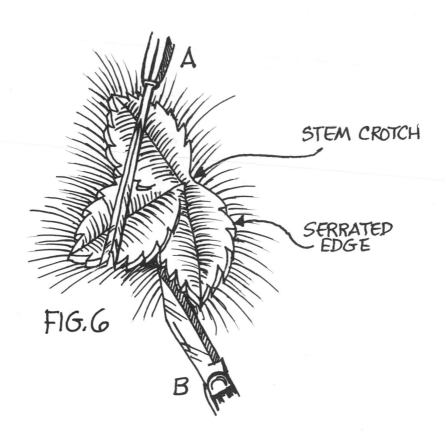

A

STEM CROTCH

SERRATED EDGE

FIG. 6

B

STEP 8. SHAPING THE STRAWBERRY FLOWER

REFER TO **YOUR** PATTERN FOR THE PROPER SHAPE OF THE PETALS. WITH YOUR JACKKNIFE, CUT STRAIGHT DOWN AROUND YOUR FLOWER CENTER & BY REMOVING WOOD FROM ITS OUTER EDGES, GRADUALLY ROUND THE CENTER INTO A DOME (FIG. 7A). WITH A FISHTAIL GOUGE (FIG. 8) CARVE FROM THE UPPER OUTSIDE EDGE OF EACH PETAL INWARD TO THE CENTER. THIS CUT GRADUALLY SLOPES DOWN TO THE BASE OF THE CENTER (FIG. 7B).

FIG. 7

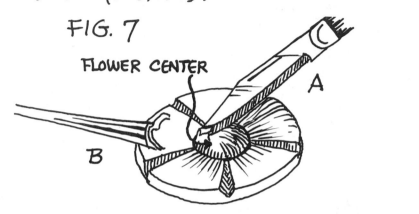

FLOWER CENTER

A

B

ANY FISHTAIL SIZE BETWEEN THESE SIZES

FIG. 8

STEP 9. FINISHING THE STRAWBERRY FLOWER

SKETCH IN THE EXACT SHAPE OF THE PETALS. WITH THE POINT OF YOUR JACKKNIFE, CUT STRAIGHT DOWN (FIG. 9A) AROUND EACH PETAL & WIDEN THE SLOTS BETWEEN THEM. CARVE AWAY YOUR BACKGROUND WITH A GRADUAL SLOPE INTO THE BASE OF THE PETALS (FIG. 9B). ON THE OUTER EDGES OF THE PETALS, CARVE THE RIDGES AWAY SO THEY ARE SLIGHTLY ROUNDED OVER. SAND THE FLOWER.

FIG. 9

PETAL SLOTS

A

B

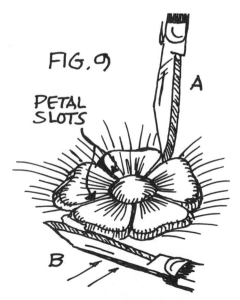

STEP 10. SHAPING THE STRAWBERRY HANDLE
CHECK YOUR SKETCH OF THE LARGE STRAWBERRY ON THE
HANDLE (SEE PATTERN), MAKING SURE IT IS BALANCED.
USE YOUR PARTING TOOL & INCISE ALONG THE BOTTOM
OF THE STRAWBERRY (FIG. 10A) & LOWER THE HANDLE INTO
THE STRAWBERRY BY REMOVING WOOD AT AN ANGLE WITH
YOUR FISHTAIL (FIG. 10B). CONTINUE INCISING & REMOVING
THE WOOD A LITTLE AT A TIME UNTIL YOU HAVE REACHED
A DEPTH SHOWN IN FIG. 10. MAKE SURE WHEN YOU ARE
INCISING ALONG THE STRAWBERRY BOTTOM YOU KEEP THE
PROPER CONTOUR WITHOUT ENLARGING OR SHORTENING THE
BOTTOM SHAPE. WITH YOUR JACKKNIFE, ROUND THE STRAW—
BERRY, WORKING FROM ITS CENTER & FALLING OFF ALL THE
WAY AROUND IT (FIG. 10C) SO ALL FLAT AREAS ARE REMOVED.

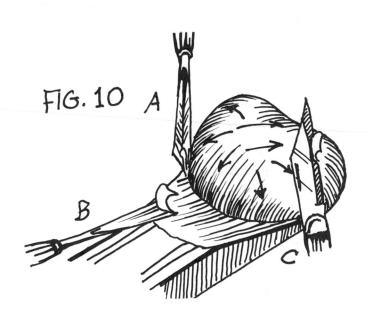

FIG. 10 A

B

C

STEP 11. SHAPING THE STEM STRAWBERRY LEAVES

SKETCH IN THE STEM LEAVES USING FIG. 11 AS A GUIDE. USING YOUR PARTING TOOL, CARVE A SHALLOW GROOVE AROUND ALL THE LEAVES (FIG. 11 A). DROP THE STRAWBERRY BACK FROM THE LEAVES WITH YOUR JACKKNIFE (FIG. 11 B).

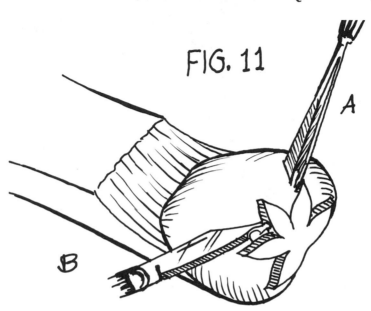

FIG. 11

STEP 12. FINISHING THE STRAWBERRY

USING A HALF-ROUND GOUGE (FIG. 12), CARVE **ELLIPTICAL** DEPRESSIONS INTO THE STRAWBERRY BODY (USE FIG. 13 FOR LOCATION OF THESE DEPRESSIONS). ALSO WITH YOUR HALF-ROUND, CARVE A CONCAVE DEPRESSION INTO EACH OF THE STEM LEAVES. CARVE THEM FROM THEIR POINTED END INTO THE TOP OF THE STRAWBERRY. SAND THE ENTIRE STRAWBERRY & ITS STEM LEAVES.

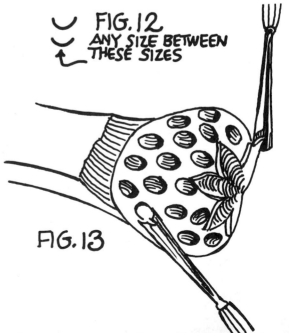

FIG. 12
ANY SIZE BETWEEN THESE SIZES

FIG. 13

STEP 13, CARVING THE VINE EDGING
REFER BACK TO YOUR PATTERN & SKETCH IN THE VINE EDGE
WHERE YOU HAVE CARVED IT AWAY. MAKE THE VINE ABOUT 1/8
INCH WIDE. USE THE POINT OF YOUR JACKKNIFE & CARVE THIS
VINE BY MAKING A DEEP 'V'. AS YOU GET TO THE LEAF STEMS,
CARVE THEM THE SAME WAY, WITH A DEEP 'V' BUT NARROWER &
TAPERING TO A POINT WHERE IT CONNECTS TO THE LEAF (FIG. 14).

FIG. 14

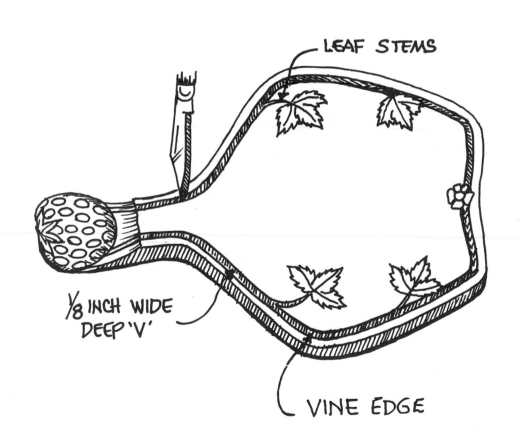

LEAF STEMS

1/8 INCH WIDE
DEEP 'V'

VINE EDGE

STEP 14. ROUNDING THE EDGE

USING A CARVER'S CHISEL, CARVE THE OUTSIDE EDGE BY ROUNDING IT OVER (FIG. 15). ROUND FROM THE EDGE OF THE VINE EDGE TO THE BACK OF THE BOARD, ELIMINATING ALL THE SAW MARKS AROUND THE EDGE. ROUND VERY SLIGHTLY THE BACK EDGE. SAND THIS ROUNDING SMOOTH & SAND THE REMAINDER OF THE BREAD BOARD, YOU ARE BETTER OFF HAND SANDING THAN USING A POWER SANDER.

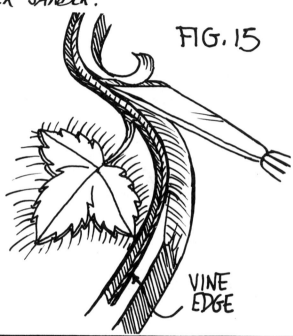

FIG. 15

VINE EDGE

STEP 15. FINISHING

I PREFER TO ADD SOME COLOR TO THIS PIECE. USING UNIVERSAL TINTING COLORS & TURPENTINE TO MAKE OIL STAINS, STAIN THE STRAWBERRY RED, THE STRAWBERRY LEAF STEM & VINE EDGE & LEAVES GREEN. STAIN THE FLOWER CENTER YELLOW BROWN & THE FLOWER PETALS WHITE. DO ALL THIS STAINING FIRST, BECAUSE YOU WILL PROBABLY GET SOME OF THESE COLORS ON THE BOARD ITSELF. TO REMOVE ANY UNWANTED COLOR ON YOUR BOARD, SIMPLY CARVE THESE MISTAKES AWAY & RESAND. THE REMAINDER OF THE BOARD SHOULD BE STAINED MAPLE OR WALNUT OR ANY STAIN COLOR YOU MAY LIKE. GIVE THE STAINED BOARD 3 COATS OF POLYURETHANE TO SEAL IT.

214

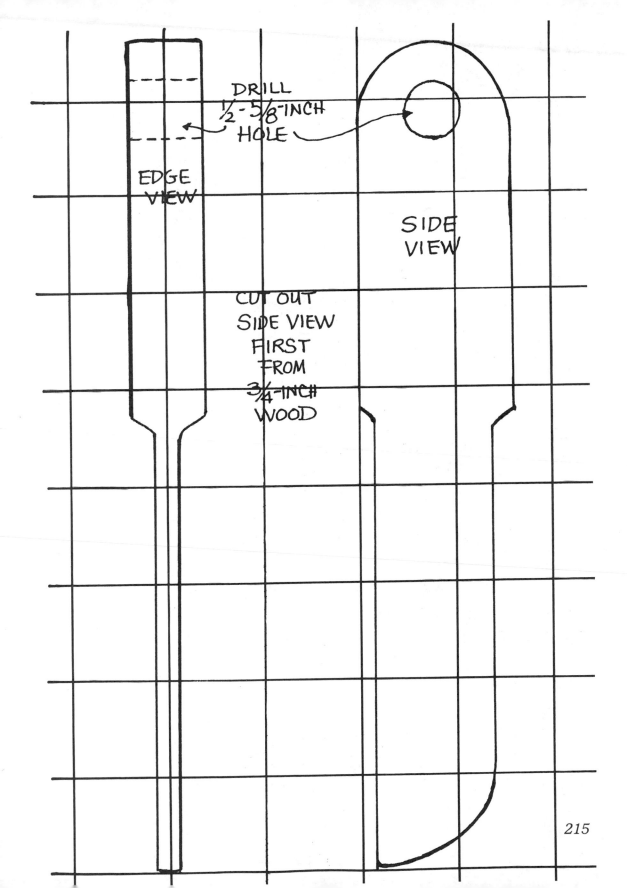

DRILL
1/2 - 5/8-INCH
HOLE

EDGE
VIEW

SIDE
VIEW

CUT OUT
SIDE VIEW
FIRST
FROM
3/4-INCH
WOOD

215

STEP 1. SHAPING THE HANDLE

CARVE AWAY THE FOUR CORNERS OF THE HANDLE EVENLY BY USING FIG. 1 AS A GUIDE.

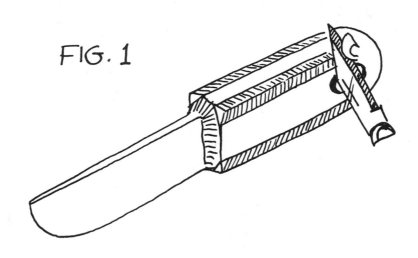

FIG. 1

STEP 2. ROUNDING THE HANDLE & CARVING THE FLOWER

CONTINUE, WITH YOUR JACKKNIFE, CARVING OFF ANY ANGULAR CORNERS UNTIL THE HANDLE IS ROUNDED ON ITS EDGES. CARVE THE HANGER HOLE USING THE SAME METHOD AS FIG. 8C IN STEP 5 OF CARVING THE SPOON. TO ELIMINATE ANY DRILL MARKS IN THE HOLE, ROLL UP SOME SANDPAPER & PUSH THROUGH THE HOLE. SKETCH YOUR FLOWER ON THE HANDLE & USE STEPS 8+9 OF THE BREAD BOARD FOR CARVING IT. SHAPE THE HANDLE INTO THE BASE OF THE FLOWER (FIG. 2) TO ELIMINATE THE SHARP EDGE.

FIG. 2

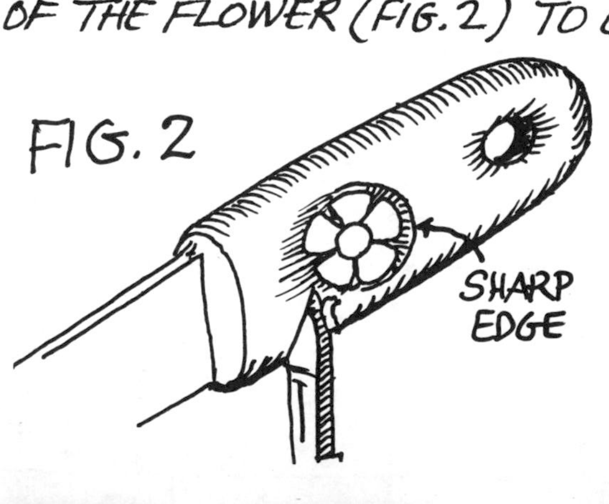

SHARP EDGE

STEP 3. CARVING THE HANDLE INTO THE BLADE

USING A SMALL HALF-ROUND (FIG. 3), CARVE THE ANGLE FROM THE HANDLE TO THE BLADE WITH CLOSE TOGETHER, HALF-ROUND CUTS (FIG. 4). TO KEEP IN PROPER LINE, SKETCH IN A LINE AROUND THE HANDLE (FIG. 4 DOTTED LINE) & CARVE INTO THE BLADE, STARTING AT YOUR LINE.

FIG. 3

USE A HALF ROUND ABOUT THIS SIZE

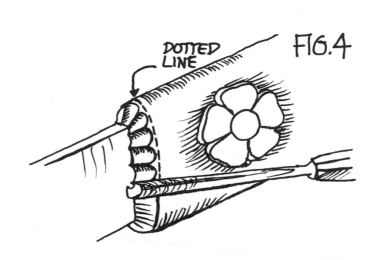

DOTTED LINE

FIG. 4

STEP 4. CARVING THE BLADE

USING THE LARGE BLADE OF YOUR JACKKNIFE, CARVE THE SIDES OF THE BLADE SO THEY TAPER FROM THE HANDLE TO THE POINT. ALSO, THE BLADE WILL HAVE A SHARP & A BLUNT EDGE (FIG. 5 END VIEW). WHEN CARVING THE SIDES (FIG. 6), THE GRAIN WILL ALLOW YOU TO CARVE UP THE BLADE ON ONE SIDE & DOWN THE BLADE ON THE OTHER. CARVE UP THE BLADE FIRST (TOWARD THE HANDLE) & DO YOUR TAPER BY GOING DOWN THE BLADE.

FIG. 5
END VIEW

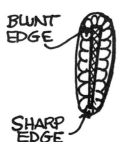

BLUNT EDGE

SHARP EDGE

FIG. 6

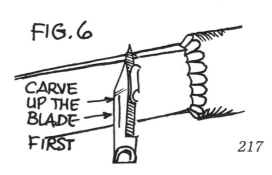

CARVE UP THE BLADE FIRST

217

STEP 5. FINISHING THE BLADE (FIG. 7)

CARVE AWAY THE SAW MARKS ON THE TOP OF THE BLADE TO CHECK A PROPER TAPER FROM THE POINT TO THE HANDLE. IF THERE ARE ANY BULGES IN THE TAPER, CARVE THEM OUT. SAND THE BLADE COMPLETELY, REMOVING ALL CARVING MARKS. AS YOU SAND, BRING THE SHARP EDGE TOGETHER WITH YOUR SANDPAPER, IT IS TOO DIFFICULT TO CARVE THE SHARP EDGE WITH YOUR JACKKNIFE BECAUSE THE JACKKNIFE WILL BITE INTO THIS EDGE & MAKE THE EDGE IRREGULAR.

FIG. 7

STEP 6. FINISHING THE KNIFE

STAIN THE KNIFE IN ANY COLOR YOU WISH. YOU COULD STAIN THE HANDLE ONE COLOR & THE BLADE ANOTHER. COLOR THE STRAWBERRY FLOWER AS YOU DID IN STEP 15 (FINISHING THE BREAD BOARD). APPLY 3 COATS OF SATIN FINISH POLYURETHANE.

218

STEP 7.   MAKING THE HANGER BOARD

USE A PIECE OF 3/4-INCH THICK WOOD 21 INCHES LONG & 4 INCHES WIDE (FIG. 8) & DRILL 1/4-INCH HOLES INTO THE BOARD AT AN UPWARD ANGLE (USE FIG. 9 FOR THE ANGLE) THAT ARE SPACED APART (FIG. 8 FOR DISTANCES). ROUND OVER ALL EDGES & SAND COMPLETELY. CUT THREE 2 3/4-INCH LONG PIECES OF 1/4-INCH DOWEL & GLUE IN PLACE. DRILL A HOLE ON EACH END 1 INCH IN FROM THE ENDS WITH A COUNTER SINK DRILL BIT. THESE HOLES ARE FOR SCREWING THIS HANGER TO YOUR WALL.   STAIN ENTIRE HANGER & POLYURETHANE THREE COATS.

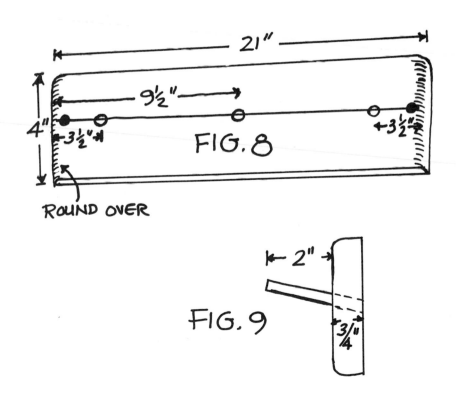

FIG. 8

ROUND OVER

FIG. 9

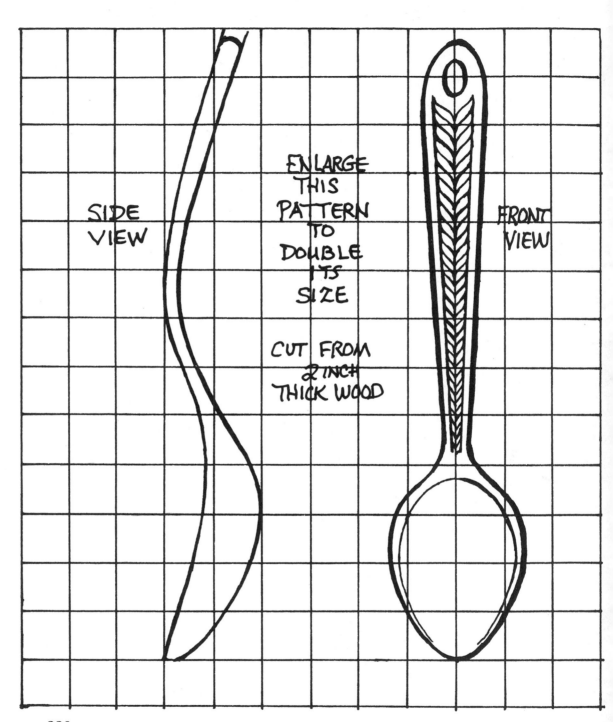

SIDE VIEW

ENLARGE THIS PATTERN TO DOUBLE ITS SIZE

CUT FROM 2 INCH THICK WOOD

FRONT VIEW

STEP 1. ROUNDING THE BOWL

WITH THE SPOON CUTOUT UPSIDE DOWN, CARVE WITH YOUR JACKKNIFE THE BACK OF THE BOWL BY HOLDING THE HANDLE & CARVING AWAY THE WOOD ON BOTH SIDES OF THE BOWL. ROUND AWAY FROM THE CENTERLINE (FIG. 1). YOU CANNOT CARVE THE ENTIRE BOWL BECAUSE YOU WOULD BE CARVING INTO (AGAINST) THE GRAIN AT THE HANDLE END. CARVE FROM THE CROWN TO THE END WHICH WOULD BE THE END 2/3 RDS OF THE BOWL, ROUND THE BOWL EVENLY BRINGING YOUR ROUNDING TO WITHIN 1/16 INCH OF THE EDGE (SEE END VIEW FIG. 2 FOR ROUNDNESS).

FIG. 1

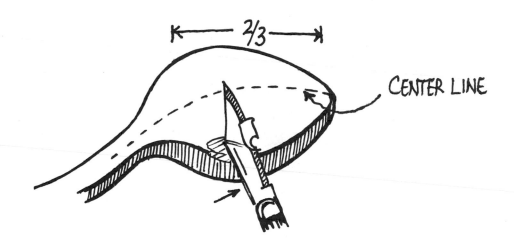

CENTER LINE

1/16 INCH
EDGE

FIG. 2
END VIEW

STEP 2. FINISH ROUNDING THE BACK OF THE BOWL (FIG. 3)
TURN THE SPOON AROUND & HOLD IT BY THE END OF THE BOWL.
WITH YOUR JACKKNIFE, ROUND THE HANDLE END OF THE BOWL
DOWN INTO THE BASE OF THE HANDLE. AFTER ROUNDING THE
BOWL, EYE IT UP TO MAKE SURE BOTH SIDES ARE EQUALLY
ROUNDED.

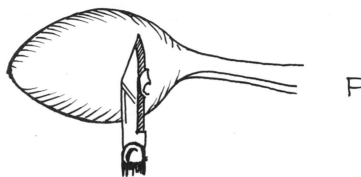

FIG. 3

STEP 3. CARVING THE INSIDE OF THE BOWL
WITH A FISHTAIL GOUGE (FIG. 4), CARVE AWAY THE WOOD FROM
INSIDE THE BOWL. YOU WILL HAVE TO CARVE IN TWO DIRECTIONS
(FIG. 5 ARROWS) BECAUSE THE GRAIN WILL CHANGE AS YOU
CARVE DEEPER INTO THE BOWL. REMOVE THIS WOOD TO COINCIDE
WITH THE BACK ROUNDING. SAND THE INSIDE & OUTSIDE OF
THE BOWL.

FIG. 4

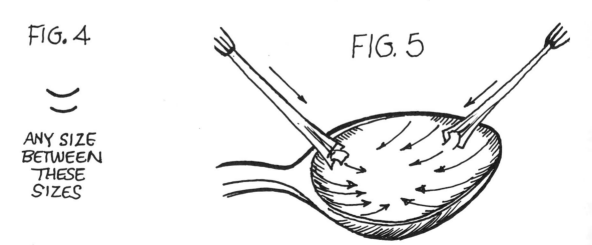

ANY SIZE
BETWEEN
THESE
SIZES

FIG. 5

STEP 4. SHAPING THE BACK OF THE HANDLE

WITH YOUR JACKKNIFE, CARVE A 45° ANGLE OFF THE EDGE OF THE HANDLE LEAVING ⅛-INCH FLAT AREA TOWARD THE FRONT OF THE HANDLE (FIG. 6). THE HANDLE BACK IS NOW ROUNDED COMPLETELY FROM THESE TWO ANGLE CUTS. THE ANGLES ARE CUT ONLY TO ESTABLISH AN EQUAL SIZE ON THE REMAINING FLAT EDGE & TO MAKE IT EASY TO GET EVEN ROUNDING. YOUR HANDLE BACK WILL BE EVENLY ROUNDED WHEN ALL SAW MARKS ARE REMOVED. FIG. 7 END VIEW SHOWS THE 45° ANGLE ON ITS RIGHT SIDE & THE ROUNDING ON THE LEFT. AFTER YOUR ROUNDING IS COMPLETED, SAND THE BACK OF THE HANDLE.

FIG. 6

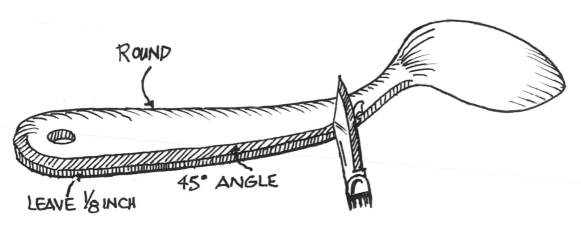

ROUND

45° ANGLE

LEAVE ⅛ INCH

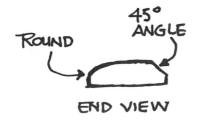

ROUND

45° ANGLE

END VIEW

FIG. 7

STEP 5. SMOOTHING THE FRONT OF THE HANDLE

WE WILL BE CARVING A WHEAT PATTERN INTO THE FRONT OF THE HANDLE, SO PRIOR TO SKETCHING THE DESIGN, THE SAW MARKS HAVE TO BE SHAVED OFF. USE YOUR JACK-KNIFE & CARVE FROM THE TOP OF THE BEND, UP THE HANDLE TOWARD THE HANGER HOLE (FIG. 8A). TO STAY WITH THE GRAIN, CARVE FROM THE TOP OF THE BEND TO THE SPOON (FIG. 8B). ALL YOU WANT TO DO IS SHAVE OFF ENOUGH WOOD TO ELIMINATE THE SAW MARKS. AS YOU DO THIS, ROUND OVER THE EDGES SLIGHTLY. THE PERFECTLY ROUND, DRILLED HOLE FOR HANGING THE SPOON SHOULD BE SHAPED, WITH THE POINT OF YOUR JACKKNIFE, INTO AN OBLONG HOLE ON BOTH SIDES (FIG. 8C). TRY TO REMOVE ALL THE DRILL MARKS ON THE INSIDE OF THIS HOLE.

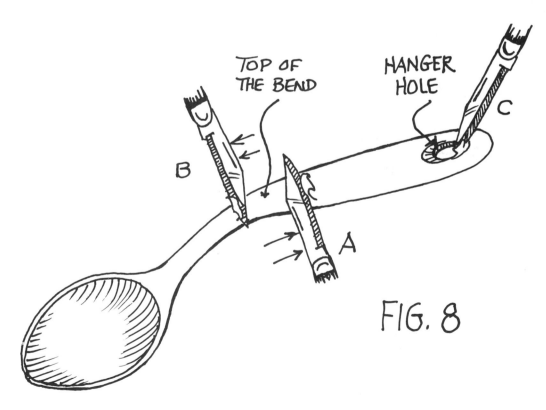

TOP OF THE BEND

HANGER HOLE

B

A

C

FIG. 8

STEP 6. LAYOUT & SHAPING THE WHEAT PATTERN

SKETCH IN THE WHEAT PATTERN ONTO THE HANDLE &, WITH A SMALL 'V' PARTING TOOL, OUTLINE ALL THE LINES DRAWN (FIG. 9). IN SKETCHING THE PATTERN, NOTICE THE DESIGN BECOMES SMALLER AS THE HANDLE NARROWS.

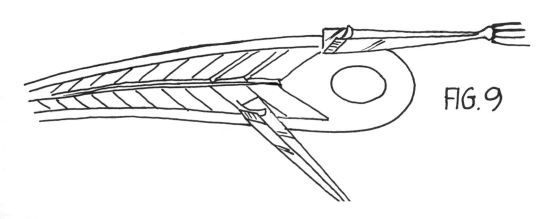

FIG. 9

STEP 7. CARVING THE WHEAT DESIGN

WITH THE POINT OF YOUR JACKKNIFE, CARVE STRAIGHT DOWN ALONG YOUR SCORED LINE, BUT TURN EACH SEGMENT'S CORNERS (FIG. 10). ROUND OVER EACH SEGMENT FROM BOTH SIDES.

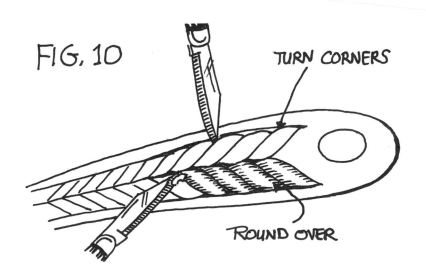

FIG. 10

TURN CORNERS

ROUND OVER

225

STEP 8. FINISHING THE SPOON

AFTER CARVING THE WHEAT DESIGN, SAND EACH SEGMENT ONE AT A TIME. MAKE SURE THE ENTIRE SPOON IS SANDED COMPLETELY. THIS SPOON WILL BE STAINED ANY COLOR YOU WISH. THE WHEAT DESIGN CAN BE STAINED A DIFFERENT COLOR FROM THE REST OF THE SPOON--FOR EXAMPLE, A WALNUT STAIN ON THE SPOON & GOLDEN OAK ON THE WHEAT. AFTER STAINING, GIVE THE SPOON 3 COATS OF SATIN FINISH POLYURETHANE.

BALL-IN-THE-BOX
Key Chain
Project No. 7

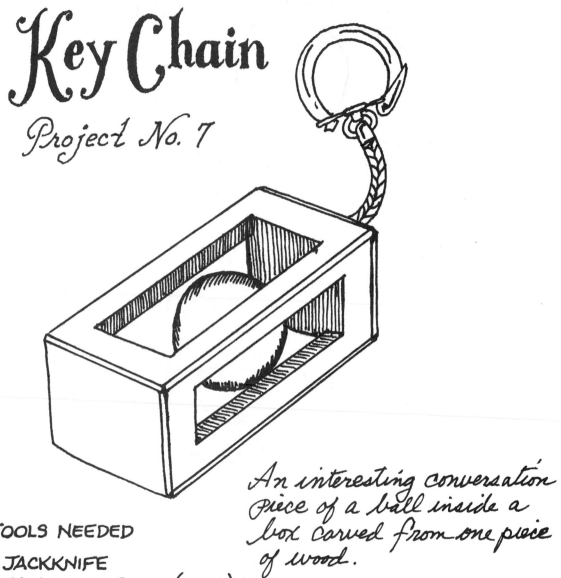

An interesting conversation piece of a ball inside a box carved from one piece of wood.

TOOLS NEEDED

JACKKNIFE
HALF-ROUND GOUGE (SMALL)
'V' PARTING TOOL (FIG. 3)

STEP 1. CUT OUT A BLOCK OF WOOD 1½ INCHES SQUARE & 3 INCHES LONG. SKETCH IN PATTERN BELOW ON ALL 4 SIDES OF THE BLOCK

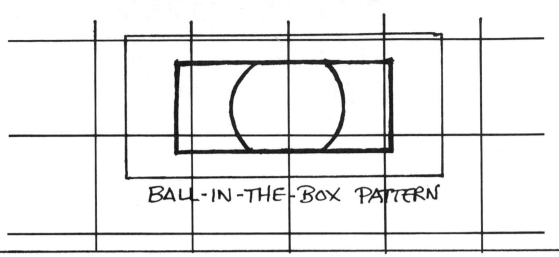

BALL-IN-THE-BOX PATTERN

STEP 2. DRILLING THE BLOCK
WITH A ¼-INCH DRILL BIT, DRILL 4 HOLES THROUGH THE BLOCK ON 2 SIDES. SEE FIG. 1 FOR LOCATIONS.

FIG. 1

DRILL 4 HOLES ON 2 SIDES

STEP 3. SEPARATING THE BALL FROM THE ENDS

THE EASIEST WAY TO REMOVE THE WOOD FROM BETWEEN THE ENDS & THE BALL IS TO USE A SMALL HALF-ROUND GOUGE & CARVE STRAIGHT DOWN AROUND THE BALL & THE ENDS. THE DRILL HOLES WILL HELP KEEP YOU IN LINE. REMOVE AS MUCH WOOD AS YOU CAN FROM ONE SIDE AT A TIME & KEEP ROTATING & REMOVING WOOD UNTIL YOU GO THROUGH (FIG. 2A), NOW USE YOUR JACK-KNIFE & WITH THE POINT OF YOUR CLIP BLADE CARVE THE INSIDE OF THE END CLEAN & FLAT. DO THE SAME TO THE ROUNDED SHAPE OF THE BALL (FIG 2B). BE CAREFUL WHEN CARVING IN TIGHT AREAS SUCH AS THIS TO AVOID CUTTING INTO THE CAGE SIDES BECAUSE, IF YOU DO, THE BALL MAY FALL OUT AFTER YOU TRIM THE CAGE SIDES ON FINAL CLEANUP.

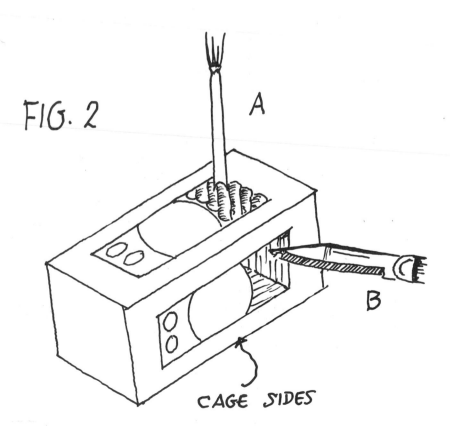

FIG. 2

A

B

CAGE SIDES

STEP 4. SHAPING THE CAGE SIDES.

THE SIDES OF THE BALL IN THE BOX ARE 1/4 INCH THICK. WE HAVE TO REMOVE WOOD ALONG THE INSIDE EDGES OF EACH CAGE SIDE UNTIL EACH CAGE SIDE IS 1/4 INCH SQUARE. USE A 'V' PARTING TOOL & CUT A GROOVE ALONG EACH SIDE. KEEP DEEPENING THIS GROOVE UNTIL YOU HAVE REACHED 1/4 INCH DEEP (FIG 3A). DO NOT REMOVE ANY WOOD FROM THE CENTER OF THE BALL & REMOVE ONLY AS MUCH AS YOU NEED FROM THE BALL SIDES TO ACHIEVE YOUR 1/4-INCH CAGE SIDES. WITH THE POINT OF YOUR JACKKNIFE, CARVE ALONG THE INSIDE EDGES OF THE CAGE SIDES TO FLATTEN & STRAIGHTEN THESE EDGES. (FIG. 3 B)

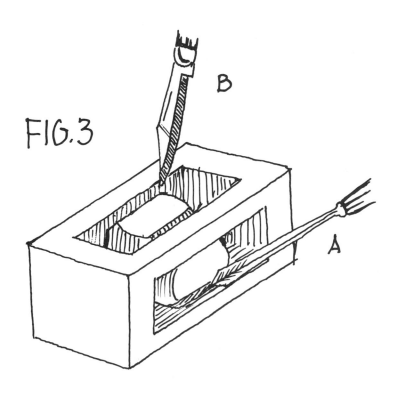

FIG. 3

STEP 5. ROUNDING THE BALL

WITH YOUR JACKKNIFE, ROUND ALL EDGES OF THE BALL TOWARD THE CENTER OF THE BOX (FIG. 4). DO NOT TRY TO COMPLETELY ROUND ONE SIDE & MOVE TO THE NEXT. ROUND EACH SIDE A LITTLE AT A TIME & EVENLY & SLOWLY UNTIL YOUR BALL STARTS TO TAKE A ROUNDED SHAPE. MANY TIMES IF YOU CONCENTRATE TOO MUCH ON GETTING THE BALL ROUNDED ON ONE SIDE, WHEN YOU ROUND AN ADJACENT SIDE THE BALL MAY BE LOPSIDED. SO KEEP CARVING AROUND THE BOX & CHECK TO MAKE SURE THE BALL IS STAYING ROUND. AS THE BALL BECOMES SMALLER OWING TO ROUNDING, YOU WILL HAVE MORE ROOM TO CLEAN UP THE CAGE SIDES. AS YOU ROUND, ALSO CLEAN THESE SIDES. CONTINUE YOUR BALL-ROUNDING & SIDE-CLEANING UNTIL THE BALL IS FREE & MOVES WITHIN THE CAGE. ONCE THE BALL IS FREE, YOU CAN CLEAN THE SIDES EASILY BY MOVING THE BALL FROM ONE END TO ANOTHER.

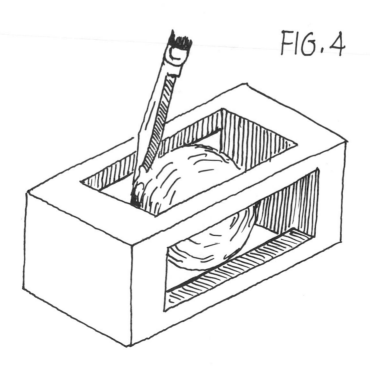

FIG. 4

STEP 6. FINISHING YOUR BALL IN THE BOX

SAND THE OUTSIDE OF THE BOX COMPLETELY. WITH YOUR JACKKNIFE, TRIM ALL OUTSIDE CORNERS INTO 45° ANGLES (FIG. 5). WITH A SMALL BRASS SCREW YOU CAN SECURE THE RING PART OF A KEY CHAIN ONTO THE TOP OF THE BOX. THERE ARE MANY DIFFERENT TYPES OF KEY CHAINS AVAILABLE. ANY OF THEM WILL DO. STAIN THE WOOD OF THE BOX ONE COLOR & THE BALL ANOTHER FOR A NICE CONTRAST. GIVE THE BALL & BOX A NUMBER OF COATS OF POLYURETHANE. PUT YOUR KEYS ON THE RING & YOU'RE IN BUSINESS.

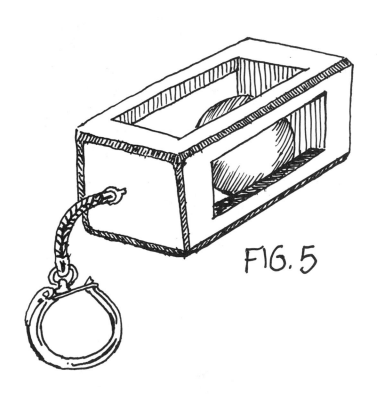

FIG. 5

Miniature
BEAVER & SHOVEL
Project No. 8

TOOLS NEEDED

HALF-ROUND GOUGE (FIG. 2)
JACKKNIFE
'V' PARTING TOOL (SMALL)
FISHTAIL GOUGE

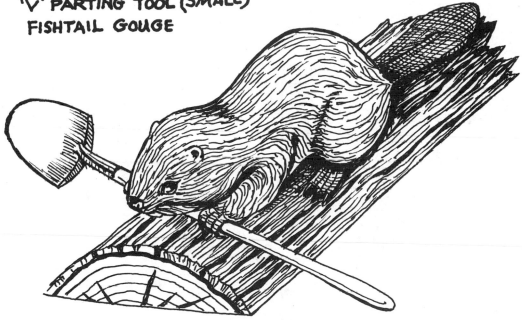

An interesting, carved mantle decoration standing on a carved log

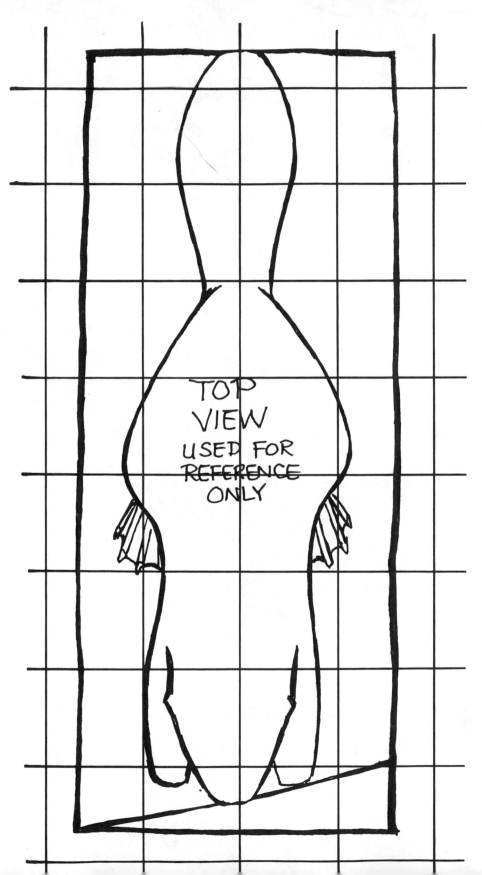

TOP
VIEW
USED FOR
REFERENCE
ONLY

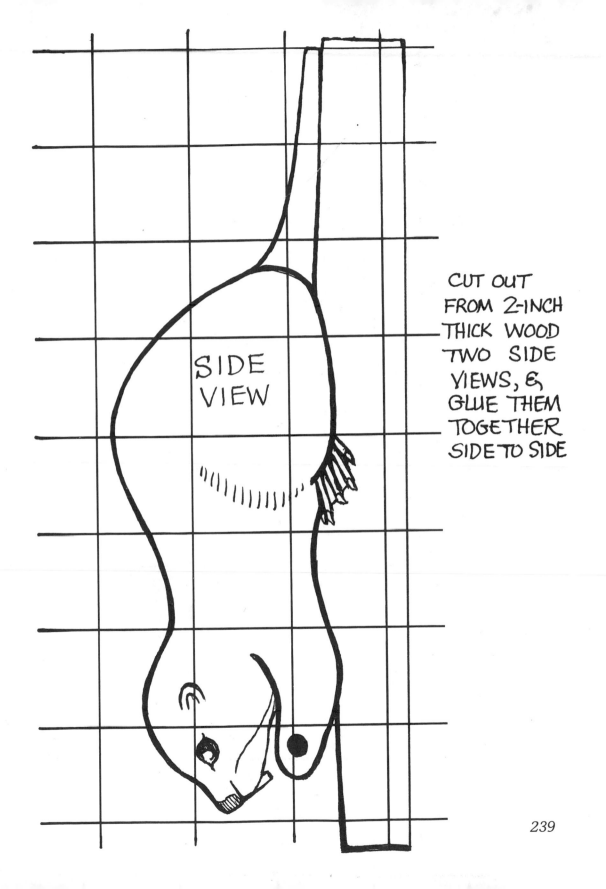

SIDE
VIEW

CUT OUT
FROM 2-INCH
THICK WOOD
TWO SIDE
VIEWS, &
GLUE THEM
TOGETHER
SIDE TO SIDE

239

SIDE
VIEW

TOP
VIEW

PATTERN
FOR
THE BEAVER'S
SHOVEL

CUT FROM
A PIECE OF
HARDWOOD
FOR STRENGTH
(BLACK WALNUT,
MAPLE, CHERRY)

240

STEP 1. TRANSFER THE TOP VIEW

USING YOUR TOP VIEW PATTERN, SKETCH THE OUTSIDE
SHAPE OF THE BEAVER ONTO YOUR GLUED-UP CUT OUT. YOUR
GLUE JOINT IS IN THE CENTER, SO SKETCH EQUALLY EACH
SIDE FROM THE CENTER. SKETCH THE SIDE LOG LINES FOR
THE BASE (FIG. 1).

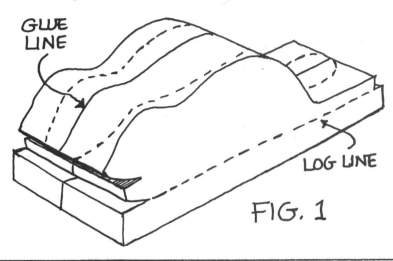

GLUE LINE

LOG LINE

FIG. 1

STEP 2. SHAPING THE BODY

USING A HALF-ROUND GOUGE (FIG. 2), START REMOVING WOOD
FROM THE TOP VIEW OUTLINE BY CARVING A GROOVE ALONG THE
LOG LINE (FIG. 3A) & ONE GROOVE NEXT TO ANOTHER. CARVE STRAIGHT
DOWN ACROSS THE GRAIN INTO THE GROOVE (FIG. 3B). CARVE THE
LOG AWAY FROM THE TAIL BY CARVING FROM THE LOG EDGE INTO
THE TAIL OUTLINE (FIG. 3C).

FIG. 3

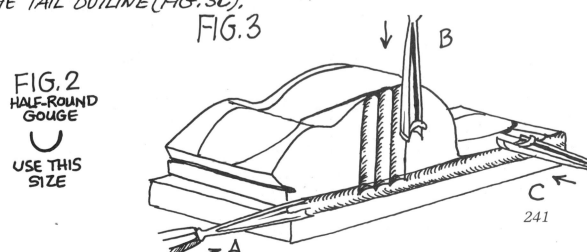

FIG. 2
HALF-ROUND
GOUGE

U

USE THIS
SIZE

B

C

A

241

STEP 3. SHAPING THE BODY (cont'd)

CONTINUE CARVING WITH YOUR HALF-ROUND DOWN THE SIDES OF THE BODY UNTIL YOU HAVE REACHED ALL YOUR TOP VIEW BODY LINES (FIG. 4A). AS YOU ENLARGE YOUR LOG, IT WILL BE NECESSARY TO CARVE STRAIGHT IN ON THE TOP OF THE LOG (FIG. 4B). THIS WILL ALLOW THE WOOD TO BE FREED AT THE BASE OF THE BEAVER. THE BEST WAY TO REMOVE THIS WOOD EVENLY IS TO CARVE IN & DOWN AS IF YOU WERE EATING AN EAR OF CORN. GO BACK & FORTH ALONG THE SIDE OF THE BODY & THE BASE. DO NOT ALLOW BOTH SIDES OF THE HALF-ROUND TO BE BURIED IN THE WOOD AT THE SAME TIME. IT IS MUCH CLEANER & EASIER TO HALF-LAP EACH CUT LIKE MOWING THE LAWN.

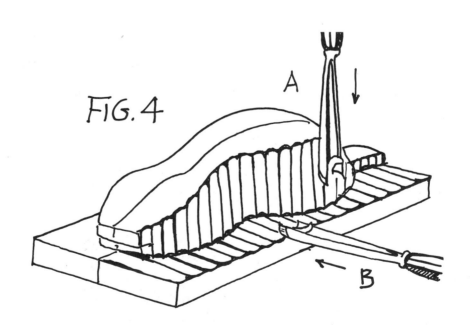

FIG. 4

STEP 4. RELIEVING THE HEAD & ROUNDING THE BODY
USING YOUR HALF-ROUND (FIG. 2), CARVE AWAY THE WOOD
FROM THE OUTSIDE OF THE HEAD OUTLINE DOWN TO THE
TOP OF THE FOOT (FIG. 5A). CARVE FROM THE BODY TO
THE NOSE (ARROW·FIG.5A). IF THIS IS DONE PROPERLY,
THE TOP OF THE FOOT WILL BE FLAT & THE SIDES OF
THE HEAD WILL BE FLAT & THE HEAD WILL BE SOME-
WHAT NARROWER THAN THE POSITION OF THE FEET (SEE
PATTERN TOP VIEW). WITH YOUR JACKKNIFE, CARVE
ALONG THE SIDES OF THE BODY (FIG. 5B) STARTING
AT THE NECK & CARVING TOWARD THE REAR. USING FIG.
5 AS A GUIDE, START BY TAKING A SMALL AREA DOWN
AT THE NECK & AS YOU GO TOWARD THE REAR REMOVE
A LARGER AREA & GRADUALLY ROUND THE SIDES.
WHEN APPROACHING THE REAR, CONTINUE CARVING
AROUND THE REAR, SKIPPING OVER THE TAIL.

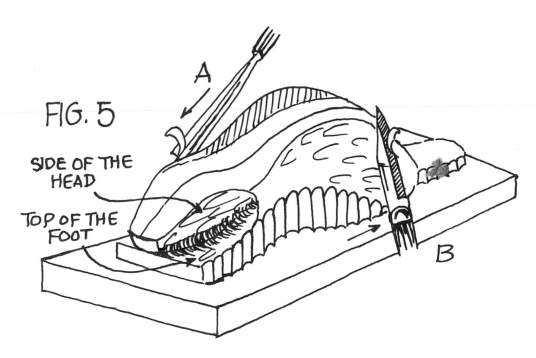

FIG. 5

A

SIDE OF THE
HEAD

TOP OF THE
FOOT

B

STEP 5. ROUNDING THE NECK & HEAD

USING YOUR JACKKNIFE, CARVE FROM THE TOP OF THE HEAD TOWARD THE BODY UNTIL YOU REACH THE BASE OF THE NECK (FIG. 6A). AT THIS POINT, THE GRAIN WILL CHANGE & YOU WILL HAVE TO CARVE FROM THE BODY TOWARD THE HEAD (FIG. 6B). IN THIS AREA YOU WILL LEARN A LOT ABOUT CHANGING GRAIN. CARVE INTO THIS AREA FROM BOTH DIRECTIONS & MATCH THE GRAIN WITH YOUR KNIFE. THIS MEANS YOU CARVE THE WOOD AWAY & ROUND THE NECK UNTIL YOU COME TO THAT ONE SLIVER OR FUZZED-UP WOOD YOU CAN'T SEEM TO GET RID OF. THIS IS WHERE MANY CARVERS GET CARRIED AWAY & BY TRYING TO MATCH THE GRAIN THEY CARVE DEEPER & DEEPER UNTIL THEY HAVE A NOTCH OR THEY HAVE LOST THE SHAPE. AFTER YOU HAVE MATCHED THE GRAIN & ROUNDED THE NECK, CONTINUE TO ROUND INTO THE TOP OF THE SHOULDERS.

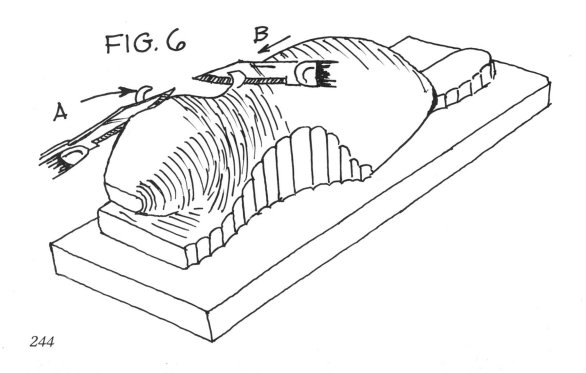

FIG. 6

A

B

STEP 6. SHAPING THE BACK LEGS (HAUNCH)

REFER TO THE TOP & SIDE VIEW PATTERNS FOR THE LOCATION OF THE HAUNCHES (THE AREA WHERE THE BACK LEGS ROUND INTO THE BODY). USING YOUR HALF-ROUND, CARVE FROM THE TOP OF EACH HAUNCH, DOWN ALONG THE SIDES OF THE BODY IN A CURVE (FIG. 7A) TO THE BASE. MAKE THIS CUT DEEP ENOUGH SO WHEN WE SHAPE THE BODY INTO THE HALF-ROUND GROOVE (FIG. 7B), YOUR JACKKNIFE CAN CARVE THE FORWARD EDGE OF THE HAUNCH INTO THE BODY SO IT BLENDS INTO THE NARROW FORWARD BODY & THE ROUNDING YOU HAVE DONE IN STEP 5.. AT THE GROOVE EDGE OF THE LEG, ROUND OVER THE LEG INTO THE BODY WITH YOUR JACKKNIFE (FIG. 7C).

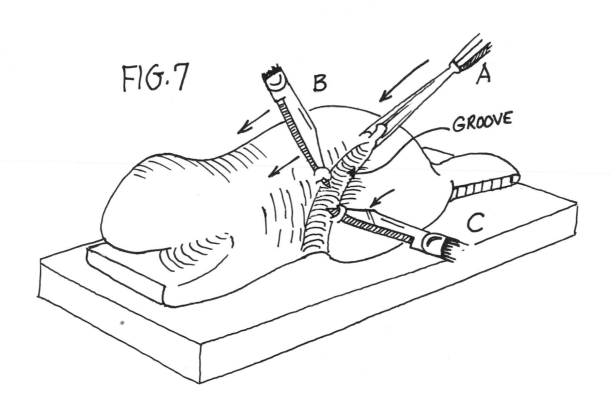

FIG. 7

B

A

GROOVE

C

STEP 7. SHAPING THE LOG BASE

SKETCH IN THE END VIEWS OF THE LOG BASE USING FIG. 8 DOTTED LINE AS A GUIDE. WITH YOUR JACKKNIFE, CARVE AWAY EXCESS WOOD TO GIVE THE BASE A SHALLOW HALF ROUND (FIG. 8A). AS YOU ROUND THE BASE INTO THE BEAVER, YOU WILL HAVE TO MAKE THE BEAVER A WEE BIT TALLER ON ITS SIDES BECAUSE OF THE ROUNDING. USING YOUR HALF-ROUND GOUGE, CARVE AT THE BASE OF THE BEAVER SO ITS SIDES ROUND UNDER & INTO THE SHAPE OF THE LOG (FIG. 8B). IN THE GROOVED AREA OF THE HAUNCH, CARVE DEEPER UNDER THE BELLY & WORK SHALLOWER AS YOU CARVE UNDER THE RUMP & FORE PAWS. DO NOT CARVE INTO THE LOG BECAUSE WE NEED A LITTLE EXTRA ROOM TO CARVE THE HIND FEET (SEE PATTERN). DO NOT CARVE UNDER THE TAIL.

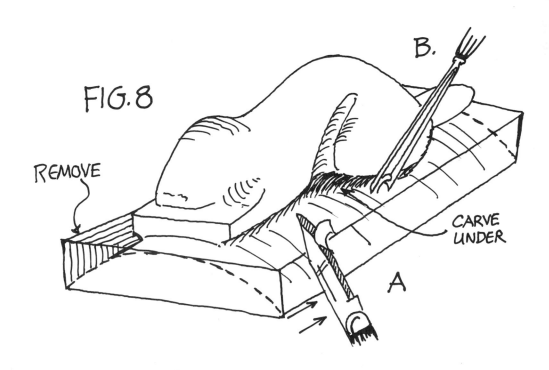

FIG. 8

REMOVE

B.

A

CARVE UNDER

STEP 8. SHAPING THE EARS & THE HEAD
USING YOUR PATTERN, SKETCH IN YOUR EARS. MAKE
SURE THEY ARE BALANCED SIDE TO SIDE. DON'T HAVE
ONE HIGHER OR LOWER OR FORWARD OR BEHIND THE
OTHER. WITH THE POINT OF YOUR JACKKNIFE, CARVE
AROUND THE EARS & REMOVE WOOD FROM THE HEAD
TO HAVE THE EARS PROJECTING FROM THE HEAD (FIG. 9A).
AS YOU DROP THE HEAD BACK FROM THE EARS, YOU WILL
HAVE TO RE-SHAPE THE HEAD ALL OVER. AT THE FOR-
WARD END OF THE EARS, CARVE THEM SLIGHTLY CON-
CAVE SO THEY WILL BLEND INTO THE SIDES OF THE
HEAD (FIG. 9). ROUND SLIGHTLY THE OUTER EDGES OF
THE EARS & USING YOUR HALF-ROUND, CARVE A CIRCULAR,
RECESSED DIVIT INTO THE CENTER OF EACH EAR (FIG. 9).
ROUND OVER THE UNDERSIDE OF THE HEAD ABOVE THE
FOREPAWS. WITH YOUR JACKKNIFE, SEPARATE THE TOP
OF THE FOREPAWS FROM THE HEAD BY CARVING THEM
EVENLY SMALLER FROM THE TOP OF THE FOREPAW
AREA (FIG. 9B). WIDEN THIS AREA TO ALMOST 1/4 INCH
BETWEEN THE HEAD & THE FOREPAWS.

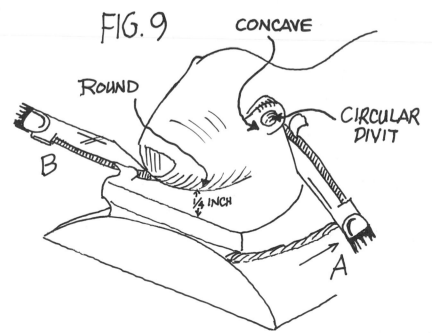

FIG. 9

ROUND
CONCAVE
CIRCULAR DIVIT
1/4 INCH
B
A

STEP 9. SHAPING THE FACE & FOREPAWS.

WITH YOUR JACKKNIFE, CARVE DOWN THE HEAD TO THE NOSE & CONCAVE THE AREA WHERE THE MUZZLE IS LOCATED (FIG.10). CARVE THIS AREA ON BOTH SIDES & THE TOP TO MAKE THE MUZZLE MUCH SMALLER THAN THE HEAD (FIG. 11). AS YOU CARVE THE SIDES, NOTICE THE CURVED CHEEK WHICH ROUNDS INTO THE MUZZLE (FIG. 11). REMOVE WOOD FROM THE SIDES OF THE FOREPAWS AS IN FIG. 10. THE FOREPAWS DO NOT POINT STRAIGHT OUT FROM THE BODY, BUT ARE CLOSER TOGETHER AT THEIR PAWS THAN WHERE THEY ATTACH TO THE BODY. USE YOUR HALF-ROUND & REMOVE THE WOOD BETWEEN THE PAWS (FIG.10) BY CARVING AT AN ANGLE STRAIGHT INTO THE BASE AS FAR AS YOU CAN REACH (FIG.11). LEAVE THE PAWS ABOUT ¼ INCH WIDE.

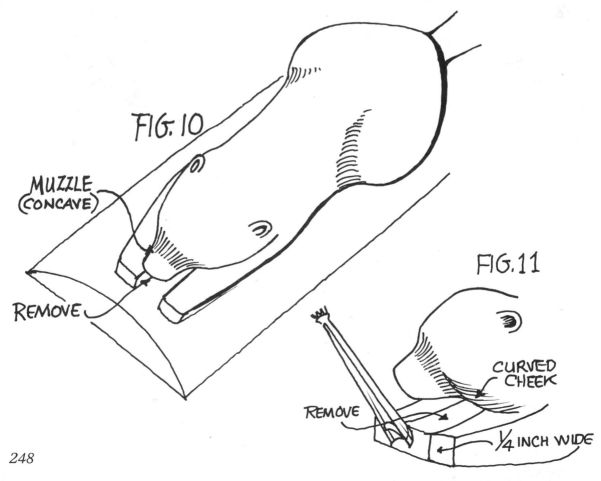

FIG. 10

MUZZLE (CONCAVE)

REMOVE

FIG. 11

REMOVE

CURVED CHEEK

¼ INCH WIDE

248

STEP 10. CARVING THE EYES & SHAPING THE FOREPAWS
SKETCH IN THE EYES BY DRAWING LINES DOWN THE SIDES
OF THE HEAD FROM THE CENTER OF THE EARS TO THE NOSE.
DRAW ANOTHER LINE ACROSS THE HEAD (FIG.12) SO YOU CAN
ESTABLISH THE EYES SIDE TO SIDE. WHERE THESE LINES
CROSS, SKETCH IN YOUR CIRCLES ON THE INTERSECTING LINES.
WITH THE POINT OF YOUR JACKKNIFE, CARVE AROUND THE
EYES AT A LITTLE OUTWARD ANGLE TO EMPHASIZE THE
LIDS. SHAPE THE EYES BY ROUNDING EVENLY INTO THE LIDS
(FIG.13). ADJUST TO SIZE OF THE LIDS BY CARVING AWAY
FROM THE LID EDGES ONTO THE SIDES OF THE HEAD (FIG.13).
CARVE DOWN THE TOPS OF THE FOREPAWS BY ROUNDING
THEM OVER (FIG.12). SLIGHTLY ROUND OVER THE END OF
THE NOSE. DO NOT CARVE BENEATH THE NOSE AREA YET.
WE STILL HAVE HIS BUCK TEETH TO CARVE HERE.

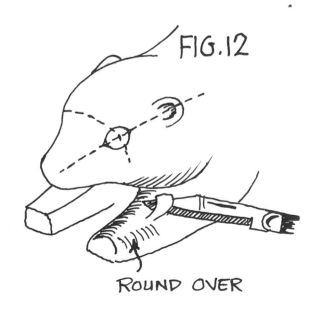

FIG.12

ROUND OVER

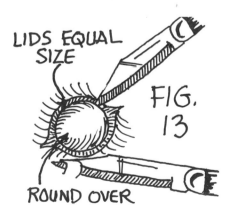

LIDS EQUAL SIZE

FIG. 13

ROUND OVER

STEP 11. THE NOSE & BUCK TEETH

USING FIG. 14, SKETCH IN THE DETAIL OF THE NOSE & TEETH. WITH THE POINT OF YOUR JACKKNIFE, CARVE STRAIGHT IN ALONG THE CURVED CHEEK LINES & AROUND THE TEETH. REMOVE THE WOOD FROM BEHIND THE TEETH WITH THE POINT OF YOUR JACKKNIFE (FIG 15A). DROP THE TEETH BACK ENOUGH TO ROUND OVER THE CHEEKS INTO THE TEETH & CUT A SHALLOW 'V' TO SEPARATE THE TWO TEETH. WITH THE POINT OF AN AWL OR OTHER POINTED OBJECT, PUSH THE POINT INTO THE NOSTRIL HOLES SO THEY ARE AS BIG AS FIG.14. CARVE DOWN THE FORELEGS, ROUNDING OVER THE ENDS WHERE THE FEET ARE. CARVE AWAY WOOD UNDER THE CHIN TO THE NECK & ROUND INTO THE FORELEGS. WHERE THE SIDE OF THE NECK & THE FORELEGS COME TOGETHER, CUT A DEFINITE 'V' & ROUND THE NECK INTO THE ROUNDED FORELEGS.

FIG. 15

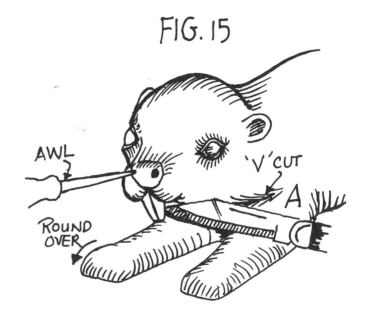

FIG. 14

NOSTRIL HOLES

CHEEK LINES

AWL

'V' CUT

A

ROUND OVER

STEP 12. SHAPING THE FOREPAWS

THE ENDS OF YOUR FOREPAWS SHOULD BE A GOOD 1/4 INCH THICK & WIDE. AS THE LEG GOES BACK INTO THE BODY, IT GRADUALLY GETS A LITTLE LARGER. USING A 3/16-INCH DRILL BIT, MOVE BACK FROM THE FRONT OF THE FOREPAWS A LITTLE MORE THAN 1/4 INCH & A LITTLE LOWER THAN THE MIDPOINT OF THE SIDE OF THE FOREPAWS & DRILL A HOLE THROUGH ONE FOREPAW & LINE UP THE OPPOSITE PAW & DRILL THROUGH THAT (FIG. 16). THESE HOLES ARE FOR THE SHOVEL & MUST BE LINED UP. WHEN THE SHOVEL IS IN PLACE, THE AREA IN FRONT OF THE HOLES WILL BE HIS FINGERS HOLDING THE SHOVEL. REMOVE THE WOOD FROM THE FRONT OF THE FOREPAWS USING FIG. 16B AS A GUIDE. THIS WILL ENABLE YOU TO CARVE HIS FINGERS AFTER THE SHOVEL IS IN PLACE. CARVE THE BOTTOM OF THE FOREPAWS AT AN ANGLE (FIG. 16A) GOING INTO A 'V' SHAPE, BRINGING THE TWO SIDES OF THE BOTTOM TOGETHER.

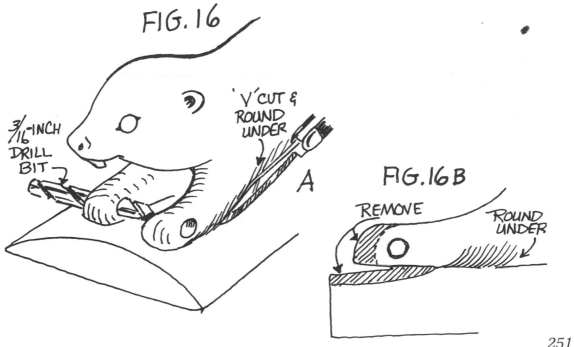

FIG. 16

3/16-INCH DRILL BIT

'V' CUT & ROUND UNDER

A

FIG. 16 B

REMOVE

ROUND UNDER

STEP 13. RELIEVING THE BASE FROM THE FEET.

TO FINISH THE PROPER SHAPING OF THE BODY TO THE BASE, USE YOUR HALF-ROUND & CARVE A GROOVE DOWN THE SIDES OF THE BODY TO ACCENT THE BACK OF THE SHOULDER OF THE FORELEG (FIG.17A). AS YOU NEAR THE BASE, ROUND THE WOOD UNDER THE BODY. SKETCH IN THE OUTLINE OF THE FEET (SEE PATTERN) & WITH THE POINT OF YOUR JACKKNIFE, CUT STRAIGHT DOWN AROUND THE FEET. CARVE AROUND THE FEET & REMOVE ABOUT 1/8 INCH OF WOOD SO FEET ARE EXPOSED (FIG.17B). DROP THE ENTIRE LOG BASE DOWN EVENLY SO THE FEET ARE RAISED. NOT KNOWING UNTIL NOW AT WHAT LEVEL THE BASE WILL BE, YOU CAN NOW ROUND THE BODY INTO THE BASE BY SMOOTH- ING & ROUNDING WITH YOUR JACKKNIFE. CLEAN UP ALL AREAS WHERE THE BODY & BASE MEET WITH A CRISP 'V' CUT. (FIG.17C). YOU MAY BE ABLE TO SEPARATE THE FOREPAWS FROM THE BASE NOW BECAUSE YOU HAVE DROPPED THE BASE THAT EXTRA 1/8 INCH (FIG.17D). LEAVE THE TAIL ALONE.

FIG.17

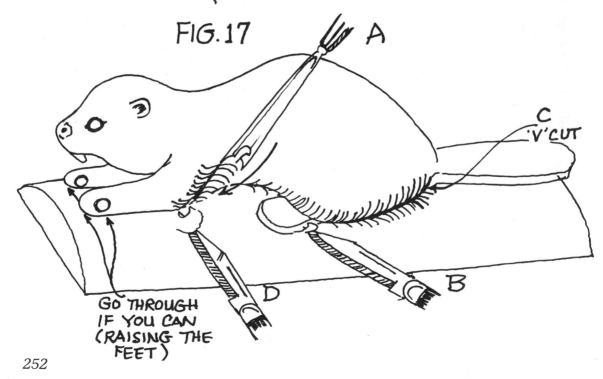

C
'V' CUT

A

B

D

GO THROUGH
IF YOU CAN
(RAISING THE
FEET)

STEP 14. CARVING THE FEET & TAIL

WITH YOUR JACKKNIFE, CARVE OFF THE TOPS OF THE FEET SO THEY ARE SLIGHTLY TURNED UPWARD WHERE THEY MEET THE BODY (FIG. 18). AS YOU CARVE DOWN THE FEET, ROUND SLIGHTLY SIDE TO SIDE (FIG. 18 ARROWS), LEAVING THE CENTER A LITTLE HIGHER THAN THE SIDES. A BEAVER HAS FIVE TOES WITH WEBBED FEET. SKETCH IN LINES TO DIVIDE THE TOES. NOTICE THE FEET ARE FAN-SHAPED, WHERE THE TOES ON THE OUTSIDE ARE SHORTER THAN THE MIDDLE ONES (FIG. 19). USING A SMALL 'V' PARTING TOOL, CARVE UP THE FEET TOWARD THE BODY ALONG YOUR DIVIDED LINES. FOLD A PIECE OF SAND PAPER & SAND THE GROOVES MADE BY YOUR PARTING TOOL (FIG. 19A), ROUNDING OVER THE RAISED EDGES OF THE TOES. WITH THE POINT OF YOUR JACKKNIFE, CARVE THE POINTED TOENAILS (FIG. 19B), USING FIG. 20 AS A REFERENCE. IF YOU HAVE ROOM BETWEEN THE TOES, CARVE THE SLIGHT ARC OF THE WEBBING (FIG. 20) & LOWER THE BASE VERY SLIGHTLY. THE TOE NAILS SHOULD BE POINTED & ROUNDED WITH A SMALL 'V' SEPARATION BETWEEN THE TOENAIL & THE TOE. WHERE THE BOTTOM OF THE FEET TURN UPWARD INTO THE BODY, REMOVE THE SMALL TRIANGULAR PIECES OF WOOD (FIG. 18) BETWEEN THE FEET, BODY & BASE. GO TO THE TAIL & WITH YOUR JACKKNIFE, CARVE DOWN BOTH SIDES FROM THE BODY, LEAVING A SLIGHT PEAK IN ITS CENTER (FIG. 19C). THE PEAK IS LARGER NEAR THE BODY & GRADUALLY GETS SMALLER AS YOU CARVE TOWARD THE END OF THE TAIL. BRING THE EDGE OF THE TAIL TO A LITTLE LESS THAN ⅛ INCH FROM THE BASE & ROUND OVER ANY SHARP EDGES (FIG. 19). YOU WILL PROBABLY HAVE TO REFER TO THE PATTERN FOR THE PROPER SHAPE OF THE TAIL PRIOR TO ROUNDING THE EDGES.

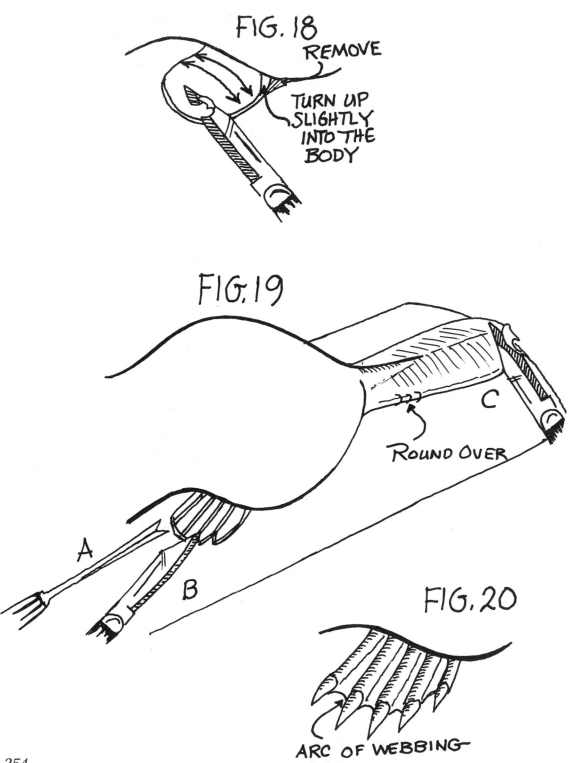

FIG. 18

REMOVE

TURN UP
SLIGHTLY
INTO THE
BODY

FIG. 19

ROUND OVER

C

A

B

FIG. 20

ARC OF WEBBING

STEP 15. SHAPING THE SHOVEL

USING YOUR HALF-ROUND, FLOW THE HANDLE INTO THE SHOVEL BY CARVING ALONG SIDE THE HANDLE ON BOTH SIDES, FORMING THE TAPERED END OF THE HANDLE (FIG. 21A). USE YOUR PATTERN FOR A GUIDE. WITH A SMALL FISHTAIL GOUGE, CARVE FROM THE END OF THE SHOVEL INTO THIS GROOVED CUT (FIG. 21B). THIS WILL GIVE THE SHOVEL A CONCAVE SURFACE, LEAVING THE TAPERED HANDLE END RAISED. WITH YOUR JACKKNIFE, CARVE DOWN THE ENTIRE HANDLE, ROUNDING IT OUT (FIG. 21C). WHEN YOU APPROACH THE TAPERED END, ROUND ONLY THE RAISED AREA ON TOP. DO NOT CARVE THE BOTTOM OF THE SHOVEL YET. SAND THE INSIDE OF THE CARVED CONCAVE SHOVEL TO GET IT EVEN & DISHED. ROUND THE ENTIRE HANDLE DOWN TO A SIZE THAT WILL FIT INTO THE FOREPAW HOLES EASILY BUT NOT TOO LOOSE. A SNUG FIT IS BEST. DO NOT TRY TO FORCE THE SHOVEL HANDLE THROUGH THESE HOLES OR YOU MAY BREAK THE FOREPAWS.

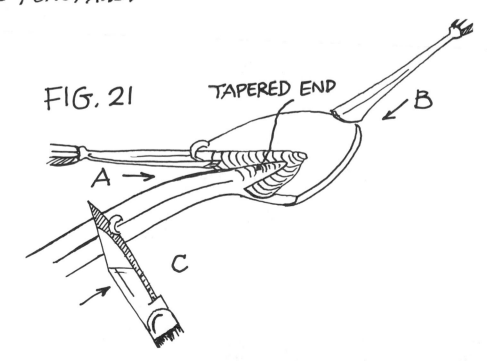

FIG. 21

TAPERED END

A →

B

C

STEP 16.   CARVING THE SHOVEL (Cont'd.)
 TURN THE SHOVEL OVER & TRIM UP THE OUTSIDE EDGES,
MAKING SURE THE SHAPE IS EQUAL ON BOTH SIDES
(SEE PATTERN). CARVE AWAY ALL SAW MARKS ON ITS EDGE.
WITH YOUR JACKKNIFE, CARVE THE BACK OF THE SHOVEL
INTO A SLIGHT DOME TO COINCIDE WITH THE CONCAVE
FRONT OF THE SHOVEL. BRING THE BACK DOWN SO THE
SHOVEL LOOKS THIN. THIN THE EDGES TO LEAVE A
VERY SMALL FLAT AREA AROUND THE SHOVEL (FIG. 22).
SAND THE BACK OF THE SHOVEL, BRINGING THE EDGE TO AN
EVEN, SHARP EDGE. INSERT THE SHOVEL INTO THE 3/16-INCH
HOLES OF THE FOREPAWS SO THE FOREPAWS ARE HOLDING
THE SHOVEL.
 WE WILL CARVE MUCH OF THE FOREPAW FINGERS WITH
THE SHOVEL IN PLACE TO AVOID BREAKING OFF WOOD
BECAUSE THE HOLES ARE FILLED & YOU CAN SHAPE THESE
FINGERS HOLDING THE SHOVEL WITH BETTER ACCURACY.

FIG. 22

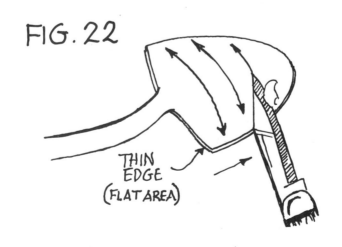

THIN
EDGE
(FLAT AREA)

STEP 17. CARVING THE FOREPAWS

WITH YOUR JACKKNIFE, CARVE THE FOREPAWS TO WITHIN 1/8 INCH OF THE SHOVEL HANDLE (FIG. 23A), WHICH IS THE THICKNESS OF THE FINGERS. THE FOREPAWS OF A BEAVER HAVE 5 FINGERS, BUT THE THUMB SIDE OF THE FIRST FINGER IS SO SHORT IT WILL NOT GRASP THE HANDLE. SKETCH IN YOUR FINGER LINES TO HAVE FOUR EQUAL SEPARATIONS (FIG. 23). USING YOUR PARTING TOOL, CARVE DOWN & OVER THE FOREPAWS, SEPARATING THE FINGERS. YOU MAY NOT BE ABLE TO REACH ONE OR TWO OF THESE LINES WITH YOUR PARTING TOOL. IN THIS CASE, VERY CAREFULLY USE THE POINT OF YOUR JACKKNIFE TO COMPLETE THESE CUTS. FOLLOWING FIG. 24 SIDE VIEW, CARVE AWAY THE WOOD FROM THE ENDS OF THE FINGERS TO THE BASE OF THE FOREPAWS AT AN ANGLE. DO NOT REMOVE THIS AREA COMPLETELY AS THE FINGERS WOULD BECOME TOO FRAGILE & BREAK AWAY. TAKE AWAY ONLY THE OUTSIDE EDGE TO SHOW WHERE THE FINGERS STOP. SAND THESE FINGERS AS YOU DID THE TOES.

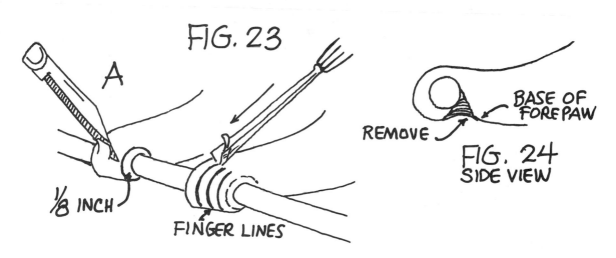

FIG. 23

A

1/8 INCH

FINGER LINES

REMOVE

BASE OF FOREPAW

FIG. 24
SIDE VIEW

STEP 18. CARVING THE FUR

SAND THE NOSE & TAIL ONLY. WITH A PARTING TOOL, CARVE THE FUR INTO THE BEAVER, FOLLOWING THE DIRECTIONS OF THE CUTS IN FIG. 25. BE CAREFUL WHEN CARVING IN AREAS LIKE THE BACK OF THE NECK & THE HEAD FOR CHANGES IN THE GRAIN. YOUR FUR CUTS SHOULD BE RIGHT NEXT TO EACH OTHER & IRREGULAR. LEAVE NO FLAT AREAS ON THE FUR, THE ENTIRE BEAVER WILL BE COVERED WITH CLOSE TOGETHER 'V' CUTS. THE TAIL WILL BE CARVED WITH PARTING TOOL CUTS IN A CRISS CROSS PATTERN. IT IS EASIER TO CARVE THE FUR WITH THE SHOVEL RE-MOVED.

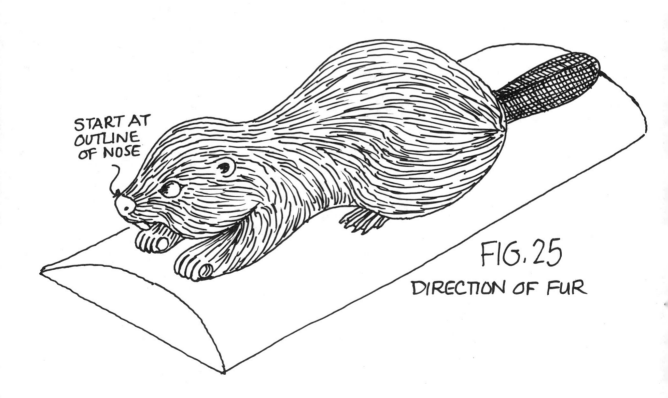

START AT OUTLINE OF NOSE

FIG. 25
DIRECTION OF FUR

STEP 19. CARVING THE LOG BASE

USING YOUR PARTING TOOL, CARVE THE LENGTH OF THE LOG BASE INTO IRREGULAR, WAVY CUTS TO EMPHASIZE THE BARK OF A TREE. DO NOT CARVE THESE GROOVES IN ANY PATTERN (FIG. 26). MAKE SOME OF THE CUTS DEEP & SOME SHALLOW. WITH YOUR JACKKNIFE, CARVE AWAY THE SAW MARKS AT THE ENDS OF THE LOG & WITH YOUR PARTING TOOL, CUT 'V' CUTS INTO THE ENDS FORMING THE GROWTH RINGS OF THE LOG (FIG. 26). YOU MAY HAVE SOME DIFFICULTY CARVING THE BARK CLOSE TO THE BODY OF THE BEAVER. USE THE POINT OF YOUR JACKKNIFE TO TRIM AWAY ANY LOOSE PIECES OF WOOD NEXT TO THE BODY.

FIG. 26

STEP 20.   FINISHING THE BEAVER

INSERT THE SHOVEL AFTER YOU HAVE STAINED THE BEAVER WITH WALNUT STAIN. IT IS NOT NECESSARY TO STAIN THE SHOVEL. STAIN THE LOG BARK WITH A COLORED STAIN DARKER THAN THE BEAVER'S. THE ENDS OF THE LOG ARE NOT STAINED, THEY ARE LEFT NATURAL. THE EDGES OF THE BARK ON THE ENDS OF THE LOG ARE STAINED THE SAME COLOR AS THE BARK. PAINT THE EYES & NOSE BLACK & APPLY A COAT OF CLEAR FINGER NAIL POLISH TO GIVE THEM A SHINY LOOK. PAINT THE BUCK TEETH A YELLOW-WHITE COLOR. SEAL YOUR ENTIRE BEAVER, BASE & SHOVEL WITH 2-3 COATS OF SATIN FINISH POLYURETHANE, OMITTING THE NOSE & EYES. YOUR BEAVER IS NOW COMPLETED.

A useful, attractive carving
project that can be completed
in a very short time.

The Carved Letter Opener

Project No. 9

TOOLS NEEDED
JACKKNIFE
HALF-ROUND
GOUGE (SMALL)

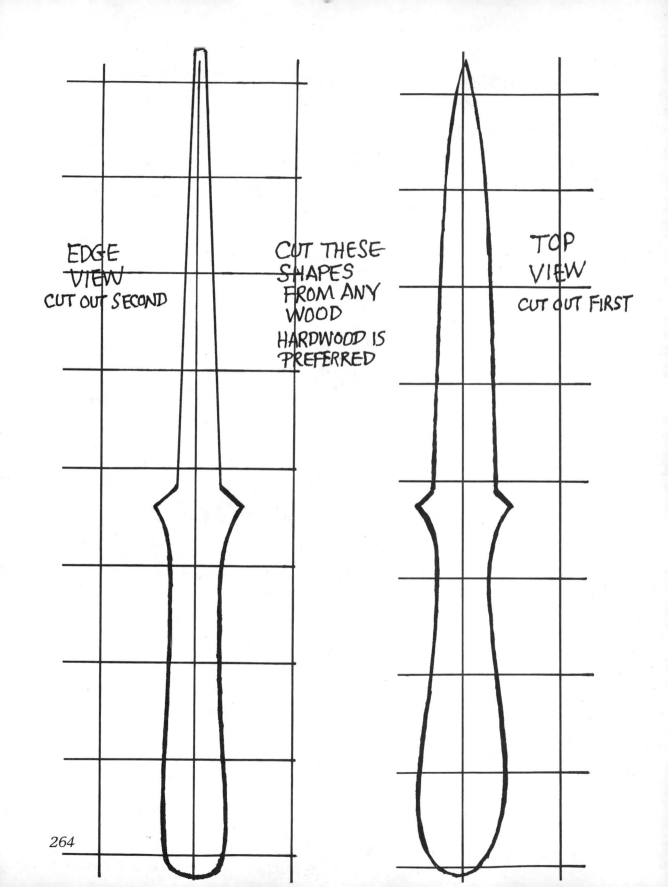

EDGE
VIEW
CUT OUT SECOND

CUT THESE
SHAPES
FROM ANY
WOOD
HARDWOOD IS
PREFERRED

TOP
VIEW
CUT OUT FIRST

264

STEP 1. SHAPING THE HANDLE

WITH YOUR JACKKNIFE, CARVE AWAY ALL EDGES EVENLY AT A 45° ANGLE (FIG. 1). BE CAREFUL WHERE THE HANDLE NARROWS NEAR THE BLADE BECAUSE YOU MAY BREAK AWAY THE HILT.

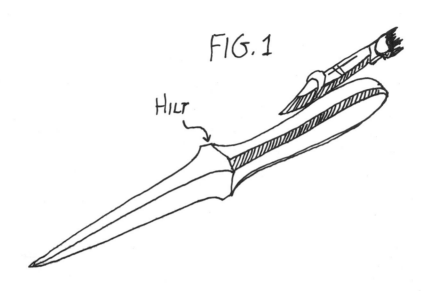

FIG. 1

HILT

STEP 2. ROUNDING THE HANDLE

BY CARVING AWAY THE 45° ANGLES, ROUNDING THE HANDLE WILL BE AN EASY CHORE. ROUND THE HANDLE BY REMOVING ALL OUTSIDE EDGES & THE HANDLE WILL AUTOMATICALLY ROUND ITSELF (FIG. 2). SAND THE HANDLE COMPLETELY.

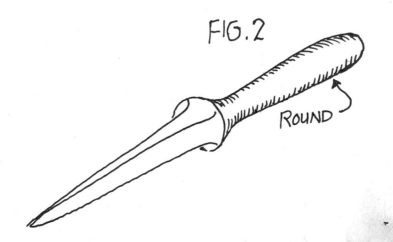

FIG. 2

ROUND

STEP 3. SHAPING THE BLADE

GO TO THE BLADE SIDE OF THE HILT & CUT STRAIGHT IN AROUND THE BLADE AT THE HILT (FIG. 3). CARVE DOWN THE BLADE, SHAPING IT INTO A DIAMOND SHAPE (END VIEW FIG. 4), LEAVING A CRISP RIDGE IN THE CENTER OF THE BLADE. DO NOT TRY TO BRING THE EDGE TO A SHARP EDGE. SAND THE BLADE TO MAKE THE EDGE SHARP BUT SLIGHTLY ROUNDED.

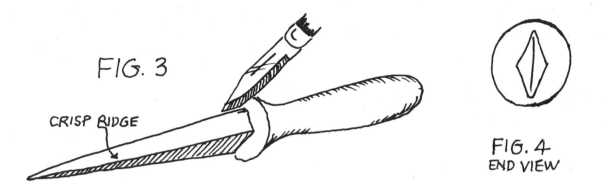

FIG. 3

CRISP RIDGE

FIG. 4
END VIEW

STEP 4. FINISHING THE HILT

MAKE SURE THE END VIEW OF THE HILT IS EVENLY ROUNDED. USE A SMALL HALF-ROUND GOUGE & CARVE THE BLADE SIDE OF THE HILT, WORKING FROM THE EDGE OF THE HILT INTO THE BLADE (FIG. 5). WITH YOUR JACKKNIFE, NOTCH THE TWO EDGES OF THE BLADE WHERE THEY ATTACH TO THE HILT (FIG. 5).

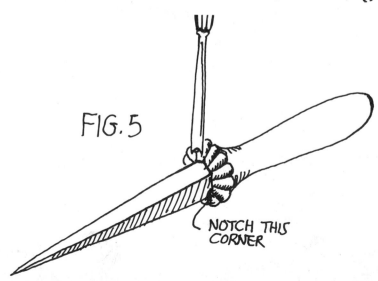

FIG. 5

NOTCH THIS CORNER

STEP 5. FINISHING THE LETTER OPENER

STAIN THE LETTER OPENER WITH TWO COMPATIBLY COLORED STAINS. WE SUGGEST USING A DARKER COLOR ON THE HANDLE & A LIGHTER COLOR ON THE BLADE & HILT GROOVES. BECAUSE OF THE OIL IN YOUR SKIN, IF THE HANDLE WERE A LIGHT COLOR IT WOULD SOON ABSORB THE OIL FROM YOUR HAND & DISCOLOR A LIGHTER STAIN. YOU CAN POLY-URETHANE THIS PIECE IF YOU WISH BUT WE PREFER TO LEAVE IT STAINED SO IT CAN PICK UP ITS LUSTER FROM THE OIL IN YOUR HANDS.

The Loon

Project No. 10

A decorative miniature carving of The common Loon suitable for your mantle.

TOOLS NEEDED • HALF·ROUND GOUGE (FIG. 2) • JACKKNIFE
PARTING TOOL (FIG. 6) • FISHTAIL GOUGE
ELECTRIC BURNING PEN

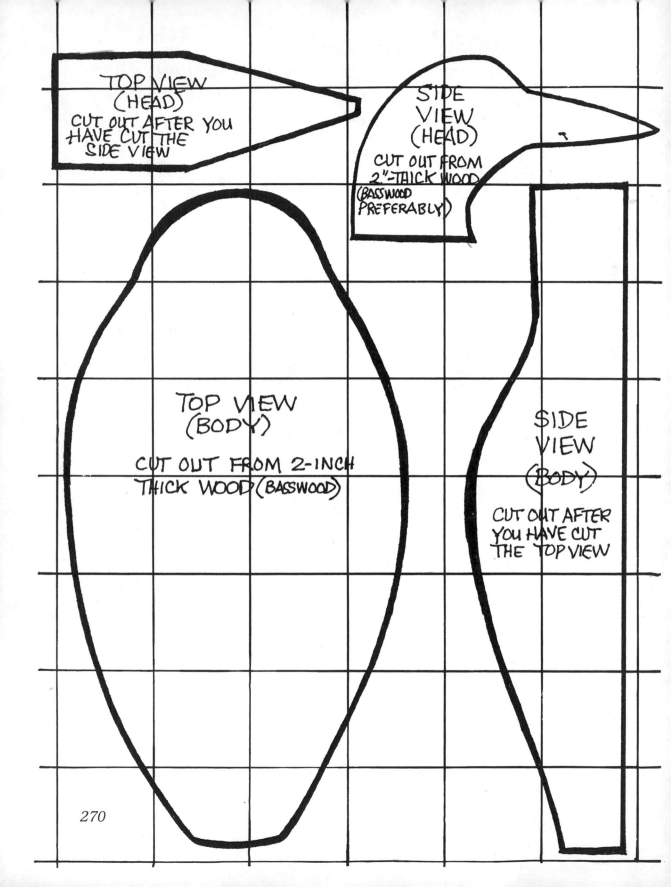

TOP VIEW
(HEAD)
CUT OUT AFTER YOU
HAVE CUT THE
SIDE VIEW

SIDE
VIEW
(HEAD)
CUT OUT FROM
2"-THICK WOOD
(BASSWOOD
PREFERABLY)

TOP VIEW
(BODY)

CUT OUT FROM 2-INCH
THICK WOOD (BASSWOOD)

SIDE
VIEW
(BODY)

CUT OUT AFTER
YOU HAVE CUT
THE TOP VIEW

270

STEP 1.   GLUE UP OF THE HEAD

AFTER SAWING OUT YOUR BODY & HEAD, YOU WILL HAVE TO CARVE AWAY THE SAW MARKS WHERE THE HEAD & THE BODY ARE TO BE CONNECTED. YOU CAN DO THIS WITH YOUR JACKKNIFE & SANDPAPER TO GET A GOOD FIT. THIS LOON WILL BE CARVED WITH HIS HEAD TURNED ABOUT 45 DEGREES TO THE RIGHT. THIS TURN WILL MEAN YOU WILL HAVE TO REMOVE SOME WOOD FROM THE CORNER OF THE NECK (FIG. 1) BECAUSE THE RISE IN THE BODY WON'T ALLOW THE HEAD TO FIT. AFTER YOU HAVE FITTED THE HEAD TO THE BODY, DRILL A HOLE LARGE ENOUGH TO FIT A 1½-INCH #10 WOOD SCREW UP THROUGH THE BODY & DRILL A SMALL PILOT HOLE INTO THE HEAD. GLUE THE HEAD & SCREW IT TO THE BODY (FIG. 1).

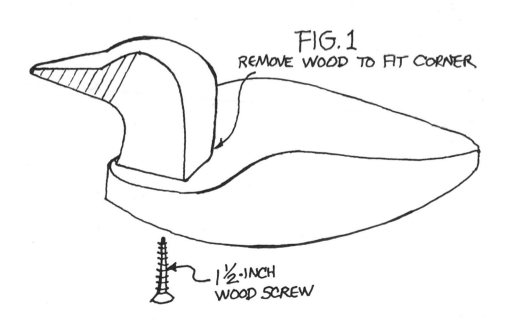

FIG. 1
REMOVE WOOD TO FIT CORNER

1½-INCH
WOOD SCREW

STEP 2. ROUNDING THE NECK

USING A HALF-ROUND GOUGE (FIG. 2), CARVE A GROOVE DOWN THE MIDDLE OF THE BACK (FIG. 3A) TO THE BASE OF THE NECK. AS YOU NEAR THE NECK, CARVE AWAY THE CORNERS OF THE NECK & CONTINUE CARVING AROUND THE NECK (FIG. 3B). WE ARE TRYING TO CARVE THIS AREA AT THE BASE OF THE NECK SO IT IS ROUND (DOTTED LINE FIG. 3). THIS WOULD BE THE AREA OF THE GLUE JOINT. IT MAY BE NECESSARY TO REMOVE WOOD FROM THE SIDES OF THE BODY (FIG. 3C) TO ALLOW YOU TO REACH THE NECK AREA WITH YOUR HALF-ROUND. BECAUSE THE HEAD IS TURNED YOU WILL HAVE SOME PROBLEMS WITH CARVING AGAINST THE GRAIN, ESPECIALLY AT THE SIDES OF THE NECK. BUT WITH DILIGENCE & REMOVING VERY SMALL PIECES OF WOOD, YOU CAN GET THE BASE OF THE NECK FAIRLY ROUND.

FIG. 2

USE THIS
SIZE

FIG. 3

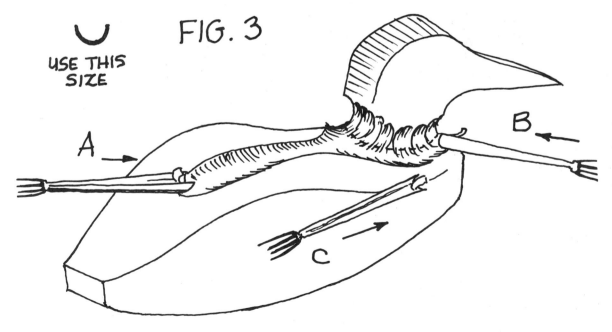

A

B

C

STEP 3. ROUNDING THE BODY & HEAD
USING YOUR JACKKNIFE, CARVE UP THE NECK ONTO THE
HEAD (FIG. 4A), ROUNDING THE NECK TO YOUR ROUNDED
HALF-ROUND CUTS MADE IN STEP 2. ROUND OVER THE
TOP OF THE HEAD SLIGHTLY. CARVE DOWN THE BEAK ON
BOTH SIDES, REMOVING WOOD TO THE SHAPE OF FIG. 5.
ROUND OVER THE EDGES OF THE BODY INTO YOUR PRE-
VIOUSLY MADE, HALF-ROUND GROOVE. CONTINUE TO
ROUND THE BODY TOWARD THE NECK & DOWN THE
FRONT (BREAST) OF YOUR LOON (FIG. 4B).

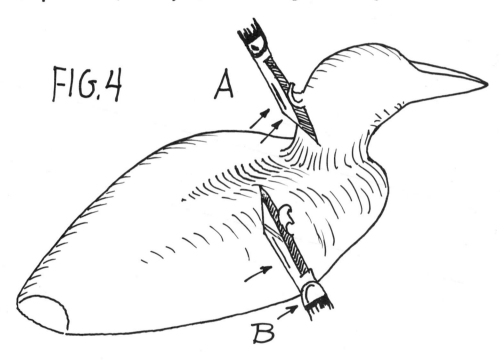

FIG. 4

FIG. 5
FRONT VIEW
HEAD & BEAK

STEP 4. SHAPING THE WING COVERT FEATHERS
SKETCH IN A CENTERLINE UP THE MIDDLE OF THE BACK
(FIG.6) & SKETCH IN THE WING COVERTS, USING FIG.6
AS A GUIDE. WITH YOUR PARTING TOOL, CARVE A GROOVE
ALONG THESE WING COVERT LINES (FIG.6A). LEAVING
THE WING COVERTS ALONE, CARVE THE BODY 1/8 INCH LOWER
THAN THE COVERTS (FIG.6B). AFTER THE ENTIRE COVERT
IS EXPOSED FROM THE BODY, ROUND OVER EACH COVERT
BACK INTO THE BODY (FIG.6C), ELIMINATING THE 1/8-INCH
DROP-OFF.

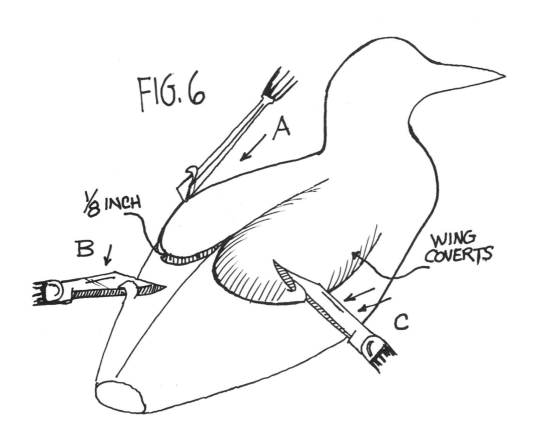

FIG. 6

A

1/8 INCH

B

WING
COVERTS

C

STEP 5. SHAPING THE HEAD & BEAK

USING YOUR JACKKNIFE, ROUND THE NECK & HEAD AS SMOOTHLY AS YOU CAN PRIOR TO SANDING. THE HEAD MAY BE A LITTLE LARGE, SO USE FIG. 7 FOR THE SHAPE & SIZE YOU ARE LOOKING FOR. WITH THE POINT OF YOUR KNIFE, CARVE DEPRESSIONS INTO THE SIDES OF THE HEAD (FIG. 7) THAT FOLLOW THE TAPER OF THE HEAD INTO THE BEAK (FIG. 8). THIN THE BEAK & SHAPE THE HEAD INTO THE BEAK AS FIG. 8 SHOWS. A LOON'S BEAK IS VERY THIN, SO DON'T THINK YOU ARE TAKING AWAY TOO MUCH WOOD AS YOU FOLLOW FIG. 8.

FIG. 7

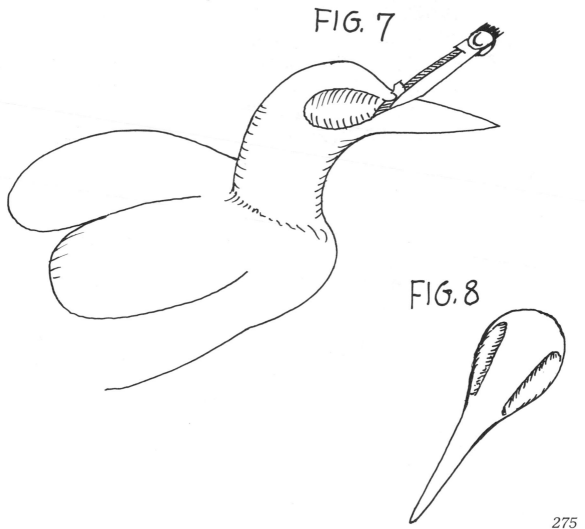

FIG. 8

STEP 6.   CARVING THE BEAK

WE HAVE TO SEPARATE THE BEAK FROM THE HEAD TO MAKE THE BEAK LOOK LIKE IT IS PROTRUDING FROM THE FEATHERED HEAD, WHICH IS A LITTLE BULKIER THAN THE SMOOTH BEAK. SKETCH IN A CENTER LINE ON EACH SIDE OF THE BEAK & STARTING AT THE HEAD END OF THE CENTERLINE, SKETCH IN THE EXACT SHAPE OF WHERE THE HEAD MEETS THE BEAK (FIG. 9 & 10). WITH THE POINT OF YOUR JACKKNIFE, CARVE A NARROW 'V' ALONG THE CENTERLINE OF THE BEAK TO SEPARATE THE UPPER & LOWER BILL. CARVE STRAIGHT IN ALONG THE BEAK-HEAD LINES & REMOVE WOOD FROM THE BILLS TO LOWER THEM FROM THE HEAD SLIGHTLY. ROUND THE HEAD BY SLIGHTLY ROUNDING INTO THE BEAK, MAKING THE HEAD LOOK PUFFY. WITH THE POINT OF YOUR JACKKNIFE, CARVE A 'V' SLOT FOR THE NOSTRIL (FIG. 9). SAND THE BEAK & THE HEAD.

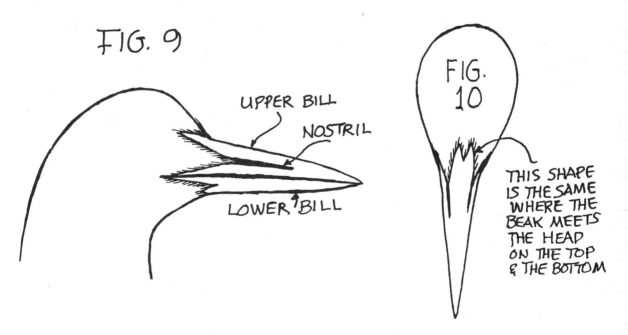

FIG. 9

UPPER BILL

NOSTRIL

LOWER BILL

FIG. 10

THIS SHAPE IS THE SAME WHERE THE BEAK MEETS THE HEAD ON THE TOP & THE BOTTOM

STEP 7. CARVING THE EYES

USING FIG. 11 AS A GUIDE, SKETCH IN THE LOCATION &
SIZE OF THE EYES. SKETCH A LINE UP THE SIDES OF
THE HEAD, FOLLOWING THE NOSTRIL LINE. SKETCH ANOTHER
LINE THAT CROSSES THE NOSTRIL LINE ABOUT IN THE
MIDDLE OF THE HEAD (FIG. 11). SKETCH YOUR CIRCLES
ON THIS CROSSING ABOUT THE SIZE SHOWN IN FIG. 11.
WITH THE POINT OF YOUR JACKKNIFE, CARVE AROUND
THIS CIRCLE & REMOVE A SHALLOW 'V' (FIG. 12). WE
ARE GOING TO CARVE THE EYE FROM WOOD, NOT INSERT
A GLASS EYE. CARVE THE EYE BY SLIGHTLY ROUNDING
FROM ITS CENTER INTO YOUR 'V' CUT SO THE EYE HAS
A DOME SHAPE (FIG. 13). CAREFULLY SAND THE EYE
WITHOUT SANDING AWAY YOUR LIDS WHICH HAVE BEEN
FORMED BY YOUR INITIAL 'V' CUT.

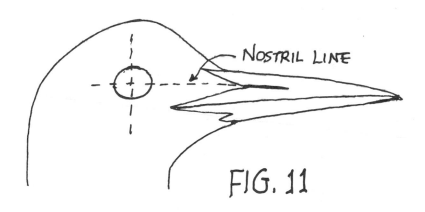

NOSTRIL LINE

FIG. 11

FIG. 12

FIG. 13
CROSS SECTION

'V' CUT   EYE

STEP 8. LAYOUT OF THE WING COVERTS

THE PATTERN OF THE FEATHERS ON A LOON IS FAIRLY SYMMETRICAL BUT NOT PERFECT. TO ACHIEVE THIS PATTERN, SKETCH IN LINES GOING ACROSS THE COVERTS TO ES- TABLISH THE ROWS OF FEATHERS (FIG.14). NOTICE THESE LINES ARE NOT STRAIGHT. USE FIG.14 TO SKETCH THESE SLIGHTLY IRREGULAR CURVED LINES. REPRODUCE THE INDI- VIDUAL FEATHERS FROM FIG.14 & SKETCH THEM ONTO THE COVERTS. NOTICE THAT THE LINES OR ROWS OF FEATH- ERS FROM FRONT TO REAR ARE NOT PERFECTLY LINED UP, BUT DO HAVE A LINED-UP LOOK. IF YOU KEEP YOUR FEATHER DRAWING ON THE COVERTS AS CLOSE TO FIG.14 AS POSSIBLE, YOU WILL BE IN GOOD SHAPE.

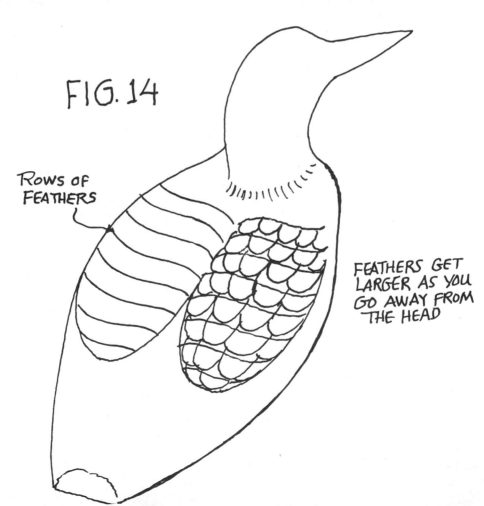

FIG. 14

Rows of FEATHERS

FEATHERS GET LARGER AS YOU GO AWAY FROM THE HEAD

278

STEP 9. SHAPING THE WING COVERT FEATHERS
USING THE POINT OF YOUR JACKKNIFE, CUT STRAIGHT
DOWN & GO AROUND EACH FEATHER (FIG. 15 A) FOLLOWING
YOUR PENCIL LINES. CARVE ALONG EACH ROW OF FEATHERS
& REMOVE WOOD TO GIVE THE ROWS A SHINGLED LOOK
(FIG. 15). WHERE ONE FEATHER WOULD OVERLAP ANOTHER
FEATHER THAT IS SIDE BY SIDE, CARVE AWAY WOOD TO
LAYER THEM SIDE BY SIDE (FIG. 15 B).

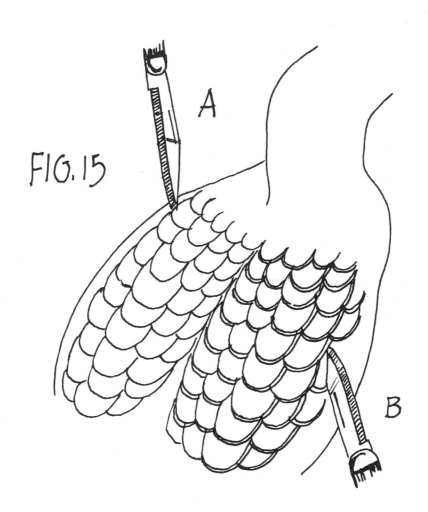

FIG. 15

STEP 10. CARVING THE COVERT FEATHERS

EACH OF THESE COVERT FEATHERS WILL BE CARVED SO THEY HAVE A SLIGHT DOME TO THEM & WILL BE CARVED DOWN SO THE EDGES ARE SLIGHTLY ROUNDED INTO ADJACENT FEATHERS. WITH YOUR JACKKNIFE, VERY SLIGHTLY ROUND THE FEATHERS OFF TO THEIR SIDES, WORKING FROM THEIR CENTERS (FIG. 16). IF THIS IS DONE PROPERLY, THE EDGES OF ALL THE FEATHERS WILL HAVE VERY LITTLE THICKNESS TO THEM, BUT EACH WILL HAVE ITS OWN DOMED SHAPE. FIG. 17 SHOWS THE DIRECTION OF ROUNDING & THICKNESS OF THE EDGE OF EACH FEATHER.

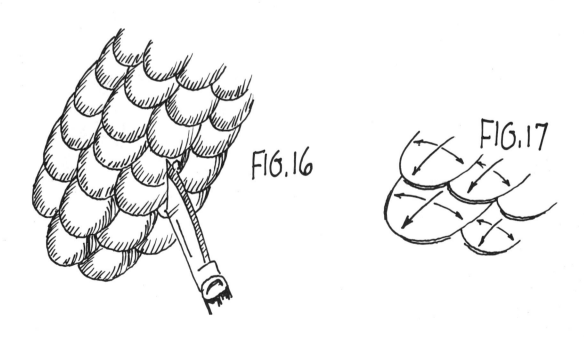

FIG. 16

FIG. 17

STEP 11. ACCENTING THE PRIMARY & SECONDARY FEATHERS
SKETCH IN THE FEATHER STRUCTURE EXACTLY AS IT
IS PICTURED IN FIG. 18., TWO SETS OF SECONDARY FEATHERS
& THE LONG PRIMARY FEATHERS. WITH THE POINT OF YOUR
JACKKNIFE, CARVE STRAIGHT DOWN AROUND THE OUTSIDE
OF THE TOTAL FEATHER AREA (DARK LINE FIG.18).
REMOVE THE WOOD AROUND THE FEATHERS BY LOWERING
THE BODY (FIG. 18A) AWAY FROM THEM ABOUT 1/8 INCH.
YOU MAY HAVE SOME PROBLEMS REMOVING THE WOOD
IN THE SMALL AREA ABOVE WHERE THE WINGS CROSS,
BUT WITH THE HELP OF A SMALL FISHTAIL OR GOUGE
THAT WILL FIT IN THERE, YOU CAN GET IT OUT WITH
LITTLE DIFFICULTY (FIG. 18 B).

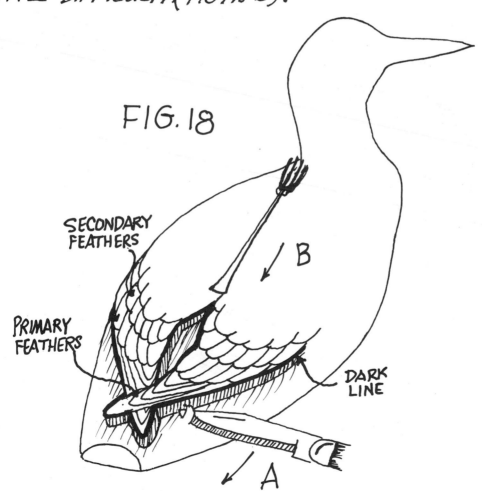

FIG. 18

SECONDARY
FEATHERS

B

PRIMARY
FEATHERS

DARK
LINE

A

STEP 12. CARVING THE SECONDARY & PRIMARY FEATHERS
WITH THE POINT OF YOUR JACKKNIFE, CARVE STRAIGHT IN ON
THE LINES YOU HAVE SKETCHED FOR THE 2 SETS OF SEC-
ONDARY FEATHERS. USE FIG. 19 AS A REFERENCE FOR EXACT
SHAPE & NUMBER OF THESE FEATHERS. LAYER BY DROPPING
DOWN YOUR 2ND SET OF SECONDARIES FROM THE 1st (FIG. 19A).
THIS WILL GIVE YOU ROOM TO LAYER EACH FEATHER LOWER
THAN THE ONE BEFORE IT (FIG. 19 B). DO NOT MAKE THE
LAYERS THICK. MAKE THEM VERY THIN BUT CLEARLY LAYERED.
CONTINUE YOUR FEATHER LAYERING ONTO THE PRIMARIES &
BE CAREFUL WHERE THE TWO SETS OF PRIMARIES CROSS.
CARVE THE TOP SET OF PRIMARY FEATHERS FIRST & THE
LOWER ONES SECOND. MAKE SURE YOUR CONTINUATIONS OF
THE FEATHER EDGES MATCH AS THE LOWER PRIMARIES
PASS UNDER THE UPPER PRIMARIES. CARVE IN AND UNDER
THE INSIDE EDGES OF ALL FEATHERS, MAKING A DEEP 'V,'
& REMOVE WOOD FROM THE BODY INTO A SLIGHT ARC
(FIG. 19 C).

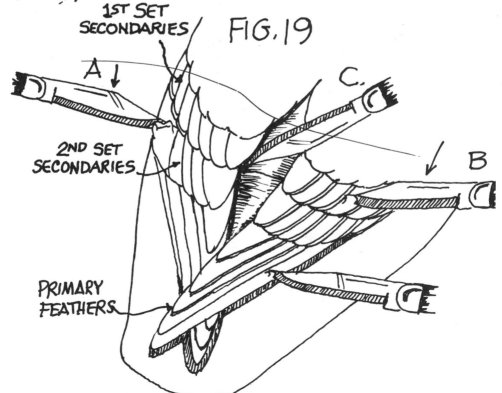

1ST SET
SECONDARIES

FIG. 19

A

C.

2ND SET
SECONDARIES

B

PRIMARY
FEATHERS

STEP 13. UNDERCUTTING THE PRIMARIES

CAREFULLY, WITH THE POINT OF YOUR JACKKNIFE, CUT STRAIGHT IN UNDER THE SIDES & TIPS OF THE PRIMARY FEATHERS & CONTINUE TO REMOVE WOOD FROM UNDER THE TIPS UNTIL THEY ARE FREE FROM THE BODY (FIG. 20). CARVE BENEATH THE TIPS & THIN THEM UNTIL THEY ARE FEATHER THICKNESS. CARVE BOTH SIDES OF THE BODY, ROUNDING INTO THE TAIL. THE TAIL WILL BE FLAT TO THE BASE (FIG. 21) BECAUSE LOONS SWIM WITH THEIR TAILS IN THE WATER. SAND THE BREAST, SIDES & ONTO THE TAIL.

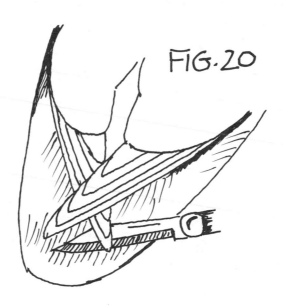

FIG. 20

FIG. 21

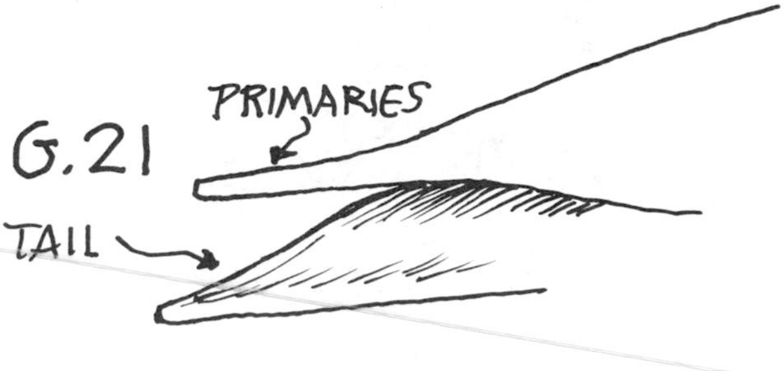

PRIMARIES

TAIL

STEP 14. BURNING THE HEAD, NECK, BREAST & SIDES
WITH THE POINT OF YOUR ELECTRIC BURNER, START AT
THE HEAD WHERE THE BEAK MEETS THE HEAD & WITH
SHORT POINTED BURNS, ACCENT THE HEAD FROM THE BEAK
(FIG. 22). DO THIS CAREFULLY BY NOT BURNING ANY
OF THE BEAK. CONTINUE YOUR BURNING FOLLOWING
THE LINE DIRECTION OF FIG. 22. BURN DOWN THE
NECK, ONTO THE BREAST & ALONG THE SIDES LEAVING
AN UNBURNED SPACE BETWEEN THE WING COVERTS &
THE BASE OF THE SIDES (FIG. 22). DO NOT BURN GREAT
LONG LINES OR BURN YOUR LINES EXACTLY SIDE BY
SIDE IN ANY STRAIGHT PATTERN. BURN WITH OVER-
LAPPING IRREGULAR STROKES & MAKE THEM ALL DIF-
FERENT SIZES & LENGTHS, BUT KEEP THEM FOLLOW-
ING YOUR LINE DIRECTIONS.

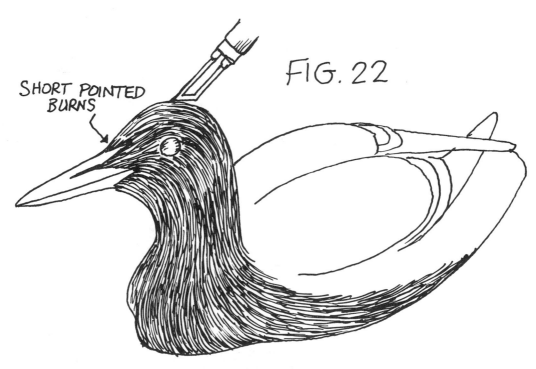

SHORT POINTED
BURNS

FIG. 22

STEP 15. BURNING THE WING COVERTS

EACH WING COVERT FEATHER WILL BE BURNED LIKE FIG. 23.
START BY BURNING 2 PARALLEL LINES IN THE CENTER OF
THE FEATHER THAT COME TOGETHER, FORMING THE QUILL.
MAKE A FEW DARKER BURNS THAT ARE SLIGHTLY CURVED
ON THE SIDES OF THE FEATHER, THESE DARKER BURNS ARE
MAINLY USED FOR A GUIDE WHEN YOU FILL IN THE REST
OF THE FEATHER. IN MANY CASES, IF YOU STARTED TO FILL
IN (BURN) THE FEATHER, STARTING AT THE TOP & BURNING IN
A ROW UNTIL YOU REACHED THE FEATHER END, THE BURN
LINES BECOME TOO STRAIGHT — THERE FORE, THE DARKER
GUIDE LINES ARE VERY HELPFUL. BURN THE FEATHERS
STARTING AT THE NECK & WORKING TOWARD THE TAIL.
WHEN FILLING IN (BURNING) THE FEATHERS, KEEP YOUR
BURN MARKS AS CLOSE TOGETHER AS POSSIBLE. WHEN
WORKING YOUR WAY DOWN THE BIRD'S BACK, USE FIG.
24 AS A GUIDE FOR THE QUILL DIRECTION. DO NOT
BURN THE QUILLS ALL IN A STRAIGHT LINE. THE IR-
REGULAR PATTERN IN FIG. 24 IS MORE NATURAL.

FIG. 23

DARKER BURNS   QUILL

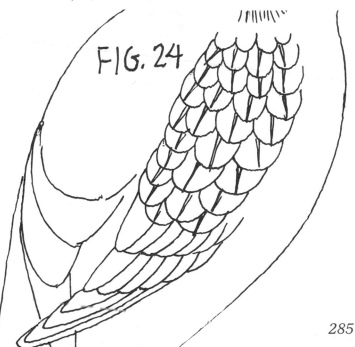

FIG. 24

STEP 16. BURNING THE PRIMARIES & SECONDARIES
MOVING DOWN THE BACK FROM THE WING COVERTS BURN THE
FEATHER DETAIL INTO ALL PRIMARY & SECONDARY FEATHERS
USING FIG. 25 AS A GUIDE. PRIOR TO BURNING, RUN THE TIP
OF THE BURNER ALONG THE UNDERPARTS OF THE PRIMARY &
SECONDARY FEATHERS (FIG. 25A). BURN IN ALL QUILL LINES
FIRST PLACED AS ILLUSTRATED IN FIG. 25. START YOUR FEATHER
DETAILING ON THE SECOND SET OF SECONDARY FEATHERS & DO
THE FIRST SET NEXT.   DO THE PRIMARIES LAST & RUN
YOUR BURNER IN THE CREASE WHEN THE TWO SETS CROSS.

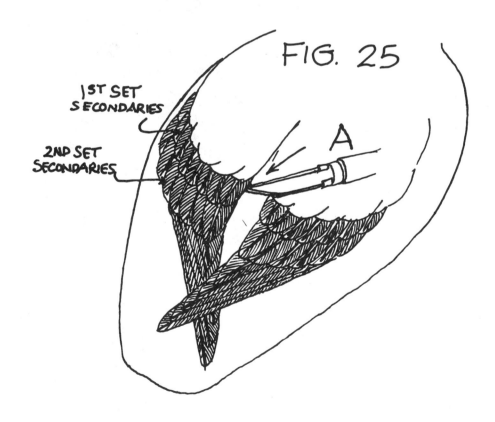

FIG. 25

1ST SET SECONDARIES

2ND SET SECONDARIES

A

STEP 17. BURNING THE SIDE FEATHERS & TAIL FEATHERS
SKETCH IN SMALL ROUNDED FEATHERS ALONG THE SIDES THAT
HAVEN'T BEEN BURNED YET. SKETCH THEM IN DOWN TO THE
TAIL & IN THE SPACE BETWEEN THE CROSSED WINGS (FIG. 26).
NOTICE AS YOU GO TOWARD THE TAIL THE FEATHERS GET
A LITTLE LARGER. SKETCH IN THE TAIL FEATHERS AS IN FIG.
26. NONE OF THESE FEATHERS HAS BEEN CARVED OR
SHAPED. WE WILL USE THE BURNER TO GIVE THE ILLUSION
OF CARVED FEATHERS ON A FLAT SURFACE. STARTING AT THE
TAIL, BURN STRAIGHT LINES DOWN THE TAIL (FIG. 27) TO
SEPARATE THE INDIVIDUAL TAIL FEATHERS. MAKE THESE
BURNS DEEPER THAN NORMAL. BURN THE INDIVIDUAL
FEATHER ON THE TAIL AS IN FIG. 27. AFTER YOU HAVE
COMPLETED THE TAIL FEATHER BURNING, START THE
BODY FEATHER BURNING AT THE TAIL & BURN UP THE
BODY ON BOTH SIDES. TO MAKE THIS FLAT AREA LOOK
LIKE FEATHERS, USE THE TIP OF YOUR BURNER & POKE
DARK BURNS AROUND THE CIRCUMFERENCE OF EACH FEATHER
(FIG 28A). BURN IN YOUR QUILLS & COMMENCE BURNING
EACH FEATHER WITH A LIGHTER BURN THAN THE FEATHER
OUTLINE BURNS (FIG 28B). YOU MAY HAVE SOME DIF-
FICULTY REACHING UNDER THE WING TIPS, BUT DO THE
BEST YOU CAN. WHEN BURNING THE FEATHERS ON
THE SIDES, ALLOW THE STRAIGHT BURNS YOU HAVE DONE
TO BLEND INTO YOUR FEATHER BURNS WITHOUT LEAVING
ANY HARD LINES. RUN YOUR BURNER ALONG THE
UNDERPARTS OF THE WING EDGES TO ELIMINATE AND
BURN AWAY ANY LOOSE PARTICLES OF WOOD OR SPLINTERS.
THESE LITTLE PIECES OF WOOD ARE DIFFICULT TO REMOVE
WITH YOUR JACKKNIFE, BUT THE BURNER JUST BURNS
THEM AWAY.

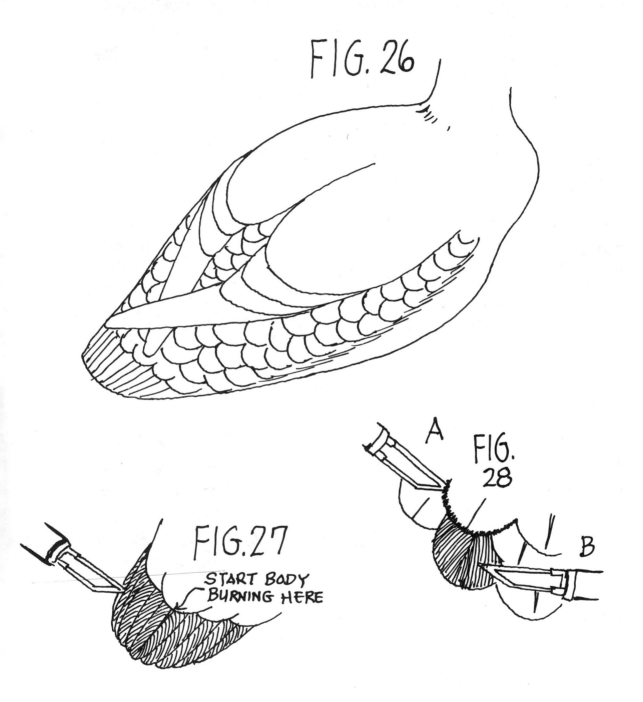

FIG. 26

FIG. 27

START BODY
BURNING HERE

A FIG. 28

B

STEP 18. FINISHING THE EYES & BEAK

USING THE TIP OF YOUR BURNER, CAREFULLY BURN AROUND THE EYES, ALLOWING THE BURNER TO SLIGHTLY FLATTEN THE LIDS & ALSO TO MAKE THE EYE LOOK ROUND. BURN A SMALL 'V' IN THE CORNERS OF THE EYES (FIG 29A). IT IS QUITE DIFFICULT TO CARVE & SAND THE EYES TO GET THEM TO LOOK ROUND. WITH THE HELP OF THE BURNER YOU CAN SMOOTH THEM A LITTLE MORE BY LAYING THE BURNER POINT FLAT AGAINST THE EYES & BY BARELY TOUCHING THE EYE, LIGHTLY PASS THE BURNER ACROSS THE EYE. WITH THE POINT OF YOUR BURNER, ACCENT THE SLOT BETWEEN THE UPPER & LOWER BEAK. YOU WILL BE ABLE TO GET THIS SLOT NICE AND STRAIGHT & A LITTLE DEEPER. WITH THE POINT OF YOUR BURNER, PUSH THROUGH AT THE NOSTRILS FROM BOTH SIDES UNTIL YOU CAN SEE LIGHT THROUGH THE NOSTRILS. MAKE SURE YOU KEEP THE NOSTRILS LINED UP SIDE TO SIDE (FIG 29B).

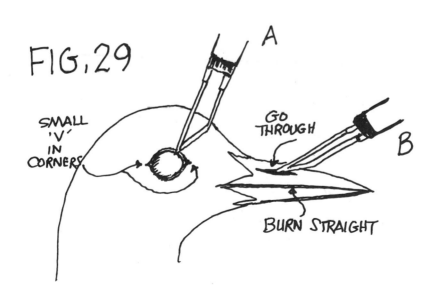

FIG. 29

SMALL 'V' IN CORNERS

A

GO THROUGH

B

BURN STRAIGHT

STEP 19. PAINTING YOUR LOON

USING FIG. 30 AS A GUIDE, PAINT THE BEAK, HEAD & BODY
WITH A THINNED-OUT, FLAT BLACK PAINT. THIN THE BLACK
TO A CONSISTENCY OF A LOOSE STAIN. AVOID GETTING
ANY BLACK ON THE WHITE NECK PATCHES OR THE BREAST
& SIDES. WIPE AWAY ALL EXCESS WET BLACK. USE A FLAT
WHITE & APPLY RIGHT FROM THE CAN TO THE NECK PATCHES,
BREAST & SIDES. BRUSH THIS STRAIGHT WHITE HARD INTO
YOUR BURNED MARKS. BLEND THE WHITE INTO THE BLACK
WITH A DRY, STIFF BRUSH. DO NOT LEAVE ANY HARD SOLID
LINES BETWEEN THE BLACK & WHITE.

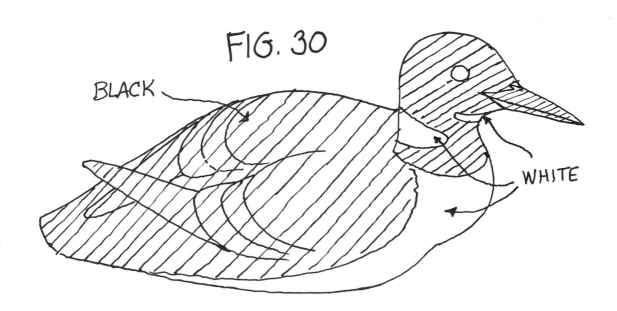

FIG. 30

BLACK

WHITE

STEP 20. PAINTING THE WING COVERTS

FOLLOWING FIG. 31, PAINT STRAIGHT WHITE, FLAT PAINT ON ALL WING COVERT FEATHERS. DO NOT TRY TO MAKE THESE SPOTS WITH SHARP EDGES. LET THEM BLEND INTO THE BLACK. EACH FEATHER HAS TWO WHITE SPOTS WITH BLACK BETWEEN THEM & BLACK REMAINS AROUND THE CIRCUMFERENCE. AS YOU GET NEAR THE NECK, THE SPOTS GET SMALLER. AT THE BASE OF THE NECK, DOT IN A SERIES OF SMALL SPOTS THAT WOULD BLEND INTO THE COVERT FEATHERS.

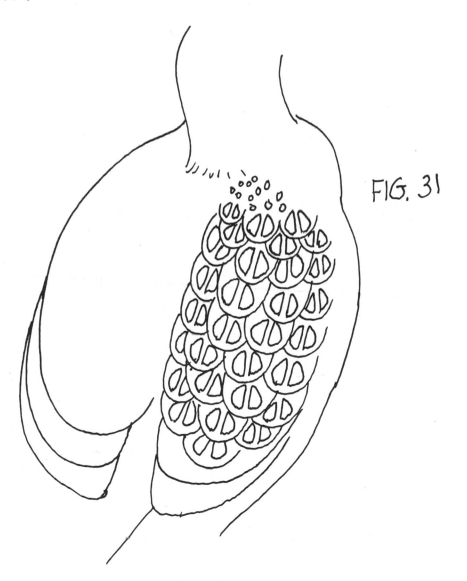

FIG. 31

STEP 21. PAINTING THE PRIMARIES, SECONDARIES & BODY WHITE
FOLLOWING FIG. 32, PAINT WHITE DOTS ON THE ENDS OF
BOTH SETS OF SECONDARY FEATHERS. ALONG THE SIDE &
TOWARD THE TAIL, DOT IN A SERIES OF SPOTS AS ILLUSTRATED.
DO NOT PAINT WHITE ON THE PRIMARY FEATHERS OR THE TAIL.

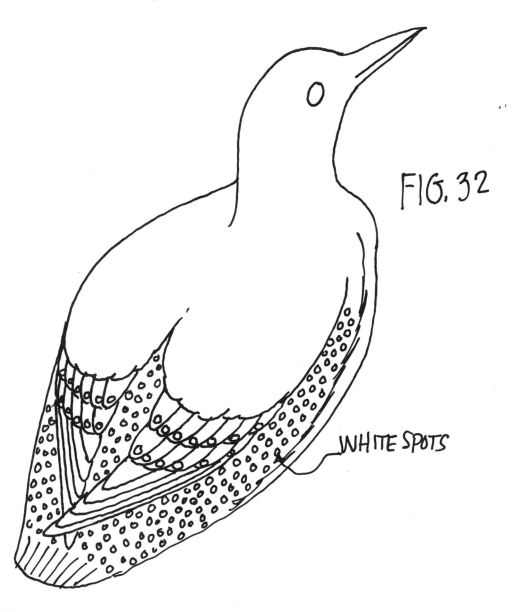

FIG. 32

WHITE SPOTS

STEP 22. FINISHING THE NECK PATCHES

(USE FIG. 32 AS A GUIDE.) THE LOON HAS BLACK STRIPES RUNNING THROUGH THE WHITE PATCHES ON EITHER SIDE OF THE NECK & UNDER HIS BEAK. USING A FINE ARTIST'S BRUSH & DULL BLACK PAINT, PAINT IN THESE STRIPES. NOTICE THE STRIPES ARE NOT PERFECTLY PARALLEL TO EACH OTHER & SOME OF THE STRIPES MAY NOT GO ALL THE WAY THROUGH THE PATCHES. THERE ARE OTHER STRIPES FORMING AT THE BASE OF THE NECK & RUNNING DOWN ONTO THE BODY.

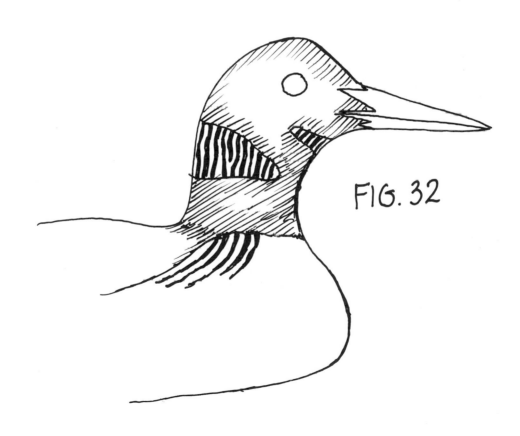

FIG. 32

STEP 23 · FINISHING THE LOON

FINISH THE EYES BY PAINTING THEM WITH RED ENAMEL & PAINT A SMALL BLACK DOT IN THE EXACT CENTER. TO GIVE THE EYES A WET LOOK, USE A DROP OF CLEAR FINGERNAIL POLISH OR HIGH GLOSS POLYURETHANE. GIVE THE BEAK A COAT OF SATIN FINISH POLYURETHANE WITH A LITTLE BLACK MIXED INTO IT. MANY DECORATIVE BIRD CARVINGS SUCH AS THIS LOON ARE MOUNTED ON A BASE THAT HAS BEEN TURNED ON A LATHE. THIS LOON WILL BE BY ITSELF MAINLY BECAUSE ONCE YOU HAVE MADE A BASE LARGE ENOUGH TO ACCOMMODATE THE LOON THE WHOLE PIECE WOULD BE TOO LARGE TO USE. FOR EXAMPLE, IT PROBABLY WOULDN'T FIT ON A MANTLE. YOUR LOON IS COMPLETED.